The Politics of Race
and Schooling

The Politics of Race and Schooling

Public Education in Georgia, 1900–1961

Thomas V. O'Brien

LEXINGTON BOOKS
Lanham • Boulder • New York • Oxford

LEXINGTON BOOKS

Published in the United States of America
by Lexington Books
4720 Boston Way, Lanham, Maryland 20706

12 Hid's Copse Road
Cumnor Hill, Oxford OX2 9JJ, England

Library of Congress Cataloging-in-Publication Data

O'Brien, Thomas V., 1958–
   The politics of race and schooling : public education in Georgia,
1900–1961 / Thomas V. O'Brien
       p.   cm.
   Includes bibliographical references (p.) and index.
   ISBN 0-7391-0060-2 (alk. paper)
   1. Discrimination in education—Georgia—History—20th century.
2. Education—Social aspects—Georgia—History—20th century.
3. Politics and education—Georgia—History—20th century.
I. Title.
LC212.22.G46037 1999
306.43—dc21   99-10348
                                                                   CIP

Printed in the United States of America

⊖™ The paper used in this publication meets the minimum requirements of American
National Standard for Information Sciences—Permanence of Paper for Printed Library
Materials, ANSI/NISO Z39.48–1992.

To the Bear

A one-room, one-teacher school in Veazy, Greene County, Georgia, October 1941. Photograph taken by Jack Delano. Courtesy of the Library of Congress, Prints and Photographs Division, Farm Security Administration Collection.

Contents

Acknowledgments

I am grateful for institutional support I received to research this project from the Spencer Foundation and Millersville University. I am also especially indebted to Charles Strickland, Vanessa Siddle Walker, Judy Monsaas, Ann Floyd, and Jonathan Zimmerman who read early drafts of selected chapters and offered helpful comments and critique. Radine Robinson proved to be an invaluable help at formatting the entire manuscript. I could not have brought this book to publication without the effort and continuous support of my spouse, Molly Townes O'Brien. Molly helped me with every aspect of this project and at every step along the way. My two sons, Cyrus and Joseph, lost their dad for hours at a time while I worked on this book; and I thank them for their patience.

Introduction

Although historians have long included schools in their political and social histories, systematic study of U.S. educational history really only began at the turn of the century at three universities in New York, Chicago, and Palo Alto. In spite of vast differences in interpretation that developed in the field, leading historians of education have lived, prepared, worked, and researched outside the South.[1] In one sense, this has conditioned those of us in the field to see the history of American schooling through "Northern eyes" (or at least non-Southern eyes). These studies have been valuable in interpreting schooling in the North and West. But, with few exceptions, they do not describe or account for the unique history of the South.[2]

In contrast to public school systems in the North, which experienced tremendous growth during the late nineteenth century, the arrival of universally available public education in the South was a mid-twentieth century phenomenon. One would therefore expect to find that the economic, ideological and social forces that impacted the rise and spread of public schooling in the South were distinct from those that guided the development of schooling in other parts of the country. More importantly, Southern public schools developed in the context of an overtly racist society. Because white Southerners made no attempt to hide their racism or the steps they took to insure white supremacy, studying the history of a Southern school system provides an important view into the inner workings of the politics of race and schooling.

This book is about the spread of universal public education in Georgia during the first six decades of the twentieth century. The impetus behind the push for universal education came in part from black leaders within the state. Even before the Civil War, black Georgians viewed the school as a key institution for achieving freedom, justice and first class citizenship. During Reconstruction black leadership set off to collaborate in the establishment of a system of publicly supported schools. By the turn of the century this drive for school opportunities—although seriously altered by the politics of race—worked alongside a regional school crusade and an economic vision of a New South, to fuel the growth of the public school system in the state.

The shape the school took, the curricula it offered, and the social purposes it aimed for in the twentieth century, however, were a far cry from what the nineteenth century black Georgians and radical Republicans might have had envisioned. Far from embodying democratic equality and inducting the state's young into citizenship, the budding Georgia public school served as a vehicle for maintaining race and class privilege. The public schools of the twentieth century became embroiled in a brand of racial politics that privileged white people over black people and rich people over poor people.

I might have written a romantic, optimistic account of the growth of public schooling in Georgia; one that celebrated the progress made in moving toward the ideal of universal schooling between 1900 and 1961. The arrival of a publicly supported system of schools, an institution that was founded on the ashes of the Civil War did in many ways signal the beginning of a new era. The expansion of and broad support for the institution in the late 1930s and especially after World War II, was no small accomplishment. The state had long been thwarted by poverty, a system of racial caste, and oligarchic politics. The school system that took hold in this environment helped to soften the grip of poverty, racial oppression, and anti-democratic elements of government on the state and its people. From this perspective, universal schooling represented a societal victory which symbolized the spread of decency, civility, and genuine equality.

From a liberal perspective, there is also reason to celebrate. In 1900 Georgia public schooling led to an educational dead end for the vast majority of Georgians. By the post-World War II period, however, schooling stretched from grade one to the university, and this extension translated into opportunities for thousands of Georgia's white and black children. Children in previously ignored or underserved groups soon found themselves in a statewide system that linked grammar school with college. Even under the system of strict segregation, black educational opportunities were improving. By 1961 Georgia's state government stepped aside and allowed its flagship university and the Atlanta public school system to begin to desegregate. In this vein, a judgment that the public school campaigns nudged the state forward toward equality, freedom, fairness and democracy seems warranted.

The more I studied the historical record with these interpretations in mind, however, the more disturbed I felt. My original goal had been to discern the ways in which the emergent system of public education ameliorated some of Georgia's most pressing social problems. As I continued, I questioned why the acceptance and wide support of this supposedly democratic institution had not done more to relieve some of the state's and region's fundamental social problems. I was distressed to find state and local policies denied open access, differentiated the curriculum, and segregated students on the basis of race and class. Ultimately my inquiry pushed me to consider a far more critical view of the public school—and the powerful few who held disproportionate influence over its growth, shape and purpose.

The account that follows suggests that while democratic and progressive impulses for universal education forced politicians to establish public education in the state—and, in the wake of *Brown v. Board of Education*, may have had marginal influence on social change that favored equality—the idea of using the public school to improve society toward democratic ends could not compete with other goals. The shape and purpose of the public school, historians David Tyack and Larry Cuban remind us, are most affected by "groups that mobilize to win support for their definitions of problems and their proposed solutions. The more powerful and prestigious the groups, the more likely it is that they will be able to buttress their reforms with laws, regulations, and accreditation requirements." Likewise, Joel Spring suggests that public school arena is best characterized by conflict, with actors working to secure what is in their self-interests. Those in power at t..e time the institution takes shape will often take steps to critically influence its social purpose.[3] Once established, it seems that public school is best suited to conserve the political and economic interests of those who shaped it rather than alter the societal configurations of which it is an outgrowth.

This text extends previous analyses by highlighting race. The factors weighed in other important studies, including politics and markets, class and social privilege, social mobility and efficiency,[4] are unable to account fully for the dynamics of change and constancy in Georgia public schooling. From the start, alongside the goals of social mobility and social efficiency, white supremacy divided blacks and whites, regardless of class. So noticeable was race in expansion of schooling that I found it necessary to argue that the Georgia public school was a calculated result of a society that prefers and empowers whiteness. In doing so, I felt it crucial to consider the political dynamics emanating from both black and white communities.

For their part, the black community in Georgia, behind the veil of segregation, debated and blended the roles public schools would play in surviving, softening, or changing the social order. The historical scholarship has begun to chronicle the belief in and appreciation for schooling and literacy in several Southern black communities.[5] Yet, in addition to mediating and accommodating the private and communal interests and survival needs of its members, leaders and intellectuals in the black community also prized broader goals of advancement of the race in the American social order and provided the catalyst for expansion. Their actions often pressured those in power to expand the enterprise, but what resulted was not always in the best interests of blacks. Black initiatives and subsequent white resistance and adjustment to them, led to a school system fundamentally flawed by the politics of race privilege. The dynamics of race politics continue to compromise the way we school our children.

*   *   *

I intend to reach two main audiences with this book. First, I am addressing students and scholars in the fields of Southern history, American educational history, and political science. Second, I hope to reach practitioners; classroom teachers studying school policy and politics, and school board members, state education officials, and other educational decision makers. It is hoped that this analysis will provide practitioners with a deeper understanding of the politics of race and schooling that they might take into account while shaping current educational programs, policies, and structures.

For this study I utilized both historical and ethnographic methods. A list of the archival records I visited is indexed in Appendix A. I also conducted numerous interviews and am indebted to the people who graciously accepted me into their homes and offices and talked so freely and openly with me about public education and racial politics.[6] Beyond the factual contributions they made in documenting what happened and when it happened, their accounts provided me with a rich variety of complex moods and attitudes that prevailed in Georgia.

In writing this narrative I also relied on the observations of many reporters who covered, wrote about and reacted to what they were part of in Georgia. To these writers I am indebted. Their names are far too numerous to mention here. As for some of the newspapers they wrote for, I found the *Atlanta Journal, Atlanta Constitution, New York Times, Savannah Morning News*, the Gainesville *Daily Times*, and the *Macon Telegraph* particularly helpful in tracing how the urban white middle class was responding to the high court's desegregation. Two black owned and operated newspapers, the *Atlanta Daily World* and the *Atlanta Inquirer*, helped me piece together the urban black response. The more conservative *World* reflected and shaped the views of Atlanta's well-educated, middle-class black community, while the *Inquirer* was helpful in understanding the response of the younger, "new guard" blacks in Atlanta. Two county weeklies, the Calhoun *Times* and the Bainbridge *Post-Searchlight*, were useful for getting a sense of the rural white response. Two weeklies, *The Statesman* and the *Augusta Courier*, published by Herman Talmadge and Roy Harris, respectively, gave me explanations of what was happening in Georgia politics and the state legislature. Both papers reflected and shaped the views of Talmadge-faction politicians who controlled state government from 1946 to 1962.

In addition to the newspapers, several periodicals were of great value. The *Southern School News*, financed by the Ford Foundation, reported state-by-state developments in Southern education as a result of the *Brown* decision. This publication reflected the views of many of the South's most respected newspaper editors, most of whom lived in the urban centers of the South, and many of whom were moderate on the issue of race. The *Race Relations Law Reporter*, chronicled the legal developments of the school/race issue.

Two lesser known journals published in Georgia—the conservative *County Commissioners Comments* and the liberal *New South*—were also quite helpful. The *Georgia House and Senate Journals*, *Georgia Laws*, and records kept by state agencies housed at the Georgia Department of Archives proved to be the best sources for determining official state action.

Finally, I am indebted to several scholars upon whose shoulders this work stands. Works by Donald L. Grant, Numan Bartley, Paul Bolster, Paul Mertz, Benjamin Muse, Neil McMillen, David Plank, Marica Turner, Paula Fass, Mark Tushnet, and Richard Kluger were particularly helpful in piecing the story together. Also essays and studies by David Labaree, Numan Bartley, James Cobb, David Tyack, Larry Cuban, Paul M. Gaston, Michael Omi, Diane Ravitch, Howard Winant, and C. Vann Woodward helped me contextualize and frame this study.

Throughout the period under study three different names were used to identify African Americans: Negro, Colored, and black. Each in its time took on a special meaning, and each in its time was accepted by the race as desirable. I have also included several primary sources that referred to African Americans as "niggers" or failed to capitalize the N in Negro. I intend no disrespect when quoting these terms. My aim is to convey accurately the times and the unvarnished racism of the speakers. When not quoting I try to use the term that was used during the time. Often, however, I use African American, black, and Negro interchangeably.

Ronald Edmonds, a pioneer of effective schools research, once argued that teaching children effectively is far more a matter of politics than of social science.[7] Edmonds's comments suggest that political histories of education do more than fill scholarly gaps in the past. These studies may play a valuable role in understanding and shaping educational policies. In short, these studies may provide decision makers with contextual information about the motivations for and consequences of school policy and thus have the potential to influence educational reform. In telling this story, I hope to contribute to and inform the debate on how to correct social injustice and to shed light on the complex and emotionally charged issues of race and schooling in America.

Notes

1. For examples of various interpretations, see the celebrationism of Ellwood P. Cubberley (Stanford), the liberalism of Lawrence Cremin (Teachers College, Columbia), the revisionism of Merle Curti (Wisconsin), Barnard Bailyn (Harvard), David Tyack (Stanford), and Michael Katz (Pennsylvania), and the neoconservativism of Diane Ravitch (Teachers College, Columbia and New York University).

2. For examples of older interpretative works, see books by Edgar Knight, Charles W. Dabney, Horace Mann Bond. For more recent works, see books by James D. Anderson, Robert Margo, James LeLoudis, Vanessa Siddle Walker, and William A. Link. Several political scientists, legal historians, and journalists have found the politics of schooling interesting, and focused on the dynamics of resistance to school desegregation. See for example works by Richard Kluger, Mark Tushnet, Numan Bartley, James Ely, and Robert Pratt. Much of the remaining scholarship on Southern schooling is journalistic in style and serves the purpose of summarizing short-term developments in Southern schooling. See for example, works by Benjamin Muse, Harry Ashmore, Calvin Trillin, and Reed Sarratt. A third area of historical script is descriptive, and was written for school administrators and others internal to the Southern system of schools. The most useful accounts in understanding the growth of schools in Georgia are works by Dorothy Orr, Oscar H. Joiner, and Melvin W. Ecke, and Haygood S. Bowden.

3. David Tyack and Larry Cuban, *Tinkering Toward Utopia, A Century of Public School Reform* (Cambridge, MA: Harvard University Press, 1995), 86; David Tyack and William Tobin, "The Grammar of Schooling: Why Has It Been So Hard to Change?" 31; *American Education Research Journal* (Fall 1994), 453-479; Joel Spring, *Conflict of Interests: The Politics of American Education* 2nd ed. (New York: Longman, 1993).

4. For a recent example, see David F. Labaree, *How to Succeed in School without Really Learning: The Credentials Race in American Education* (New Haven: Yale University Press, 1997).

5. Scholars have chronicled how blacks developed and maintained linkages between schooling, the development of good character, and social mobility within a segregated system. As Vanessa Siddle Walker and others have found, Southern black school communities blended the academic, personal, moral, social, and spiritual goals held for their members, and thus blurred lines that connected the public, private, and spiritual good as well as the institutions primarily responsible for advancing those goods. See Vanessa Siddle Walker, *Their Highest Potential* (University of North Carolina Press: Chapel Hill, 1996). Another student recently found that it was not unusual for some upcountry blacks in Georgia to understand "family" as extending beyond kinship lines and provide care, discipline or shelter to individuals in the greater community. Compared to the more rigid boundaries that defined white families, black family-school-community boundaries were permeable and

fluid, and thus strengthened the black community's "constructions of collectivity." See Ann Short Chirhart, "Torches of Light: African American and White Female Teachers in the Georgia Upcountry, 1910-1950" (Ph.D. diss., Emory University, 1997), 92-94. Siddle Walker has many examples of how this mediation played out. She refers to one principal who regularly reminded students that they should focus not on the "log cabin they came from but where they were going," and urged boys not to "marry pretty little things, but women who would help them in their efforts to get ahead," pp. 111–12.

6. Following leads in the secondary source literature, private papers and correspondence, and contemporaneous newspaper accounts, I located and interviewed 21 people between 1991 and 1995. The interview data was corroborated with two traditional sources whenever possible before an interpretation was made. Those interviewed are listed in Appendix B.

7. Ronald Edmonds, Effective Schools for the Urban Poor, 37 *Educational Leadership*, (October 1979), 15-23.

Chapter 1

Jim Crow and the New South Creed: The Foundation of Georgia Public Education

We know, looking at history, that the damage done by the Civil War in property losses was great. The poverty which followed was harsh, often brutal. But the corrosive damage done the spirit and soul of the South was through lack of education. The children, the grandchildren and the great-grandchildren of the adults of those postwar years did not have a fair chance.
　　　　　　　　　　　　　　　　　　　　　　　　　　　　　　－Ralph McGill, 1958

The establishment of universal, tax-supported public education is often cited as a mid-nineteenth century phenomenon. In many areas of the Deep South, however, the establishment of public schooling would not be secure for another hundred years. Even during the early twentieth century, while Northern progressives completed the construction of a sequential, integrated school system from kindergarten to the university, many rural areas in Georgia lacked any schools. Those schools that did exist in rural areas held classes for only a few months a year and were often staffed by teachers who had only three or four years of formal education. Visiting a one-teacher school in rural Georgia in the late 1930s, Gunnar Myrdal, the famed sociologist and author of *An American Dilemma*, "hardly believed his eyes and ears" when he saw the primitive school building, the "lack of practically all equipment," the untrained teacher, and the "bottomless ignorance of the pupils." Likewise in 1946, Benjamin Fine, the education specialist and reporter for the *New York Times* was "shocked" to find "education in the rough" in a one room school not far from Atlanta, where a seventh grade girl was the only teacher.[1]

Poverty certainly played a role in the delayed growth of public education in the South. It was, however, the white South's dedication to race privilege that most

1

profoundly stunted the growth of publicly funded education. The establishment of universal, publicly supported education in Georgia would be a long process, mired in the politics of race and distorted by the economic vision of the New South Creed.

The New South Creed

Still war-torn at the end of the nineteenth century, Georgia was among the nation's poorest states, overwhelmingly agricultural, rural, and thinly populated. Post-Civil War economic devastation persisted well into the twentieth century. Economic growth would not accelerate until after World War II. Nevertheless, even before the turn of the century, a growing business-class of white Southerners had embraced the "New South Creed," a vision of economic development that aimed to regenerate the South through industrialization, urbanization, and economic diversification.[2] Boosters of the New South billed Georgia as the land of economic opportunity for Northern capitalists and pointed to abundant natural resources, low taxes, and cooperative state and local governments.

Another key component of New South attractiveness for investment was the availability of low-wage labor. Poverty was extreme in much of rural Georgia; in many cases the poor barely subsisted. Lax enforcement of state child-labor and compulsory school attendance laws, which passed in Georgia in 1914 and 1916, respectively, gave cotton farmers, textile mill owners and Northern investors a ready supply of cheap labor. The plantation tradition, sharecropping, child-labor, and a lack of unionism worked to keep wages low. Investors and capitalists of the 1920s interested in the labor-intensive industries of textiles, turpentine, lumber and wood, fertilizer, cotton seed oil, and railroad machines found Georgia an attractive business option.[3]

Incoming industrialists of the 1880s "were less interested in schools or hospitals than in low taxes, and responsible leadership was less important to them than freedom from regulation." Employers counted on "getting maximum productivity out of workforces consisting largely of ex-sharecroppers, females, and children, none of whom were likely to complain about wages and working conditions or otherwise develop a well-defined sense of class consciousness."[4]

Georgia politics, like the politics of other Southern states, were oligarchic and antidemocratic. Powerful elites included planters and upper-income farmers, professionals, and a growing group of industrialists. The Southern urban middle class was small in number and politically weak. The poll tax worked to keep poor whites and blacks impotent politically. In Georgia, the poll tax worked alongside a peculiar "County Unit System" which placed a great deal of the political power in the hands of rural county elites. As a result of this system, the political power base became even more concentrated in the countryside while Georgia's cities grew in the twentieth century.[5]

Although poor whites and urban whites were politically weak in Georgia, blacks were politically powerless. At the end of Civil War Reconstruction, beginning in Mississippi and spreading north and east, state legislatures began a campaign to disenfranchise the freedmen. Schemes that required landownership, literacy qualifications, the payment of a poll tax, and ultimately the "white primary" succeeded in prohibiting blacks from registering to vote. At the same time antiblack propaganda that linked the race to vile lawlessness became commonplace, giving whites of all classes a pre-chosen scapegoat. White supremacy was justified by antiblack propaganda and enforced by white violence against blacks. Within this context, at the turn of the century, segregation laws took hold throughout the South.

Jim Crow

As Civil War Reconstruction ended, the white South developed a system of legal and cultural apartheid.[6] In 1877 a new Georgia Constitution provided for free, common schooling open to all, but segregated by race.[7] During the 1890s and early 1900s racial segregation laws, called "Jim Crow" laws, patterned in the North, appeared on the books of every Southern state.[8] The constitutional validity of Jim Crow was ratified in *Plessy v. Ferguson*, a 1896 U.S. Supreme Court decision that upheld a Louisiana law requiring segregated-but-equal passenger cars on trains. Subsequent decisions approved the application of the *Plessy* "separate but equal" doctrine in all public accommodations, including education.

The logic of separate railway compartments in the *Plessy* decision would in no time apply to all types of social arrangements. Jim Crow spread to steamboat travel, theaters, boarding houses, retirement homes, barbershops, waiting rooms, hospitals, housing, amusements, water fountains, soda fountains, restaurants, taverns, cemeteries and even cadavers for medical schools. Three years on the heels of the *Plessy* decision a 1899 U.S. Supreme Court decision gave the sanction of federal law to an up-and-coming tradition: separate and unequal elementary schools for white and black children and separate and nonexistent funding for white and black high schools. In the case *Cumming v. Board of Education*, the high court found that it was acceptable for a local school board in Richmond County, Georgia, to abandon its state-apportioned financial support of the black high school while continuing to support two white high schools, one for males and other for females.[9]

Under the Jim Crow system, the plight of blacks in the United States, particularly in the South, fell to new lows. The white South made little pretense of upholding the "equal" aspect of the "separate but equal" doctrine.[10]

The Beginnings of Public Schooling in Georgia

Before the Civil War, Georgia law permitted but did not require the establishment of schools. Instead of patterning a system based on the New England common school model, Georgia lawmakers in the nineteenth century opted for a two-tier system of private academies and pauper schools. The academies served prosperous white Georgians who chose to educate their children within the state, while the poor schools were intended to provide basic literacy to the state's poor white population. While both institutions received a small amount of money from the state, academies also required the payment of tuition. Only those children whose parents could afford the fee and the loss of labor attended. By 1850, 219 charters had been issued for academies in the state.

For the most part, the pauper school was a failed experiment. Insufficient funding, clumsy administration, and half-hearted attention from the state, combined with locals' cultural beliefs to sink the institution. For their part poor whites, isolated, illiterate, undernourished, and plagued by illness, valued rugged individualism and autonomy, not outreach. Most not only distrusted outside influence, but opposed declaring themselves paupers to qualify for poor school funds, which would place "a definite stigma on themselves and their children." They preferred to be left alone and go without training.[11] These values, and an unwillingness to part with their children's labor, led to near extinction of the pauper school. Although the state had divided the school fund between academies and the pauper schools, the disappearance of the latter allowed local authorities to pass along the money to the semiprivate academies that charged tuition and were not affordable to the poor.[12]

Prior to Emancipation there were, of course, no state or local provisions made for the formal schooling of the state's black population, free or enslaved. Eighteenth century black codes gave slaves the right to religious instruction but levied fines against anyone who taught a slave to write or read. By the nineteenth century, due in part to fears of insurrection, laws were tightened and blacks who taught other blacks to read were fined and whipped. Whites who were caught teaching blacks were fined and jailed. After Nat Turner's revolt and the publication of *David Walker's Appeal*, larger cities and towns often passed ordinances to bolster state law.[13]

Antebellum blacks who risked the acquisition of literacy often did so at great peril. Black children in Savannah who attended clandestine schools, for example, hid their books in their clothing. Discovery of their study could cause the school to close, or worse. Slaveholders and their overseers often took the law into their own hands and sometimes removed the thumb or finger of a slave who was caught in the act of instruction. Still, the codes were randomly enforced and often evaded and disregarded. It was not unheard of, for example, for slaveholders who relied on their slaves to conduct business or to bring their goods to market to openly encourage and support their literacy and numeracy.[14] Some planters, it seems, were willing to school their slaves if it meant increased efficiency within the existing social order.

Most felt, however, that any promotion of learning would threaten the stability of the slave economy. Training of any kind would only spoil slaves and free blacks and lead to discontent and social unrest.[15] These same attitudes persisted into Reconstruction. According to W.E.B. DuBois, blacks were disliked and feared in direct proportion to their intelligence and capacity. Schools where blacks were taught were burned, and so-called nigger teachers were ostracized and threatened.[16] Until the economic devastation of 1866 "scarcely any white persons could be found who were willing to 'disgrace' themselves by 'teaching niggers,'" observed a white educator in Savannah. "But, as times grew hard, and money and bread scarce," one local educator was flooded with applications from whites, "a vast majority [who] were unable to write grammatically or spell the most simple words in our language correctly. Not a few appeared to think that 'anybody can teach niggers.'"[17]

In the midst of oppression, Georgia's blacks worked to develop their own institutions, improve their economic conditions, gain the right to vote, and educate their children. Blacks had long associated literacy with freedom and social advancement and thus persisted to vie for it. In 1866 a group of black leaders formed the Georgia Education Association, an association that encouraged the recently freed slaves to establish schools in their counties. Black Georgians of all ages were enthusiastic to secure an education and by 1867, 191 day schools and 45 night schools for blacks had been established in the state. Former slaves became a dynamic force in the movement for universal, publicly supported education.[18] Their efforts along with those of Northern "scalawags and carpetbaggers" were instrumental in the passage of the Georgia Constitution of 1877, which provided for publicly supported common schools. As W.E.B. DuBois noted,

> It is fair to say that the Negro carpetbag governments established the public schools of the South. Although recent researches have shown many germs of a public school system in the South before the war, there can be no reasonable doubt that common school instruction in the South, in the modern sense of the

term, was founded by the Freedmen's Bureau and missionary societies, and that the state public school system was formed mainly by Negro Reconstruction governments.[19]

Embroiled from its inception in the politics of race, the Georgia Constitution of 1877 provided for separate schools "for the white and colored races." Even so, whites continued to be suspicious of the institution that had its origins in Reconstruction politics. Battles over school funding in the first few years after passage of the law providing for public education were won by resistant whites who succeeded in suspending public school operations for several years.

The Constitution of 1877 allowed counties to establish a system of elementary or common schools, but forbade counties from levying a local tax to further support them or to extend the system to include secondary schools. These restrictions made Georgia, until 1920, the only state to bar the development of the state supported high school.[20] Lawmakers in 1872 were careful to put in place a protective clause that exempted five urban counties that had already established secondary schools from this restriction.[21] These city school systems—with relatively abundant wealth and the ability to tax on the local level—grew independently from the rest of the state. Changes in state law in 1889 and 1904 allowed for the establishment of independent school districts in other counties.

Under the law that supported independent school systems, Georgia's urban elites and small middle class established publicly supported white schooling from first grade to the university in cities and larger towns, but not in rural areas. Rural counties received a stipend from the state for common schooling, but were unable by law and reluctant by their cultural values to move beyond "an English education only" until the legislature allowed for establishment of high schools in 1911.[22]

Early Twentieth Century Public Schooling

Formal schooling throughout the state in the four decades bracketing 1900 was only a small and incidental part of child's life. As Benjamin Mays recalled, schooling "was not considered essential in those days, not even by or for whites."[23] The two-to-five month school term revolved around the cycle of the agricultural calendar. The masses of poor southern children of both races learned most of their lessons while working in the field or laboring in the mill.[24]

Roy V. Harris, who would later become one of the state's most powerful and influential political figures, grew up in rural Glascock County, Georgia, and began attending a public school in 1903. He went to a one-room field school for white children that met only a few months a year. Harris remembered, "School started late after the crops had been gathered and closed early at cotton chopping time." In 1907, after moving to a larger town that maintained "a complete grammar school and a high school," Harris recalled the schools "were still inadequate."[25]

Forty miles away, across the state line in rural Greenwood County, South Carolina, a dark-skinned boy named Benjamin Elijah Mays, who would grow up to become the president of Morehouse College in Atlanta, lived and worked on a forty-acre two-mule farm with his mother, father and seven brothers and sisters. The Mays family, like other families in the Black Belt, were sharecroppers. The family worked the land all year, picked cotton in the fall, and could count on a yearly pay off of $600 at market—about half the money it would take to make it through the year, and to pay for rent, food and clothing. Unlike Harris's town, Greenwood County had no high schools at the turn of the century for whites or blacks. Mays recalled going to an ungraded primary school for about four months during the winter, two months less than white children in the county.[26]

Willie Mae Wright recalled her school in Carroll County, Georgia, as "one big old room, made out of big logs. It had a big heater right in the middle of it, and all the boys had to tote firewood and pile it up in the back corner of the room. There was about fifty of us in that room," she recalled, "and classes went up to fourth grade." One teacher handled those fifty pupils and taught a smaller group of children in grades five, six, and seven in another wooden building nearby.[27] In the first two decades of the twentieth century, there were no public schools for blacks beyond grade seven in Carroll County, or for that matter in any other county in Georgia, save Clarke County. Rural blacks attended school for about four months during the winter, two months less than white children in the county. "It would never have occurred to the white people in charge of the schools that they should allow school to interfere with work on the farms," Benjamin Mays recalled.

The recollections of Harris, Mays, and Wright point out the incidental role of schooling in the Deep South well into the twentieth century. While Northern communities could boast of a full system of common schools in rural areas, graded "egg-crate" elementary schools, and high schools in urban areas, Georgia's "public" schools still charged tuition, met only a few months a year and lacked basic standards for teacher preparation. High schools for whites were established in a few independent districts and served only a few children, operating to protect race and class advantages. Elites and a small mobility-conscious middleclass gravitated to affluent independent district systems and roped off in-town attendance zones from the rest of the county. Here they levied a district-only property tax and maintained a public high school. With wealth concentrated in the districts and with the control of state law, elites skillfully extended their class advantages over poorer whites and blacks.[28] First, the ability to tax and spend only within district boundaries enabled in-town whites to prevent dilution of their investment across the county and concentrate state and local revenue on an unabridged grammar through college system of education for their own children. Because the law prohibited the counties from establishing institutes beyond the common schools, but allowed independent districts to maintain high schools at their discretion, this class of whites monopolized the only avenue to higher education.[29] Finally, by effecting law that excluded blacks and poor whites from district high schools, elites were able to maximize the *exchange value* of the high school credential. This guaranteed the scarcity of a high school diploma, and gave the children of elites a competitive advantage in the job market.[30]

The Black Struggle for Schooling

While poor rural whites often rejected formal schooling, Georgia's blacks saw it as a vehicle for upward mobility and social progress. Blacks hoped and whites feared that schooling would lead to equality between the races. White political support for black schooling was almost non-existent. Efforts to build and support blacks schools were frustrated by white responses that ranged from passive indifference to violent resistance.[31]

Between 1880 and 1936, behind the veil of segregation and in the face of enormous obstacles, black communities, with some help from northern philanthropy, established schools which succeeded in educating thousands of black children.[32] Schools outside of the Black Belt and in cities were the most successful. In 1912 Atlanta had eleven common schools which enrolled about half of the city's 10,000 school-age black children. In Augusta, Miss Lucy Laney's private Haines Institute taught 860 black grammar and high school pupils.[33] Attempting to quench the demand for literacy, black public school teachers in city schools often taught double shifts in overcrowded classrooms with as many as sixty children.

Booker T. Washington and Industrial Education

The rise of Booker T. Washington and his crusade for "industrial" public education for blacks represented a compromise between black hopes and white fears for education. Backed by a core of Southern elites and Northern philanthropists, Washington called for an education for blacks that would fit them for useful employment. He called on blacks to "cast down their buckets" and work with Southern businessmen and planters in ways that did not challenge political equality and segregation. Embracing the ethos of New South thinking, Washington called on whites and blacks to work together to move the South forward economically. His now well-known challenge to blacks in Atlanta in 1895 was "to earn a dollar in a factory," and till a field. "Our greatest danger," he argued will be if blacks forget they will "prosper in proportion as [they] learn to dignify and glorify common labor and put brains and skill into the common occupations."[34] Washington believed that hard work and the accumulation of property were the keys to resolving the problems of race and class. His was a liberal faith in social progress through the marketplace.[35]

Washington's strategy assumed there were gradual, linear, and chronological linkages between social efficiency, social mobility and democratic equality.[36] His strategy relied on a series of hypothesized causal relationships that social efficiency would lead to social mobility and ultimately democratic equality. Specifically, Washington believed that blacks must first establish themselves as reliable workers who could labor productively on the bottom of the socioeconomic pyramid for goals envisioned by New South leaders. He assumed that once their efficiency had been demonstrated region-wide, those blacks who showed merit could mobilize to improve their social and economic positions. From this "better class of blacks," individuals would be accepted to participate in the democratic process. The success of his strategy would depend on an enlightened governing class and economic leaders who would emerge from the racist oligarchy to assist these transitions. It was a strategy based on the assumption that whites would have no good reason to deny hard-working blacks a share of the economic and political power and privilege.

Washington's bottom-up, gradualist strategy depended on linkages that were either not there or failed to operate. Instead, Washington's ideas translated into an industrial education that fit hand-in-glove with what Southern leaders desired in terms of a white supremacist industrial economy. Industrial education by design prepared blacks for unskilled and semiskilled work as factory workers, laundresses, domestics, mechanics, and other jobs at the bottom of the social structure. Industrial education was schooling that met the goal of social efficiency, and accepted the existing political and social arrangements of power and privilege in Southern life. The road to economic self-sufficiency did not lead in a linear fashion to greater democratic equality.

With backing from many quarters, Washington's brand of industrial education emerged as the dominant publicly supported curriculum for blacks at all levels during the early twentieth century. To be sure, there were schools and colleges that rejected Washington's "Hampton-Tuskegee" model and educated hundreds of blacks in a more traditional or classical curriculum, but these institutions were generally cut off from Northern philanthropy and state allotments, and thus had to rely on precious few resources from the black communities where they were centered.[37]

Even the industrial education model did not garner sufficient public support. Opportunities for any schooling were limited. In 1914, the state only had one four-year public high school for blacks located in Athens.[38] During the school campaigns in the progressive period and 1920s, white dominated local school boards provided expanded school opportunities for white children, while limiting those for black children.[39] Despite pleas for more equitable funding, the vast majority of counties made no expenditures for Negro schools except for salaries of teachers, which were well below those offered to white teachers. Consequently, many blacks held classes in churches, cabins, barns, or abandoned houses with very little in the way of chairs, benches, or desks. Reporting on the conditions of black common schooling in 1927, one observer wrote that more than one-half of Georgia's "colored children are taught in churches, lodges and dwellings." Many of the structures were old, unheated, poorly lit, one-teacher schools, with "plank benches which sometimes have no backs." The facilities, she concluded, were "unfit for teaching purposes." A meager stipend from the state supplemented by fund-raising in the black community paid teachers salaries, which was often "as low as $15 per month," plus "ten and fifteen cents per pupil, which is paid by the patrons." In 1924 local county boards of education owned 2,876 white schools worth $11 million and 961 black schools worth $1 million. Meanwhile, philanthropy and black communities themselves established another 1,687 schools in the state.[40]

By 1924 roughly 68 percent of all black children of common school age were estimated to be enrolled in a common school. Only in a few of these schools did the school term extend more than six months. In most rural areas black schools lasted only four months and instruction rarely went beyond grade five.[41]

County elites and superintendents often rationalized unequal disbursement, reasoning that black schools received financial assistance from Northern philanthropic organizations like the General Education Board, Rosenwald, and Jeanes Funds. This was disingenuous, as outside funding provided only a fraction of the total expenditure on black schooling. Negro schools throughout the South, had precious few textbooks and supplies, no libraries or transportation, offered no lunches, employed no janitors, and were usually heated only by wood. In 1929 nine Georgia counties had no black schools at all, and only a handful had high schools.[42] That year the state Director of the Division of Negro Education estimated an average of $10.26 spent on educating each black student, while $42.64 was spent on each white student.[43]

Disparities were most apparent in the black belt, where low numbers of wealthy whites lived among numerous poor blacks. The state school fund was apportioned in accordance to the reported number of school-age children, regardless of race, but left to the discretion of the local officials how the money would be used. Wealthy whites, often the grandchildren of antebellum planters, used the state funds for white schools at a rate several times that used for black schools. In 1910, for example, whites in the Georgia Black Belt spent only $1.61 for each child compared to $19.23 spent on each white child.[44]

Elites in the Black Belt and in other counties with high percentages of blacks, maintained their stronghold on school governance, and invoked policies that greatly favored white school children, white teachers, white children's school buildings and facilities, including libraries. Some went so far as to discourage black and poor white children from attending school in order to better serve more affluent whites who were enrolled.[45] In 1905 the value of school houses for whites was estimated at $4 million, while the black school houses were worth $585,000. As one observer wrote in 1925, many whites "would not even permit [blacks] to be educated; others think they should be given the kind of education that would make them economically efficient."[46] No voice in the white community advocated an education for black democratic equality and social mobility.

Schoolmen and Other Reformers

With class and race mobility paralyzed, state-level school reformers sought to centralize their administrative power over county systems. In the first third of the twentieth century, state school commissioners and governors called for adequate publicly supported schooling for blacks and poor whites. Grounding their argument in white supremacist ideology and the New South vision, reformers asserted that the right type of education for Georgia's blacks would improve the quality of life for all Southerners and not threaten the social order.

For Marion L. Brittain, who served as State Commissioner from 1910 to 1922, the major obstacle to bringing efficiency to the state and humanitarianism in the form of industrial education to blacks and poor whites was the decentralized politics of Georgia's common school system. Brittain, a quintessential schoolman in pursuit of the "one best system," favored the election of the county board by "popular vote," but urged the legislature to allow county boards to appoint the superintendent.[47] He thought that the law requiring the election of county superintendents "dragged the head of the county school into politics" and denied rural children "the right to get the best county school superintendents possible."[48]

Local politics, controlled by elites, hindered what Brittain considered to be progress along the educational path. To remedy self-interest driven localism, Brittain sought to insulate superintendents from the voting population by making them accountable only to the elected board. Brittain worked for a shift in power from local elites to an cadre of expert schoolmen. Brittain envisioned the schoolmen, as if following a calling from God, evangelically pushing forward for the good of all.

As part of the effort, then, these schoolmen, needed to share a common philosophy, develop and share strategies to subdue skeptics, and find the means to support each other in their quest for the "one-best system." In short, the situation required schoolmen to be professionally affiliated and organized so that school reform might be expertly and scientifically managed. This, Brittain felt, would lessen the grip of self-interests fostered by local politics, and thus begin a process of extracting the school from politics.

Nevertheless, Georgia's school reformers, operating within the context of Jim Crow and the New South Creed, adopted very modest goals for improvement in education for blacks and poor whites. Schooling for citizenship was a radical idea, so extreme, indeed, that most public discussions left out its mention. The few times that it was considered publicly, it was tagged on at the end of a closing sentence, and took the form of abstract dogma not unlike scripture about the afterlife. A liberal education, such as the one that DuBois had argued for in his "talented tenth" proposal was unthinkable. At the turn of the century Allen D. Candler, the two-time Governor of Georgia viewed political power in the hands of blacks as "a constant menace" that "tainted society." Candler opposed higher education for blacks, asserting, "He should be taught the trades, but when he is taught the fine arts, he is educated above his caste and this makes him unhappy."[49]

White reformers called for better funding of the Hampton-Tuskegee model of industrial education. A succession of nine state school commissioners from 1895 to 1958 asked local superintendents and legislators not for racial impartiality but rather for "better treatment for the colored race." Georgia's state school leaders pleaded for "justice and common sense" for blacks. Uplift meant not equality or the end of oppression, but compassion for blacks, which took the form of a religious paternalism. "Let us adapt our program to the needs of the people," wrote State Commissioner Gustavus R. Glenn in 1898, "and above all things let us give them that industrial education which will prepare them to be self-supporting citizens."[50] They typically justified public support for black education in economic terms. "As long as the Negro remains in ignorance," reported Glenn in 1895, "he is a standing menace to everything we hold dear."[51] Glenn's call for improved education for blacks exemplified the racist beliefs of the paternalistic school reformers.

By nature he is impulsive, sympathetic, emotional, and easily excited; he is instinctively loyal and generous. If the good qualities of his head and heart are wisely directed by proper educational processes he can become a most powerful factor in aiding the Southern people to work out their great industrial problem. It is a great mistake to assume that education hurts the colored man and unfits him for service. I believe the time has now come to add industrial features to our school system. The colored people especially need a system of education that will increase their industrial usefulness.[52]

In spite of rhetoric about training for blacks, few progressive boosters of industrial education were inclined to embrace equipping Georgia's blacks with definite trade skills and technical know-how. That brand of vocational training, as we will see, was reserved for the white masses. Industrial education, then, meant first and foremost instructing blacks to be self-sufficient at the bottom of the social order and to be deferential to white authority. Moreover, it meant socializing blacks so that they would be competent, hardworking, and responsible workers, satisfied with their position at the bottom of the social order.

From this vantage point, industrial education needed very little in the way of resources and equipment. It meant obedience, punctuality, thrift, and accommodation to "superior" and "more intelligent" whites who had set forth their vision of regional progress. Far from the state-of-the-art agricultural, trade, and business skills education that was envisioned for rural whites, black industrial education would instill a neo-slave-style discipline and healthy habits of living. As part of the curriculum blacks would learn primitive and intermediate "technologies" such as gardening, domestic work, basket-weaving, canning, and homemaking. The curriculum would also provide lessons on sanitation, personal hygiene, and disease prevention. Finally, industrial education would instill in them the value of property, and teach them take pride in and improve the physical appearance of their schools, homes, and communities. Rather than a curriculum designed for economic and political empowerment or social mobility, industrial education aimed to lift the Negro in ways that would diminish the economic and cultural drag he supposedly placed on the South. The essence of the program would be on the development of habits consistent with the New South vision.[53]

Notwithstanding the modest pleas of governors and progressive school leaders, whites in general were insulted by the desire of blacks to secure literacy, and incensed by those who sought a liberal education. If whites were to support any type of black schooling, it would have to, as a prerequisite, accept and promote white supremacy in both form and function. The most obvious goal would be to improve social efficiency and its design would have to limit the mobility of blacks. In short, it would have to be a curriculum congruent with the existing social order.

The Power of Migration

Blacks held at the bottom of the social order—by disfranchisement, undereducation, segregation, malnutrition, and more brutal forms of oppression, such as lynchings and beatings—realized that safety and economic opportunity might come about if they voted with their feet. Although Georgia's population increased from 2.2 million in 1900 to 3.1 million in 1940 (due in large part to high birthrates), its black population as a percentage of the total shrank from 46.7 percent to 34.7 percent over the same period. In search of safety and survival more than social mobility, blacks migrated in record numbers to urban areas in the region and then to the North and Midwest. Between 1915 and 1918 more than 60,000 black Georgians, frustrated by their economic circumstances, and attacked by whites, left their homes in Georgia. Another 135,000 left between 1920 and 1930. By 1950, nearly half of all Southern blacks were living in or near cities. In Georgia, between 1940 and 1950, there was a 29 percent decrease in the percentage of black farmers and a 23 percent increase of blacks in urban areas.[54]

Migration out of the region in the early twentieth century became so acute that many Georgia industrialists and businessmen realized labor shortages would result, causing not only short-term financial loss, but also collapse of the New South vision. Commerce officials warned that one out of every five labor-intensive jobs was unfilled in 1917. That year an Atlanta fertilizer company was forced to cut production after it lost more than two-thirds of its black labor force.[55] The flight of poor whites, only one notch above blacks on the socioeconomic scale,[56] only added to the concerns of businessmen and industrialists. New South advocates joined with the press, state and local governmental officials and myriad organizations, in determined but only marginally successful efforts to stem the flight of labor.[57] The alarm was accompanied by the formation of several indigenous biracial organizations, such as the Atlanta-based Commission on Interracial Cooperation (CIC), founded in 1919, and its affiliate, the Association of Southern Women for the Prevention of Lynching (ASWPL). These groups organized moderate and liberal middle-class Georgians who were opposed to the more brutal forms of racial oppression. Motivated by an abhorrence of violence, these groups set the pattern for future race-moderate organizations.

Businessmen and politicians had earlier turned the other way when white-on-black violence erupted. But with the demise of the cotton crop in the 1920s because of boll weevil infestation and the flight of the region's labor surplus, New South advocates realized that business interests were in jeopardy. The mob-bug-labor triad put the plans for progress and prosperity envisioned by New South leaders at risk. They began to consider changing their laissez-faire attitude about lynching and their policy of keeping wages and taxes low at all costs. Driven by self-interest, they warned would-be migrants that the North was no promised land, and assured them better wages, fairer treatment and improved schools. As historian Donald Grant accurately concluded, "Coercion had failed, so worried businessmen and planters turned to conciliation and persuasion in an effort to stem the migration."[58] Between 1910 and 1918 average wages (including room and board) for Georgia black farmhands rose from $18.00 a month to $32.60 a month, while white wages throughout the South doubled.[59]

Actions taken by Governor Hugh Dorsey illustrate how the effort to restrain migration aided school reform. Elected in 1917, the business-friendly Dorsey became an outspoken critic of violence against blacks.[60] During his campaign Dorsey pledged to improve public schooling in the state, and after his election he met with an interracial group of community, state and federal leaders to discuss Georgia's impending labor shortage.[61] Black leaders petitioned Dorsey to improve black schooling, put more blacks in positions of power in state government, raise black wages, and curb white-on-black violence that had not diminished since the Atlanta riot of 1906.

In July of 1919, with school reform legislation pending, black community leaders again pressured Dorsey and other state officials, requesting higher teachers salaries, longer school terms, new buildings, a state-supported normal school for blacks, more agricultural schools, more equitable funding for black schools, appointment of a black state supervisor, and appropriations for summer teacher training. Responding to school reformers, blacks, and business interests, Dorsey's administration took action in 1919 and pushed through the legislature the Elders-Carswell Bill and Barrett-Rogers Act, legislation that called for a new school code, six months attendance, and enforcement of the three-year-old compulsory attendance law.[62] The laws also provided for the levy of local taxes to operate and maintain schools, the issuance of schoolhouse bonds, defined the duties of local boards of education, and placed budgetary responsibilities on state and local officials. The legislation also set up grants for consolidation, lifted the ban on transportation, and gave the power to license teachers to the state board of education.[63] As a result, the state school fund jumped from $9.3 million in 1919 to nearly $12 million in 1920 and had increased by another 5.3 million dollars by 1921.

In 1921, Governor Hugh Dorsey continued to call for an end to lynching, mob violence, individual acts of cruelty and peonage and resolved to tighten laws and punish offenders. "In some counties the negro [sic] is being driven out like a wild beast," he declared in a widely circulated pamphlet. "In others he is being held like a slave. In others no negroes [sic] remain." He also called for higher pay and better schools for whites and blacks, promising to enforce compulsory school attendance laws and to encourage interracial cooperation.[64] Still, Dorsey and state educators were unable to articulate a cogent argument to challenge the way in which the money was spent at the local level. The 1919 legislation continued the practice of apportioning the state school fund to counties on the basis of their entire school-age population and allowed county authorities to divide and supplement the fund as they desired. This arrangement gave white county authorities the flexibility to spend school funds in ways that primarily benefitted white schools.

While Dorsey's determination to do away with violent forms of black oppression has been documented and celebrated, it could be argued that the real issue that concerned him was the loss of the state's abundant labor supply to the North and West. The crusade against lynching, adjustment of wages, and school reform in the 1920s perhaps did not come about solely because of white altruism or the evangelist efforts of school reformers. The move away from brutal oppression came about in part because the industrialists and other elites found it necessary to make concessions to continue to realize profits.

Resistance and Accommodation: Lessons in Black Schools

Caught in the midst of the politics of race and schooling were the black teachers and students. The black teacher, in preparing her pupils, mediated a socialization process that both reinforced and resisted the caste system. The message teetered back and forth between accepting the social structure and one's place in it, to softening it so as to allow for increased individual mobility. The school, through its teachers, parents and community, connected and redefined the values of industry, self-sufficiency, individualism, religious piety, and localism. Black educators demanded that their pupils be punctual, obedient, well-groomed, efficient and frugal, and refrain from dancing, gambling, profanity and alcohol.[65]

This focus on industry fit nicely with the New South's push for social efficiency and seemed like a logical and reasonable curriculum to offer to black students. Even in private schools, teachers may have perpetuated black subservience to white interests. Lucy Laney and Beulah Rucker Oliver were two women who directed private schools for black children. Like many black schoolteachers, Laney and Oliver were strict disciplinarians and known for employing corporal punishment when children "rocked the boat." Lifting the rod served as both a warning and promise of more severe physical retribution to come if the child failed to understand his or her "place" in the social order.

While preparing their charges to bow to authority helped to assure the children's immediate survival in the existing social order, it did little to prepare them for long-term self-empowerment. Corporal punishment, doled out by some parents and teachers like Oliver and Laney, was no doubt a form of "tough love." "Mama would always visualize some awful things when you got out of line," Oliver's daughter recalled, and take you "all the way to prison."[66]

"I'm whipping you because I love you," assured Oliver, and "I don't want somebody else to have to do it."[67]

Still, these whippings reinforced the greater circumscriptions of obedience and servility and thus served to advance the long-term interests of white elites disproportionately to and sometimes against the interests of the masses.

On the other hand, certain aspects of the school-community milieu threatened the social order. Notwithstanding the corporal discipline system, Lucy Laney's Haines Institute, offered a somewhat classical schooling in addition to industrial training. Rucker's pupils studied black heroes. These lessons were more likely to arouse a democratic worldview that questioned systems of authority and power. The school's reinforcement of the church's support of equality among men, classical features of the school curriculum, and the study of black heroes and accomplishments, entertained possibilities of a different social order, some of which could combine with other forces to challenge the political and economic power of elites. Further, teachers often emerged as distinguished leaders in the community and helped their young charges acquire not only literacy and numeracy but also self-confidence and direction.

In other communities, however, white county elites and all-white school boards, with control over the state allotment, chose who taught in the black public schools. It was not uncommon for the most able teachers to be bypassed as some county patricians did not want good black teachers. The "colored teacher," reported Myra Logan in 1927, "is often selected by some influential white man in the community from among poorly prepared Negroes who have worked for him."[68] This situation often led to abysmal instruction that by design and tradition mis-served black students. Thus, black schools and teachers could serve either to reinforce or challenge the existing power relations. Sometimes they did both.

The Jeanes Fund

Black teachers rarely received regular publicly supported supervision. At the county level, superintendents usually ignored blacks schools. The state's white teacher-supervisors also concentrated their time and energies on white schools. Black schools did not appear to "enter into the minds" of Georgia's white state or local educators.[69] The quality of schooling offered in the isolated, rural black schools was uneven at best.

In 1908, the Jeanes Foundation, a Northern philanthropic organization, began a campaign to change the situation. The fund provided money to hire teacher-supervisors for black, rural schools. Jeanes teachers, with few exceptions, were Southern black women with experience in the industrial training model. Jeanes teachers, under direction of the state agent, but subordinate to the county superintendent, were charged with entering black rural schoolrooms and introducing lessons on simple home industries and economics, sanitation, personal cleanliness, and gardening. Jeanes teachers also supervised rural teachers, and assisted county officials with reports on attendance, and the care of school buildings and property. Although the General Education Board assumed responsibility for paying the salary of Jeanes teachers, county superintendents oversaw their work.[70] Jeanes teachers were paid at a better rate than a regular teacher and carried considerable prestige in the black community, factors that led reactionary whites, including some county superintendents, to oppose the program.

Key support for the program came from the Georgia Department of Education. The Department established the Division of Negro Education, which employed a state agent to direct and organize black schooling state-wide. Instructed by the State Department of Education to work in the "best interests of the Negroes," through the emphasis of "instruction in hygiene, manual and domestic science, and agriculture," the state agent became the liaison for county and state schoolmen and philanthropic foundations, and emerged as the critical link to public funding for black schools.[71] Georgia's state agents were white, progressive middle-class men.

Progressives favored the addition of Jeanes teacher-supervisors as a method for improving black instruction. Jeanes teachers were carefully chosen based on their abilities to recognize the "deficiency in training and cultural attainment of the average Negro teacher"[72] and to sympathize with blacks' "backward rural conditions."[73] One extension teacher who worked in three communities wrote of "reorganizing the cooking and sewing classes and the Improvement League." Another Jeanes supervisor, who taught in a different school every two to three days, won praise from her county superintendent for teaching "plain sewing and basketry."[74] Another county supervisor in the Black Belt reported that the Jeanes teacher had organized industrial clubs in ten schools where the children are "making mats from shucks, rag rugs, pillows, pine-needle baskets, [and] spreads," and converted "a shed of a room" into a kitchen to house a cooking class. Jeanes teachers often raised money from within the rural black community for new schools. They also inspired teachers and students "to make our schools the most attractive places in the county."[75]

In her work, the Jeanes supervisor drew attention to the black educational effort. Notwithstanding its improvement of the black community's level of literacy and health, the Jeanes program by design reflected the county elites' goal of efficiency and theme of white supremacy. Supervisors not only focused on pedagogy, rudimentary health and industrial training but also penetrated the black community and aroused interest in their programs. Once there they solicited money, resources, and labor for black schooling to supplement and offset the contributions made by the Jeanes Fund and the state. In this arrangement, the Jeanes supervisors served not only as mentors, master teachers, and community organizers, but also as agents of reinforcement for the social, economic, and racial status quo. Jeanes teachers could and did, at times, foster the more radical goals of softening or destabilizing the social order, but did so covertly and at great peril.[76]

The Rise of Vocational Education:
A Conservative Move for Social Efficiency

In the 1920s and 1930s, school leaders in Georgia began to promote the expansion of vocational education. Providing vocational training in the public school, they argued, would produce better workers, increase the state's agricultural production, and augment the campaign for new business and industry. School leaders promoted the expansion of a vocational curriculum for white schools only that was superior to the industrial education provided in the black schools.

The state superintendent's 1920 Annual School Report in Georgia is typical of the reports filed in the 1920 and 1930s. It reveals a commitment in vocational education for white children and continued "praise" but little in the way of funding for black industrial education. The report cited the establishment of nearly 50 schools for wagon repair, blacksmithing, carpentry, textiles, dressmaking, machine shop, shoemaking, cooking, weaving, spinning, auto engines, locomotive assembly, and electricity.[77] By 1930, the Georgia state school superintendent bragged that no state in the union, save Texas, had more people in vocational classes.[78]

Training for the vocations fit nicely with upper-income farmers' worldview on race and class as well as the New South's goal of social efficiency. As well-to-do planters considered mechanizing their farms, they envisioned a small cadre of reliable and responsible workers to operate their expensive machinery. This work would "draw a white man's pay."[79] Southern industrialists wanted an abundant supply of semiskilled workers competing for jobs. A labor surplus would keep wages down and discourage unions from taking hold. For both groups vocational education was consistent with realizing greater profits. At the same time, it put poor whites just one notch above blacks in social position and thus maintained the region's tradition of white privilege.

To be sure, poverty among rural whites was pervasive throughout the state and region, and training in the vocations was seen as a benevolent means for increasing self-sufficiency and social betterment. State Superintendent Mauney Douglass (M.D.) Collins supported a progressive curriculum that featured vocational education, health and physical education, home economics and art and music appreciation.[80] Collins, a devout Baptist and dedicated schoolman with rural roots, approached the job of schooling the New South with a populist bent.[81] Elected to office in 1933, Collins was aware of the campaign for new industry, the strength and conviction of New South advocates, and their desire for, among other things, efficiency, with which he agreed. Collins, however, also wanted to extend schooling to Georgia's rural white children and to offer them a chance for a better quality of life, even if it meant more spending more money on schools and teachers, and consequently more taxes.[82]

For Collins vocational education and a progressive curriculum that offered instruction in nutrition and hygiene, physical education, and home economics held the key to a better quality of life for Georgia's rural folks. At the start, Collins foresaw not so much an improved social standing for rural whites but a healthier and more productive life. The state's poor county folk had survived tenant farming, the boll weevil, mill work, and the Depression. The region was still plagued by poverty, malnutrition, pellagra, hookworm, and rickets. At its inception, vocational education was designed not to provide rural whites with a chance to climb the social ladder—where they might attain more money, power and status—but instead to provide an upgraded, modernized life that kept pace with the technological, economic and structural changes. Advocates of vocational training and progressive education in the South promised more economic security, better family and community relations, better health, and more a productive use of leisure.

Collins' efforts to expand the practical curriculum coincided nicely with a nationwide school campaign of the day, and gave his school crusade a progressive twist. In the 1920s and 1930s many states had turned to "foundation" programs that sought to remedy funding disparities among districts. Since the property tax was the primary means of funding schools, uneven property values resulted in far better schools in the cities than in rural areas. Collins was active in the National Education Association, and his regular contact with like-minded schoolmen across the country outfitted him with a rhetoric of equality and efficiency and cemented his commitment to equalization. One of his many slogans was "equal educational opportunity for all the children of all the people."

Collins understood the connection between better schools and teacher salaries; they went together as he saw it, "like grits and gravy." In the mid-1930s he recommended "the equalization of educational opportunities for all the children of the state through a system of schools which is more adequately supported by state funds." Increased involvement by the state, he asserted, would lessen the difficulty of support "from the over-burdened local units"[83] He called for new legislation for schools, asserting that "legislation, like a woman's hat, becomes out of style,"[84] and argued that Georgia had some of the best schools in the country, but also some of the poorest. "We need an educational program largely supported by the state so that every child in Georgia may be guaranteed a minimum school term, a well qualified teacher and a social atmosphere conducive to happiness, character training, love for home, church, school and native land." Collins called on "school people and lay groups" to "work together in planning programs of education that will improve the quality of living in Georgia."[85]

In calling for improved educational opportunities, Collins stressed geographical but not racial disparities. All of Georgia's children, *"no matter where they live,"* he argued, should be given an equal educational opportunity. His goals were inclusive of the rural poor and a noticeable improvement from earlier school policy in their promises to upgrade the condition of rural life. At the core, however, they were consistent with past school reforms in maintaining white advantage. His administration persisted in short-changing black students, particularly those of high school age.[86]

His real challenge was to find ways for poor Georgians to tread water during the Depression without offending the political elites or challenging planters and industrialists, with their profits-at-all-costs motives.[87] Collins's solution called for modernizing and upgrading public school vocational training. All secondary schools, he argued, should offer vocational work, and teachers should be prepared and competent not only in helping school-age children acquire practical job-related skills but also in "helping adults to study the economic life of the community to discover how better economic values can be realized." Reminiscent of the New South slogan "Expenditures Produce Prosperity," Collins adopted the slogan "Education doesn't cost, it pays."[88]

By 1937 the school campaign in Georgia began to bear fruit. The state legislature passed an act that required a seven month school term, provided free textbooks (to white children), created a state board of education, and significantly expanded programs in vocational education. Over the next decade, as high school enrollments in the state increased by 32 percent, secondary instruction in agriculture, food processing, home economics, and "distributive education" more than doubled. Trade and industrial education blossomed in the period, as secondary schools instituted joint efforts with local businesses and industries to "individualize" instruction for each "student's chosen occupation." On the eve of U.S. involvement in World War II, roughly 34 percent of all the South's high school students were in vocational tracks.[89]

Under segregation, Southern high schools funded vocational instruction for whites at nearly twice the rate as for blacks. The few black public high schools which had the means to create vocational tracks were restricted to the least prestigious programs. When a middle track in business education emerged in the 1930s (called "distributive education," which included study in merchandising, personnel administration, and business management), whites were seven times more likely to be enrolled than blacks.[90]

On several counts, vocational education was a necessary and welcomed, if limited, contribution to the public good. Although it could do little for displaced tenant farmers, it was of some value to their children.[91] Skills learned in the vocational tracks helped the sons, daughters, and grandchildren of sharecroppers and millworkers and the growing numbers of poor migrating to urban areas with transitions into a new labor market. Progressive educators hailed it for its capacity to "meet the needs of the child." In the opinion of middle-class reformers, training in the vocations was more desirable than uninterrupted day or night labor in the field or mill. Northern industrialists, who found allies in these reformers, applauded its removal of youngsters from the mills, not for humanitarian reasons, but for its impact on their competitors' labor costs. And local political and economic power brokers, who sought to mechanize their farms or attract new industry to the South, came to realize and appreciate the economic value of healthier and better-trained workers.

Still, it was a curriculum that reflected the politics of privilege of rich over poor and white over black. Vocational education and the progressive curriculum promised very little in changing the traditional distribution of wealth or power, or offering much in the way of mobility to Georgia's forgotten black and poor white children. Notwithstanding the democratic rhetoric of "personal choice," and "meeting the needs of the child," the vocational and progressive programs worked against open access to a common curriculum and preparation for the political process. By differentiating the curriculum and directing poor children toward the world of work, school programs mirrored the economic and racial stratification of Southern society, and gave whites an advantage in competing with blacks for work in farming, industry and semiskilled trades.

Notes

1. Gunnar Myrdal, *An American Dilemma: The Negro Problem in Modern Democracy*, 20th Anniversary ed., 1966 (New York: Harper Row, 1944), 902; Benjamin Fine, quoted in *Atlanta Journal*, 6 December 1946, 11; also, see *Atlanta Journal* 15 December 1946, 1-B.

2. James C. Cobb, *Industrialization and Southern Society, 1877-1984* (Louisville: University of Kentucky Press, 1985); Paul M. Gaston, *The New South Creed: A Study in Southern Mythmaking* (Baton Rouge: Louisiana State University Press, 1970).

3.Charles E. Wynes, "Postwar Economic Development," in Kenneth Coleman, ed., *A History of Georgia*, 2nd ed. (Athens: University of Georgia Press, 1991), 225-38.

4. Quoted from James C. Cobb, *The Selling of the South: The Southern Crusade for Industrial Development, 1936-1980* (Baton Rouge: Louisiana State University Press, 1982), 3. See also Wilbur J. Cash, *The Mind of the South*, (New York: Knopf, 1941), 149; Wynes, "Postwar Economic Development," 231.

5. For discussions of Southern politics during this era, see, generally, C. Vann Woodward, *Origins of the New South*, 1877-1913 (Baton Rouge: Louisiana State University Press, 1971); George B. Tindall, *The Emergence of the New South, 1913-1946* (Baton Rouge: Louisiana State University Press, 1967); Dewey Grantham, *The South in Modern America: A Region at Odds*, (New York: HarperCollins, 1994), 1-133; John W. Cell, *The Highest State of White Supremacy* (New York: Cambridge University Press, 1987), 103-154. For more on the county unit system and Georgia politics, see V. O. Key, Jr., *Southern Politics in State and Nation* (New York: Knopf, 1949) 106-129; John Dittmer, *Black Georgia in the Progressive Era, 1900-1920* (Urbana: University of Illinois Press, 1977); Donald L. Grant, *The Way It Was in the South, The Black Experience in Georgia* (New York: Birch Lane Press, 1993), 206-339.

6. John Hammond Moore, "Jim Crow in Georgia," *South Atlantic Quarterly* 66 (Autumn 1967), 554-565; *Plessy v. Ferguson*, 163 U.S. 537 (1896); *Brown v. Board of Education*, 347 U.S. 483 (1954).

7. In 1870, the Georgia legislature passed "An Act to Establish a System of Public Instruction." The law provided for a state school commissioner, a state board of education and 136 county boards of education. State laws establishing separate-but-equal public schools were included in the Act of 1870 and then again in the State Constitution of 1877. Acts and Resolutions of the General Assembly of the State of Georgia, Session of 1870, Title VI, Section 32, Paragraph I; State Constitution of 1877, Article VIII, Section I, Paragraph I; Robert H. Hall, "Segregation in the Public Schools of Georgia," *Georgia Bar Journal* 16 (May 1954), 421-26; Lawrence R. Hepburn, *Contemporary Georgia*, ed., (Athens: Carl Vinson Institute of Government, 1987), 176; Dorothy Orr, *A History of Education in Georgia* (Chapel Hill: University of North Carolina Press, 1950), 184-203.

8. Prior to the Civil War and the passage of the Thirteenth, Fourteenth and Fifteenth Amendments to the U.S. Constitution, the validity of segregated public education had been upheld in a Massachusetts case, *Roberts v. City of Boston*, 5 Cushing Reports, (1849). Richard Kluger, *Simple Justice* (New York: Vintage, 1977), 74-5. For more on Jim Crow segregation in the North and its move to the South, see C. Vann Woodward, *The Strange Career of Jim Crow* 3rd. ed., (New York: Oxford, 1974); Moore, "Jim Crow in Georgia."

9. *Cumming v. Richmond County Board of Education* 175 U.S. 528 (1899); Louis R. Harlan, *Separate and Unequal: Public School Campaigns and Racism in the Southern Seaboard States, 1901-1915* (New York: Atheneum, 1969), 213; Kluger, *Simple Justice*, 83.

10. C. Vann Woodward, *The Strange Career of Jim Crow*, 69; W.E.B. DuBois, *Black Reconstruction in America* (New York: Atheneum, 1992), 487-525.

11. Orr, *History of Education*, 80-81.

12. Claude Purcell, "Introduction," in Oscar H. Joiner, ed., *A History of Public Education in Georgia 1834-1976* (Columbia, SC: R. L. Bryan, 1979), x, 25; Orr, *History of Education*, 78-80.

13. Grant, *The Way It Was*, 49, 60-61.

14. Grant, *The Way It Was*, 62.

15. Grant, *The Way It Was*, 53, 61-64.

16. DuBois, *Black Reconstruction in America*, 646.

17. Professor Vashon, quoted in "Legal Status of the Colored Population in Respect to Schools and Education: Schools for Blacks in Georgia." Reprinted in U.S. Office of Education, *The History of Schools for the Colored Population* (New York: Arno Press and the New York Times, 1969), 340-341.

18. Molly Townes O'Brien, "Private School Tuition Vouchers and the Realities of Racial Politics," 64 *Tennessee Law Review* (Winter 1997), 1295.

19. DuBois, *Black Reconstruction in America*, 664.

20. Orr, *History of Education*, 260, 265.

21. Atlanta, Savannah, Augusta, Macon, and Brunswick were located in the exempted counties.

22. Joiner, *Public Education*, 193.

23. Benjamin E. Mays, *Born to Rebel* (Athens: University of Georgia Press, 1971), 3.

24. James L. Leloudis, *Schooling the New South: Pedagogy, Self and Society in North Carolina 1880-1920* (Chapel Hill: University of North Carolina Press, 1996), 230-31.

25. *Augusta Courier*, 9 September 1949, 2; *Augusta Courier*, 29 September 1949, 1.

26. Mays, *Born to Rebel*, 3-5. The term "Black Belt" refers to rural areas in the deep South where rich soil allowed land owners to cultivate cotton, tobacco, and other cash crops. To plant, tend, harvest, and bring the crops to market for profit, cheap labor was required. Consequently, the Black Belt was typically populated by large numbers of poor blacks and a few wealthy white landowners.

27. Elizabeth Kytle, *Willie Mae* (McClean, VA: EPM Publishers, 1958, reprinted in 1991), 16.

28. "Since the Constitutional Convention of 1877," griped state Superintendent M. L. Brittain "we have suffered from parsimonious tax laws. Nearly all states permit and most require the local communities to do something or else refuse the advantages of state funds

intended to equalize conditions. Our Constitution does not only not do this, but penalizes progress in this direction by not even permitting counties to tax themselves..." Brittain, as quoted in Hines Lafayette Hill, "Negro Education in Rural Georgia," (Masters Thesis: Emory University, 1939), 42.

29. For a description of a wealthy, white independent system, see Haygood S. Bowden, *Two Hundred Years of Education, 1733-1933: Savannah, Chatham County, Georgia* (Richmond: Dietz, 1932), 251-381.

30. David F. Labaree, "Public Good, Private Goods: The Struggle Over Educational Goals," *American Educational Research Journal* 34 (Spring 1997), 53-57; Orr, 176-77, 219, 227, 250; Joiner, 216, 223.

31. James D. Anderson, *The Education of Blacks in the South, 1860-1935* (Chapel Hill: University of North Carolina Press, 1988); Donald Spivey, *Schooling for the New Slavery: Black Industrial Education, 1868-1915* (Westport, CT: Greenwood Press, 1978); Harlan, *Separate and Unequal*; John Dittmer, *Black Georgia in the Progressive Era, 1900-1920* (Urbana: University of Illinois Press, 1977).

32. Dittmer, *Black Georgia*, xi.

33. Grant, *The Way It Was*, 231; Dittmer, *Black Georgia*.

34. Booker T. Washington, as quoted in Joseph Newman, *America's Teachers,* 2nd ed. (White Plains, NY: Longman, 1994), 160-61.

35. Steven E. Tozer, Paul C. Violas and Guy Senese, *School and Society: Educational Practice as Social Expression* (New York: McGraw Hill 1993), 84-101.

36. These terms come from the framework developed by David F. Labaree. See David F. Labaree, *How to Succeed in School without Really Learning* (New Haven, CT: Yale University Press, 1997), 15-52.

37. Willard Range, *The Rise and Progress of Negro Colleges in Georgia, 1865-1949* (Athens, GA: University of Georgia Press, 1951), 66-91; William Link, *The Paradox of Southern Progressivism* (Chapel Hill: University of North Carolina Press, 1992), *243-247;* Louis R. Harlan, *Booker T. Washington, The Wizard of Tuskegee* (New York: Oxford University Press, 1983), 33, 129. See generally James D. Anderson, *The Education of Blacks in the South.*

38. Coleman, *A History of Georgia*, 325.

39. Harlan, *Separate and Unequal*; Dittmer, *Black Georgia*. Dittmer writes that while schooling for blacks was thwarted at every turn, "one is impressed not so much by its shortcomings as by its achievement against overwhelming odds." Ibid. at 162.

40. Myra Logan, "Negro Education in Georgia," *Atlanta University Bulletin*, February 1927, 7.

41. Logan, "Negro Education in Georgia," 7. See also Hines Lafayette Hill, "Negro Education in Rural Georgia," (Masters Thesis: Emory University, 1939), 53.

42. 60th and 61st Annual Reports of the State Superintendent to the General Assembly. See, generally, Anderson, *The Education of Blacks in the South.*

43. Disparities of the same magnitude continued well into the 1930s and 1940s. Seventy-Sixth and Seventy-Seventh Annual Reports of the Department of Education to the General Assembly of the State of Georgia.

44. Dittmer, *Black Georgia,* 143.

45. Hill, "Negro Education in Rural Georgia," 43.

46. Paul L. Haworth, The United States in Our Time, 1865-1924 (New York: Scribner, 1925), 536.

47. Brittain's goals fit within a national trend toward removing power over schooling from political figures and placing it in the hands of professional school administrators. See, generally, David Tyack, One Best System (Cambridge, MA: Harvard University Press, 1974); Raymond E. Callahan, Education and the Cult of Efficiency: A Study of the Social Forces that Have Shaped the Administration of the Public Schools (Chicago: University of Chicago Press, 1962).

48. Joiner, Public Education, 191.

49. Governor Allen D. Candler, 25 April 1901, quoted in Dittmer, Black Georgia, 142. During his inaugural address in 1900, Candler had warned that Georgia would not prosper unless blacks were disfranchised. Grant, The Way It Was, 201-202.

50. Gustavus R. Glenn, as quoted in Hill, "Negro Education in Rural Georgia," 33-34.

51. Glenn in Hill, "Negro Education," 31.

52. Glenn in Hill, "Negro Education," 31.

53. Southern Education Foundation, Jeanes Supervision in Georgia Schools; A Guiding Light in Education, (Atlanta: Georgia Association of Jeanes Curriculum Directors and the Southern Education Foundation, 1975); Donald Spivey, Schooling for the New Slavery, Black Industrial Education, 1868-1915 (Westport CT, Greenwood, 1978); James D. Anderson, The Education of Blacks in the South, 1860-1935 (Chapel Hill: University of North Carolina Press, 1988).

54. John C. Belcher and Carolyn N. Allman, The Non-White Population of Georgia (Athens: Institute of Community and Area Development, 1967), 4; Grant, The Way It Was in the South, 300-326; Swanson and Griffin, Public Education, 24-25; See, generally, Nicholas Lemann, The Promised Land; Great Black Migration and How It Changed America (New York: Vintage, 1992).

55. Grant, The Way It Was, 293.

56. Grantham, The South, 85.

57. Grant, The Way It Was, 290-292, 295; Swanson and Griffin, Public Education, 17.

58. Grant, The Way It Was, 293.

59. Grant, The Way It Was, 293.

60. Dorsey was a product of Georgia's closed political system and, like his predecessors, he was poised to protect the interests of industry. He also aware of the progressive impulses that resonated in the state and realized there might be some common ground business and reformers.

61. Grant, The Way It Was, 294.

62. Between 1910 and 1930, the school attendance percentages for 5-to-9 year-olds rose from 39.5 percent to 59.7 percent for blacks and 55.2 percent to 67.67 for whites. For children ages 10-14 attendance rose from 62.1 percent to 82.7 percent for blacks and 81.7 to 88.6 for whites. Bureau of the Census. 16th U.S. Census (1940), (Washington, DC, 1943), 201.

63. Joiner, Public Education, 211-213.

64. "A Statement from Hugh M. Dorsey as to the Negro in Georgia," Atlanta, 22 April 1921. See also Coleman, *History of Georgia*, 290.

65. Ann Short Chirhart, "Torches of Light: African American and White Female Teachers in the Georgia Up Country," 1910-1950 (Unpublished Dissertation, Emory University: 1997), 39, 44-45.

66. Chirhart, "Torches of Light," 80.

67. Chirhart, "Torches of Light," 80.

68. Myra Logan, "Negro Education," 11.

69. Myra Logan, "Negro Education," 7-12.

70. Southern Education Foundation, *Jeanes Supervision*.

71. M.L. Brittain, quoted in Southern Education Foundation, *Jeanes Supervision*, pp. 24-25.

72. Joiner, *Public Education*, 253.

73. Orr, *History of Education*, 319; Southern Education Foundation, *Jeanes Supervision*, 18.

74. Southern Education Foundation, *Jeanes Supervision*, 26.

75. Miss Maude Miller, February 1932, Miss Maggie L. Perry, January 1931, as quoted in Southern Education Foundation, *Jeanes Supervision*, 128-129.

76. Link, *The Paradox of Southern Progressivism*, 245-246.

77. 49th Annual Report of the State Department of Education to the General Assembly of the State of Georgia for 1920.

78. 58th and 59th Annual Report of the Department of Education to the General Assembly of the State of Georgia for 1930.

79. Gunnar Myrdal quoted in Arthur M. Ford, *Political Economics of Rural Poverty in the South* (Cambridge: Ballinger), 1973, 27.

80. Sixty-Sixth and Sixty-Seventh Annual Reports of the State Department of Education to the Georgia General Assembly for 1937 and 1938.

81. M.D. Collins Collection, Georgia Department of Archives, Atlanta, Georgia, Record Group 12-2-144, Box 2.

82. James C. Cobb, *Industrialization and Southern Society, 1877-1984*. (Lexington: University Press of Kentucky, 1984), 104. Collins lamented in his first three annual reports (1933-35) about the inattention and short shrift Georgia rural schools were getting.

83. Sixty-Fourth and Sixty-Fifth Annual Reports of the Department of Education to the General Assembly of the State of Georgia for 1935 and 1936; *Augusta Courier*, 21 March 1949, 4, 5.

84. *Georgia Education Journal*, November 1933, 13.

85. *Georgia Educational Journal*, September 1934, 13.

86. *Augusta Courier*, 21 March 1949, 4, 5; *Augusta Courier*, 19 September 1949, 1; James Hilliard Broughton, "A Historical Study of Selected Aspects of the Equalization of Educational Opportunity in Georgia, 1937-1968" (Ph.D. diss., University of Georgia, 1969), 130.

87. Arthur M. Ford, *Political Economics of Rural Poverty in the South*, Cambridge: Ballinger, 1973), 18, 21.

88. Collins, quoted in *Augusta Courier*, 21 March 1949, 4-5; *Augusta Courier*, 19 September 1949, 1.

89. Joiner, *A History of Public Education in Georgia*, 286, 348. Swanson and Griffin, *Public Education*, 38-39, 56-57.

90. Swanson and Griffin found that in the 1939-40 school year in rural counties in seven states, whites received $52 per pupil while blacks received $26 for agriculture. Also that year they found that in rural counties in eight states, whites received $21 per pupil while blacks received $10 for home economics. No rural county data was available for industrial education or distributive education, but when state totals were figured (that considered rural, rural-urban, and metropolitan counties), whites received $23 per pupil and blacks $13 per pupil for industrial and trade education. Whites also received an average of $82 per pupil for distributive education. No numbers were available for blacks in distributive education. Swanson and Griffin, *Public Education*, 57.

91. Ford, *Political Economics*, 91.

Chapter 2

Inroads into the Jim Crow System

Democratic equalization of opportunity in a changing world must mean the provision of equal facilities for all children at all times.
    –Horace Mann Bond

The NAACP

Even before progressives began their crusade for the expansion of schooling for whites, black Georgians showed a determination to acquire literacy and numeracy and fashion educational opportunities for their children. For blacks, disfranchised shortly after Reconstruction and trapped at the bottom of the socioeconomic structure, schooling had long been considered the key to looking after an array of public and private interests.

A major movement to improve educational opportunity for blacks began in the 1930s, organized largely through the efforts of the National Association for the Advancement of Colored People (NAACP).[1] The NAACP valued the goal of democratic equality and saw the public school as the essential arena for liberation. The association, as its name suggests, was committed to removing political and economic barriers that impeded social mobility for blacks. To this end it sought to end inequality in all aspects of American life, including, but not limited to schooling.

To carry out the school campaign the association devised a strategy that was two pronged: One campaign sought admission for qualified blacks into graduate and professional schools in the South where no black graduate schools existed. The second campaign targeted facilities, expenditures, programs, length of school term and teacher salaries, seeking to make headway within the "separate but equal" doctrine that was established in *Plessy v. Ferguson* in 1896 and *Cumming v.*

29

Richmond in 1899. The *Cumming* decision in particular had provided a legal rationale for the growth of white but not black public high schools. By 1923 Georgia had used the logic of *Cumming* to establish 275 accredited public high schools for whites, but only 2 for blacks.[2]

The architect of the two-pronged strategy was Charles Hamilton Houston, World War I army officer, Phi Beta Kappa graduate from Amherst College, and graduate of Harvard Law School, where he was the first black elected to the *Harvard Law Review.* Among Harvard's best law students, Houston continued his legal studies with Felix Frankfurter, earning a doctor of juridical science at Harvard and later a doctor of civil law from the University of Madrid. In 1929 Houston answered the call of Howard University President Mordecai Johnson to serve as the dean of the Howard University Law School and make it respectable. Johnson had apparently been stung by Supreme Court Justice Louis Brandeis's remark that briefs written by black attorneys were often identifiable because of their poor quality. Houston took the position and proved to be more than a scholar-professor who could insist on high-quality briefs. In the words of Jack Greenberg, Houston, "in six energy-filled years transformed it from a law school with a part-time faculty and student body into an accredited institution that became a West Point of civil rights, producing an annual crop of lawyers rigorously trained to do battle for equal justice."[3] During his deanship Houston worked part time for the NAACP and became special counsel in 1935. That year he recruited one of his top students from Howard Law School, Thurgood Marshall, to work as his assistant. On the recommendation of Houston, Marshall took over as special counsel in 1938.

The NAACP experienced some early successes. The first challenge played out in Maryland state court in 1935 and resulted in the admission of Donald Murray, a recent graduate of Amherst College, to the University of Maryland Law School in Baltimore. Then in 1939 the Legal Defense and Education Fund (LDF), the litigation arm of the NAACP, won in federal court, when Supreme Court ruled in *Missouri ex. rel. Gaines v. Canada* that equal protection of the laws required that Missouri either provide a separate and equal law school for a qualified black applicant or admit him to the state's flagship white law school.

At the same time that the NAACP was working to gain admission for black students to white graduate schools, it was also carrying on a campaign to equalize funding for existing black schools. The equalization campaign was most successful in the areas of teacher salaries and length of school term. As late as 1940, Southern black teachers were paid roughly half of what their white counterparts earned. But over the next decade black teacher salaries increased an average of 152 percent. In Georgia black salaries increased by 228 percent. Still, by the end of the Second World War, Georgia and five other Southern states were spending an average of

$44.84 on a black child's education for every $80.29 spent on a white child.[4]

Notwithstanding the gains made under the equalization campaign, there was a growing sense among some LDF staff that a new approach was needed. The suggested approach was for a more calculated drive to end discrimination by seeking racial integration as a remedy and leaving equalization as a fallback. As Thurgood Marshall put it in 1947, the idea was to be "constantly hitting on segregation" while allowing for equalization as one type of relief.[5] Though subtle, it was a critical strategic change. Ultimately it meant that the LDF would stop seeking enforcement of the "separate but equal" doctrine. To win support for this change would take all the political savvy Marshall could muster.[6]

The National Debate within the NAACP

Before World War II, there was no real consensus within the black community—nationally or within Georgia—on whether to push for desegregated schools. A sharp tactical debate raged within the black community and the NAACP. As the debate ensued, tactical differences began to shape competing ideologies about the merits of race integration versus black self-pride. Two of the most prominent black intellectuals of the day, W.E.B. DuBois, a founding member of the NAACP, and E. Franklin Frazier, saw limitations and problems in desegregating the common schools.[7] Early in his academic career DuBois had acknowledged that "segregation was a menace to democracy and bred misunderstanding and racial hatred." By 1934, however, while supporting the theory of integration, he called for policy that would improve and build black institutions which would honor and respect black culture. At a conference at Howard University, which marked his break with the NAACP, DuBois argued that the segregated black community was a fact of life. All-black common schools along with other black institutions, provided a means for the proper education of blacks. If blacks attended schools run by whites, they would be "miseducated and crucified" by the dominant white culture, DuBois reasoned.[8] In spite of his feeling that segregated schools were undemocratic, DuBois accepted them as "engrafted in the customs and mores of the nation" and urged black leaders "to make them the best schools possible."[9]

Another voice in the black community who opposed integrating public common schools was Horace Mann Bond, the young president of Fort Valley State College for Negroes. A fast-rising scholar of schooling for blacks, Bond held that the answer to solving the problem of inferior schooling was through the gradual equalization of educational expenditures financed largely through federal aid.[10]

Most blunt in his assessment of inferior schooling was Carter G. Woodson, who had published *The Mis-Education of the Negro* in 1933. Going well beyond DuBois and Bond, Woodson argued the racist American system of schooling had even failed whites, and the Negro should "carry out a program of his own."[11] Woodson argued that education for blacks designed by and under the control of whites would "mis-educate." His main point dealt with what he perceived to be the failure of white-controlled black education to produce a corp of black leaders to advance black intellectual and social interests.[12] Woodson favored junking the system almost in its entirety.[13]

Ignoring the arguments of Woodson, Bond and DuBois, Charles Houston had already started training a band of black lawyers to challenge the segregated system. Houston and Marshall believed that removing the wall of race was ultimately the best guarantee of equality. Writing in the *Crisis* in 1935, Houston reiterated the NAACP's official position.

> The ultimate objective of the association is the abolition of all forms of segregation in public education whether in the admission or activities of students, the appointment or advancement of teachers, or administrative control. The association will resist any attempt to extend segregated schools.[14]

Nevertheless, Houston and Marshall were not yet prepared to abandon the equalization strategy that had won them major gains in teacher salaries. Of particular importance was the fact that another major organizational objective of the NAACP was the building of local branch memberships by appealing to black schoolteachers, the largest group of black professionals in America. James Weldon Johnson, the NAACP's executive secretary, had worked diligently to recruit members which by 1920 numbered ninety thousand with about half coming from the South. By 1948 membership had grown to roughly one-half million.[15]

Teachers and principals, who swelled the ranks of the NAACP in the late 30s and 40s, actively supported the equalization campaign, particularly the drive for equal salaries. But integration was a different matter. First, it might be rejected by the courts and put equalization in jeopardy. Second, if it was successful, it might put black jobs in jeopardy. Understandably distrustful of white boards of education and other policy-makers, black teachers and principals feared desegregation would mean they would be replaced by white teachers. It was a great risk.

To temper the official NAACP position Houston added a pragmatic corollary:

> Where segregation is so firmly entrenched by law that a frontal attack cannot be made, the association will throw its immediate force toward bringing Negro schools up to an absolute equality with white schools. If the white South insists

upon separate schools, it must not squeeze the Negro schools to pay for them.[16]

It was this equalization corollary that drove NAACP strategy until the middle 1940s. The strategy to pursue access and thus integration eventually won out over warnings about cultural imperialism. But the arguments of DuBois, Woodson, and other critics would endure and inform the continuing debate about black schooling.

By the end of the Second World War there was a sense among some of the membership of the NAACP that the two-pronged-equalization-default strategy needed sharpening. Some, like Carter Wesley, an influential attorney and newspaper editor, agreed with Woodson and DuBois and leaned on Marshall for a more aggressive equalization approach. Walter White, the NAACP's executive secretary, pushed for a speedy frontal attack on segregation laws.[17] Moved by both internal organizational factors and his own reading of the fast and furious social and legal changes under way, Marshall effected a subtle but critical strategic change. Ultimately it meant that the NAACP would stop seeking enforcement of the "separate but equal" doctrine.[18]

The Debate in Georgia

In Georgia, the debate within the black community over black school reform was polyphonous. Accommodationists like Benjamin Jefferson Davis, Beulah Rucker Oliver, and Joseph Winthrop Holley, saw the road to freedom in Washingtonian terms. Others, like John and Lucenia Hope, W.E.B. DuBois, Benjamin Mays and Grace Hamilton, were less optimistic about the African American's chances of advancement in the existing social order and calculated ways to change it. This second group of leaders saw abundant integrity in the black community and demanded political inclusion and the right of access.

With religious zeal accommodationists embraced various forms industrial education for social efficiency. Conservative followers of Booker T. Washington were inclined to accept the existing social structure and theory of white supremacy. Inspired by their faith in education, God, white virtue, the free market, and a rural cultural construction that valued self-sufficiency, frugality, and sobriety, Georgia's black accommodationists viewed self-help and self-sacrifice with paternalist assistance from whites as the means of racial uplift.

Beulah Rucker Oliver, who founded the State Industrial and High School outside of Gainesville in 1912, for example, stressed the values of self-sufficiency and hard work, while at the same time accepting her socially inferior position in order to solicit funds from local charities.[19] Benjamin Jefferson Davis, who worked as the editor of the *Atlanta Independent* and the *National Baptist Review*, argued that black progress was dependent on white progress. Only after "developing industrial efficiency" and establishing a "reputation as for industry and reliability" would blacks and whites prosper.

Joseph Winthrop Holley felt much the same way. Holley was the founder and president of the Albany Bible and Manual Training Institute (later renamed Albany State College), one of only a few black institutions that received steady annual financial support from the state. Perhaps the most extreme conservative among Georgia blacks, Holley argued that the educational requirements of a people "only a few years out of the jungle are not the same as those of people who have had thousands of years of civilization back of them." The state should not force a black youngster, he continued, "to fit himself for service in a field where the door is closed," but rather train him in "a field where there is a prospect of his getting work."[20] Holley saw the power and "greatness of the white race" not in their skin color, but in "the character that lay beneath it." Whites had "developed the qualities that God has been able to use powerfully," and if blacks also "wanted to be great and serviceable to mankind," they "should emulate the character of the white man and not try to become like him in color."[21] Linking uplift to self-help and evangelical protestantism, Holley urged blacks to rise above their station by gently nudging, but not impatiently shoving the white man. "The uplift of a people," wrote Holley, "is a gradual process from within."[22]

Other Georgians scoffed at the gradualist approach. DuBois, who had returned to Atlanta University in 1934 after serving more than twenty years as editor of the NAACP's *Crisis* in New York, had arguably become the nation's best known black radical intellectual. Early in his career he demanded the right to vote, civil equality, and open educational access for blacks "according to ability."[23] He challenged the Booker T. Washington's accomodationist economic approach to racial injustice, arguing suffrage, political power, and a liberal education were essential for black advancement. DuBois saw open access to schooling and citizenship education as critical to the black struggle, acknowledging that "segregation was a menace to democracy and bred misunderstanding and racial hatred."[24] Since the publication of the *Souls of Black Folk* in 1903, DuBois had developed complex opinions on racial integration, and argued that no "general and inflexible rule" should be laid down. By 1934, however, while supporting the concept of open access, he called for economic policy that would improve and build black-controlled institutions which would honor and respect black culture.

Most blacks in Georgia placed themselves between the accommodationists and DuBois, but beginning in the post-World War II period, moderate blacks began to see integration as more promising strategy for fostering democracy and social mobility. Some, like Benjamin Mays, president of Morehouse College, saw integration as a means of taking the self-serving white community and its institutions as hostage. Since his childhood days in South Carolina Mays had witnessed how the cotton culture used segregation and disfranchisement to advantage whites and at the expense of blacks. Mays had experienced inferior schooling, unequal wages for equal work, and political exploitation. In the 1940s and 1950s he saw segregation as the key obstacle to black advancement. Blacks, Mays felt, could only get the social and economic benefits of Georgia's publicly supported institutions by tethering themselves to whites and thus forcing the burgeoning state education enterprise to provide their children with not *equal* but the *same* books, facilities, resources and pay.[25] Whites would make sure that their own children's schools were stocked with good teachers, well-run and well-supplied. If black children were in the same schools, they would reap the same public and private benefits. Whites, in the end, would not cut public support of their own children's benefit, he believed. Thus, open access to schools and classrooms where whites were taught was critical to the struggle for equality.

DuBois disagreed with Mays, opposing school integration. Integration, he argued, would not adequately address the economic and cultural dimensions of racial injustice. To concentrate on political equality without a clear articulation of economic equality, he reasoned, would lead to frivolous and limited gains in the education arena while simultaneously injuring black children. In DuBois's way of thinking, black children in the integration chess game, would no longer be nurtured in an admittedly financially starved, but caring community-school-church triangle. Rather they would be sacrificed as pawns on the frontlines of the race battle. Taking the white communities hostage with an integration-at-all costs approach would lead to the loss of black collective school-church-community cultures which had flowered behind the veil of segregation. Despite his awareness that Jim Crow segregation was a powerful and dangerous instrument of oppression, DuBois still saw more danger than promise in the quest for racial integration.

Seeds of Change

World War II

While the NAACP carried out its double-barreled campaign, other forces were making inroads into the Jim Crow system. During the Second World War many of the seeds for change were planted, seeds that quickly matured and irreversibly altered the country's racial dynamics and concepts of justice. The war transformed the South in numerous and profound ways and altered its relationship and role with the rest of the nation.[26]

The war created a need for labor in defense industries and at military bases. Munitions factories in Macon and Milledgeville, shipyards in Savannah and Brunswick, and numerous military bases across Georgia, created more jobs than could be filled by whites alone. By 1941, President Roosevelt, under pressure from black labor leaders, had banned discrimination in defense industries. Although employment discrimination continued almost unabated, some black workers gained a foothold in jobs where they had been previously excluded.[27] As the need for farm labor in the South declined, blacks migrated from the countryside to the cities in search of work. As blacks settled in cities across the South, their numbers increased and so did their earning power and their potential political power.[28] For example, by 1948 Atlanta blacks had developed a bloc vote that was used effectively in municipal elections. Soon after, a political coalition developed between Atlanta's black community and Atlanta's politically powerful white business community, which controlled city government.[29]

The Soldier Problem and Illiteracy

Prior to the war it was generally safe for white politicians and policy makers to ignore blacks. War time efforts to recruit soldiers and develop a massive war-support machine with engineers, mechanics, pilots, and radio operators, exposed the high cost of ignoring a large part of the nation's population. It became apparent that the deficiencies of the education enterprise created a national security risk. Blacks, immigrants, rural dwellers, and others outside the mainstream were often illiterate or too ill to be drafted. Blacks who sought to enlist in the service were rejected at a rate twice that of whites due to illiteracy, with Southern rural blacks heading the list. In Georgia, 46.9 percent of white registrants (second highest in 48 states) and 57.8 percent of colored registrants (seventh highest in the 48 states) were classified as not fit for service.[30] Those who were accepted were often placed in noncombat, unskilled service commands in part due to their "low educational level and meager administrative and technical experiences."[31]

Blacks' low scores on the battery of army mental tests further exposed the literacy problems; 80 percent of all enlisted blacks (compared to 30-40 percent of enlisted whites) tested out in the lowest two categories on the Army General Classification Test. Though it was not made public until after the war, other Army data collected between 1941 and 1946 found, among other differences, a 24 percent gap difference in high school graduation rates between black and white enlistees.

Studies of black illiteracy gave statistical confirmation for what had been obvious to, but beyond the scope of, the NAACP for decades: glaring and obvious disparities between the races at all levels of education across the country, particularly in the South.[32]

While the war exposed deficiencies that would fundamentally alter American education and schooling in the remaining half-century, it also provoked a climate of urgency that demanded short-term pragmatic solutions to immediate political and military problems. Recruiting, training and maintaining dependable armed forces headed the list. The army, the largest of the four divisions, came under intense political pressure from all sides to meet personnel demands. After raising the recruitment of illiterates to 10 percent, the army developed a centralized remedial reading program for illiterate, but otherwise mentally adequate, recruits. The pressure to improve education came from the top, bottom, left and right. President Roosevelt insisted that blacks be deployed proportionately in all parts of the service. The black press and black enlisted men expressed frustration and a growing resentment of being assigned to low-status, non-combat commands. Ironically, pressure also came from at least one Southern white demagogue politician who complained that regional quotas and literacy requirements had taken high numbers of whites and left the majority of blacks at home. Mississippi Senator Theodore Bilbo urged Congress to "develop the reservoir of the illiterate class" for a more equal distribution.[33]

The Double V

For many black soldiers in Europe, the South Pacific, and in the States the war brought both hope and despair. Although they fought, ate, slept and traveled in segregated and often unequal units, there was a growing sense among black troops that a "Double V" was in the cards: a victory in Europe over a ruthless fascist dictator who was hell-bent on exterminating an entire race, and a victory at home over racial discrimination, where segregation enforced age-old patterns of racial dominance, white privilege and in some cases outright hatred. It was as if the war had found a black man's skeleton in Uncle Sam's closet that identified Sam as a hypocrite. How could the symbol of world freedom fight for democracy and self rule and against a race-hate monger abroad and tolerate a reactionary oligarchy that pitted race against class at home?

American war-time propaganda and its slogans—"brotherhood," "freedom," and "democracy" — acted on the public conscience to favor social change. By war's end, the war-time rhetoric was internalized not only by many blacks, but also by growing numbers of whites who agitated against racial discrimination. By the mid-1940s, Howard Odum, the distinguished Southern sociologist, commented that masses of white Americans, especially those from outside the South, but also a significant number from within the South, were convinced that "something should be done about the [white] South's treatment of the Negro."[34] Gunnar Myrdal, another sociologist of international repute who had just completed his massive study on the discrepancy between American ideals and practice, shared Odum's optimism. He predicted that the social forces of increased government intervention brought on by the New Deal, economic stimulus from the war, emerging black suffrage and the decline of racism as a political ideology, would bring about the convergence of the American ideal with American practice. Intellectual moderates seemed to agree that the war might irreversibly alter race relations in the region.[35]

Indigenous Initiatives: The Push for a Biracial Approach

The emphasis on democratic equality that developed in the post-war period downplayed economics, stressed legal rights and converged on biracialism. In concept, as a first step toward racial justice, the region's middle-class leaders from both races would work together and speak in one authoritative voice. Once organized, these community and state activists could go about the task of documenting and explaining inequalities. Gradually blacks, from the middle class down, would gain access to the universities, and public schools, the Democratic primary and other Southern political institutions. The biracial coalition of middle-class liberals and moderates believed that biracial understanding would lead to a full comprehension of injustice which would, in turn, lead to access and ultimately full integration. Eliminating Jim Crow, by gaining access to previously all-white institutions became the principal remedy against oppression and the chosen path to first class citizenship.

Active in the new biracial movements were a cadre of black intellectuals and civic and community activists including Grace Hamilton, executive secretary of the Atlanta Urban League, Benjamin Mays, and Georgia's first black political boss, Austin T. Walden. Liberal-minded, moderate, and accustomed to working within the restrictions of de jure segregation, Georgia's middle-class black leaders not only saw Georgia as a bastion of racial privileging and white supremacy but also recognized it as home to a small, but critical mass of well-meaning, middle-class whites with whom they believed they had much in common.

Perhaps no one in Georgia typified this more than Grace Hamilton. A one-time student of DuBois, Hamilton came to believe that black advancement could not be realized without the active support and cooperation of the "best class" of whites. Appointed to direct the Atlanta Urban League in 1942, she worked resolutely to build and serve on several interracial coalitions and document racial inequalities in housing and schooling in Atlanta. By the mid-1940s, she had established an integrated Atlanta Urban League board, composed of several of the city's more liberal black and white community leaders. Elegant, conciliatory, and persistent with whites, strong-willed and forceful, and sometimes high-browed with blacks, Hamilton's tireless efforts typified the black bourgeoisie's "inside agitator" approach pressing for racial justice.

Hamilton, like most middle-class black activists in post-war Georgia, was by DuBois's (and today's) standards, a gradualist who felt that whites needed to be nudged but not pushed. In contrast to Holley, however, Hamilton had a shorter time frame in mind and thus defined gradualism more sharply. Moreover, Hamilton felt the nudging required white collaboration to succeed. Hamilton believed liberal and moderate whites had good intentions and would help remedy racial inequality once they fully understood it in concrete terms. The work at hand, as Hamilton saw it, was to organize these well-meaning citizens into interracial organizations, invigorate their interest in fairness, investigate injustices, and propose solutions. These biracial organizations would bring their findings to like-minded communities in the cities and across the state. As greater and greater numbers of citizens gained a working knowledge of racial inequalities, the enlightened critical mass would grow, ultimately crowding out narrow-mindedness, hate, self-interest and white supremacy.[36]

The preference for a biracial approach that stressed integration over DuBois's reconceptualization of black improvement through economic self-sufficiency and pluralism was dominant in black middle-class thought and action during the post-war period.[37] Most leaders of the biracial movement held views on segregation that coincided with those of Thurgood Marshall, who felt that once the legal barriers fell, "the whole [race relations] picture would change."[38]

The Southern Regional Council

As part of the indigenous biracial effort to do something about the treatment of blacks, the Commission on Interracial Cooperation (CIC), founded in 1919, was reorganized as the Southern Regional Council (SRC) in 1944. The reorganization meeting came in response to a call by a group of black leaders, who, in 1943, challenged their white counterparts to create a new regional organization to address the problems in the South in "an affirmative way."[39] This call prompted some of

Georgia's white community leaders—including Protestant, Catholic, and Jewish clergy; labor leaders; two college Presidents; and "the conscience of the South," Ralph McGill, editor of the *Atlanta Constitution*—to meet and deliberate and subsequently to confer with several Southern black leaders.[40] The conferences resulted in the founding of the SRC in early 1944.[41]

The SRC set as its overriding goal the development of a greater participatory democracy in the South and pursued this goal indirectly through collecting and disseminating information about the region's problems. Rather than challenging head-on the distribution of the region's wealth and power, the SRC accepted and advanced the liberal notion that societal progress could be addressed through educational means, which included conducting research, publishing findings in popular and scholarly periodicals, and supporting the expansion and equalization of public schooling. Viewing institutions such as the media, school, and church as key gatekeepers that might be employed to remedy societal ills, the SRC set off to collect facts about the region's racial problems and economic stagnation. The SRC then made interpretations of these facts available to private citizens and public officials. To carry out its agenda for social progress the SRC sought to appeal to that part of the Southern mind that was rational and analytical. In this way, the SRC differed little from its predecessor.[42] Public schools, colleges, and universities naturally fit into this strategy. SRC members included a handful of activists and clergy, such as Jesse Daniel Ames, Martin Luther King Sr., and Williams Holmes Borders; but most members were academicians and journalists; Howard Odum, Gordon B. Hancock, Charles Johnson, Benjamin Mays, Ralph McGill, Arthur Raper and later Benjamin Muse and Howard Zinn.

The SRC took a behind the scenes role in eroding the color line in the South. One of the organization's tactics in the area of education was to sponsor and conduct academic research that would document the disparities between black and white educational facilities. By appearing scholarly, and avoiding a direct attack on segregation, the SRC sought to display an objective image to the greater Southern community. The idea was to influence and appeal to that large group of Southerners who may not have endorsed breaking with the "tradition of segregation," but who did favor "fair play" via equal resources for blacks. The first step, as the SRC saw it, was to point out statistically the inequality of resources available for blacks. The second step was to support the removal of the legal barriers that were thought to be largely responsible for the disparities. This approach, though more conservative than the NAACP's national strategy by war's end, complemented the NAACP's and Urban League's local strategy in Georgia.

Because of the SRC's preoccupation with maintaining an image of objectivity, it initially did not take a stand on racial segregation. John A. Griffin, who joined the Council in 1945, recalled that this equivocation in the late 1940s may have caused one of the SRC's better known members to quit:

> We had one member, a Georgia writer named Lillian Smith, who had written a best seller [called] *Strange Fruit*. Smith was very impatient with the Council's position on integration, and after an exchange with the agency's executive director, Guy Johnson, quit the SRC. By 1949 the SRC came out in favor of integration. The early idea was to work for fair play, but not integration. In the meantime, the [NAACP] was winning battles against segregation, primarily in higher education.[43]

Highlander Folk School and the
Southern Conference on Human Welfare

The work of the SRC was part of a broader indigenous social reform effort that had been under way in the South for nearly two decades. The Highlander Folk School in Monteagle, Tennessee, founded by Myles Horton and Don West in 1932, became a training school for social activists until 1961, when it was ordered closed by the Tennessee legislature for allegedly violating Tennessee's segregation statutes.[44] Until mid-century Highlander worked with poor and oppressed Southerners to find ways to gain power over their circumstances and, ideally, to rebuild the social order in a way that would end poverty, prejudice, and economic exploitation. In contrast to the SRC and CIC—organizations that adhered to a moderate, progressive philosophy—Highlander Folk School was one of a few centers for a new radical movement that took issue with systematic social injustice and legally imposed racial segregation.[45] For its first twenty years Highlander helped workers unionize. In the early fifties Highlander zeroed in on race relations as its raison d'etre. It was, in essence, a residential adult training camp for up-and-coming labor and civil rights leaders. Horton, a native of Tennessee and the eldest son of two sharecroppers and part-time schoolteachers, had, as a child, developed an enduring belief in the transformative power of education. During his college years at Cumberland University Horton joined the YMCA. There he learned firsthand about the degradations blacks suffered under the grip of Jim Crow and the power industrialists held over their hired workers. Working as a student YMCA secretary and later as a student at Columbia's Union Theological Seminary in New York, Horton began reading the pragmatism of John Dewey and William James and the leftist writings of Harry F. Ward in an effort to bridge what he began to see as a vast abyss between Christian theory and practice. While at Union Horton studied under Reinhold Neibhur, a self-described "Christian Marxist" theologian from Chicago who rejected the then fashionable liberal notion of inevitable social progress. Using Marxist theory, Neibhur attacked the New Deal, seeing it as a "prop to continue capitalism."[46] Horton went on to develop a personal friendship with Neibhur, who later provided advice and financial support for Horton's radical activities. Horton also was influenced by the lectures and writings of social reconstructionists George Counts, Eduard C. Lindeman and Joseph Hart.

In late 1930, Horton went to the University of Chicago to study under sociologist Robert E. Park, an eminent teacher and scholar who was deeply interested in issues of social justice, particularly the African American experience. During his career Park had worked with Booker T. Washington, Charles S. Johnson, E. Franklin Frazier and Horace Mann Bond.[47] Park's interest in the study of the "marginal man," as well as his theory of social change—which involved the mechanisms of crisis, conflict and mass movement—were no doubt of special interest to Horton. He gained increased confidence in the notion that education, particularly adult education for the poor, could provide the means to mobilize the poor and powerless toward improving their condition. His social and intellectual interests led him to Chicago's south side and to Hull House, where he befriended Jane Addams. Addams, like Park and Dewey, implicitly challenged the radical thinking of Ward and Neibhur by embracing the vision of a true democracy and social uplift through her work in Chicago and elsewhere. Although Horton ultimately rejected Addams's vision, he found great satisfaction in talking with her and learned a great deal about contextual conflict and the practical politics of social change.

Horton was part of a loosely-knit collection of militants and social reconstructionist organizations that constituted leftist work and thought in the South in the periods between the Great Depression and the Civil Rights Movement. James Dombrowski and John B. Thompson, classmates of Horton at Union, were among the ranks, as were Howard Kester, Don West, Ward Rodgers, and Claude Williams, activists who had studied the "social gospel" under theologian Alva Taylor at Vanderbilt University. In 1934, two years after Highlander was founded, Kester and M.L. Mitchell, the son of Tennessee sharecroppers, organized a biracial coalition of field hands known as the Southern Tenant Farmer Union, that, by 1938 had over thirty thousand members in seven Southern states.[48] Kester, who investigated lynchings for the NAACP and the American Civil Liberties Union, also headed up The Fellowship of Christian Churchmen, a biracial alliance of men and women working for social reform.

Radicalized in the mid-thirties by the fallout of the Great Depression, the appeal of the Soviet Union's collective socialism, and the rise of Nazism in Europe, the militants came to regard capitalism as flawed and took aim at transforming it into socialism "by means of a dictatorship of the proletariat."[49] The "radical gospel" movement emerged at the vanguard of Southern progressivism in the 1930s and 1940s. Organizing unions, educating community and union leaders, attacking segregation and pushing moderates and liberals to do the same, these radicals sought to use Christianity and, to a lesser extent, the church, as a means to bring social justice to the region.[50] Throughout the thirties, working sometimes together but usually in tandem or alone, these radicals succeeded in setting up labor training schools, folk schools, unions and workshops to affect social change.

The high-water mark for the Southern radicals in the mid-thirties was followed by a 20-year period of decline during which the numbers of active radicals dwindled. In the late 1930s, however, the radicals were swaying progressives and other moderates to reexamine their region and the economic and racial inequalities that persisted. The coming together of radicals, progressives and moderates in Birmingham in the fall of 1938 for the Southern Conference of Human Welfare marked the beginning of what John Egerton has called the "most significant attempt by Southerners, up to that time, to introduce a far-reaching agenda of change and improvement" to the South.[51] The four-day conference in November, attended by 1,200 reform-minded liberals, including Eleanor Roosevelt, Hugo Black and Frank P. Graham, aimed to "modernize the South and liberalize the region's Democratic party."[52] The conference took several bold stands; it called for the repeal of the poll tax and went on record to oppose some types of social and racial discrimination. It endorsed the right of labor to organize, anti-lynching laws, and a Fair Employment Practices Commission. It also backed policy proposals that called for federal aid to education.

Historians concur that the contributions of the Southern radicals and liberals were modest at best, futile at worst. Overlooked, however, is the effect that these early attempts to promote racial and economic parity had on Southern middle-class moderates, who as a group were far more numerous, and politically much more powerful, at least potentially. While most moderates were unwilling to accept proposals that sought to solve the region's economic and racial problems through direct political action, the actions by the radicals and liberals forced many moderates to acknowledge that these regional problems existed and required some type of attention. The radicals and liberals, in spite of falling short of accomplishing their greater societal goals, had sensitized the greater South's "vital center" to several of its most pressing social problems. This democratic sensitization, the effects of World War II, and the calculated drive by the NAACP, would soon converge on a massive public school expansion program and identify the school as the arena of reform.

Truman

If the work of sensitizing the South's vital center fell on the region's radicals and liberals, then the job of legitimizing that center turned out to be the work of the federal executive.[53] The two, of course, were not unconnected. Before and during most of the war key people in Roosevelt's New Deal were progressive, even radical-minded Southerners. Mark Etheridge of the Fair Employment Practices Committee (FEPC), Clark Forman of the Public Works Administration and the administration's "advisor on Negro affairs," Will Alexander of the Resettlement Administration, Mary McLeod Bethune of the National Youth Administration (NYA), and Aubrey Williams of the Federal Emergency Relief Administration and NYA, all had ties to the Southern left.[54] During Roosevelt's lengthy watch, several symbolic and behind-the-scenes changes took place in the federal government's policy on race issues. Roosevelt added black leadership in the federal bureaucracy and military and supported educational assistance programs through New Deal programs.[55]

With the death of Roosevelt, however, and the emergence of Harry S. Truman on the scene, some predicted a relaxation if not a reversal in progressive federal policy. White Southern politicians believed that Truman, unlike his predecessor, would easily "pass a litmus test on white supremacy."[56] The grandson of Kentuckians and Confederates, the young Truman had a history of making racial slurs and developed a reputation for privately cracking demeaning "nigger jokes."[57] As a senator from the border state of Missouri, he rarely voted with Southern conservatives on filibusters and states' rights issues, but seemed poised to reject "social equality" between the races. Writing to his daughter in 1939 he described waiters at the White House as "an army of coons," and in 1941 expressed to her his regret that "a white man like Lee had to surrender to old Grant."[58]

There were other signs, however, that Truman would not be the conservative South's redeemer. In 1940, while campaigning for the U.S. Senate in Sedalia, Missouri, for example, he addressed a nearly all-white courthouse crowd about his beliefs in the "brotherhood of man; not merely the brotherhood of white men, but the brotherhood of all men before the law." He continued,

> If any class or race can be permanently set apart from, or pushed down below the rest in political and civil rights, so may any other class or race when it shall incur the displeasure of its more powerful associates, and we may say farewell to the principles on which we count our safety.[59]

In 1944, during his campaign for vice president, Truman declared his support for a permanent Fair Employment Practices Committee (FEPC), a federal anti-lynching law, and abolition of the poll tax. With the sudden death of Roosevelt, President Truman determined to turn the civil rights rhetoric and symbolism of his party into action. Within two months of taking the presidential oath, Truman wrote Adolph Sabath, chair of the House of Representatives Rules Committee, and urged him to get behind a bill that would make permanent the FEPC. At the same time he wrote a letter of protest to the House Appropriations Committee which had cut off funds to the wartime FEPC. This letter, which stated it was un-American to discriminate on the basis of race, creed or color in employment was Truman's first stand as President for civil rights.[60]

Truman's most decisive stands for civil rights took place after the war. Black soldiers returning to the South after serving in World War II encountered not only pervasive discrimination but also violence. Racist beatings and lynchings took place across the South. Several vicious attacks on returning soldiers attracted national attention and provoked outrage.[61] In 1946 Truman commissioned two major studies that condemned all forms of discrimination, particularly racial discrimination. The report of the Commission on Higher Education, released in 1948, argued:

> [the nation's economy] could no longer [support] long-standing policies denying large numbers of Americans access to educational opportunity on the basis of race, class, gender, and national origin . . . and, the nation's reputation abroad could ill afford the stigmata conferred by such policies[62]

Truman's Committee on Civil Rights was even stronger in its condemnation of discrimination. Reporting in 1947, the committee called for federal policies that would guarantee rights not only for blacks but also for other groups that had been victims of long-standing patterns of discrimination: Jews, Roman Catholics, native Americans, Hispanics, Filipinos and Asians. The report "rejected out of hand the assumption that separate facilities for the races could ever be equal," and recommended "the elimination of segregation based on race, color, creed, or national origin from American life."[63]

In February 1948, Truman sent to Congress a proposal calling for legislation prohibiting lynching, outlawing the poll tax, and establishing an FEPC and a Commission on Civil Rights. In 1950, he instructed his Department of Justice to argue for the overturn of the separate-but-equal doctrine. Though Truman's proposals were largely deflected by a resistant Congress, the President proved true to his word in areas where he had firm control. Truman set in motion a far-reaching executive order that abolished racial segregation in the armed services. The armed forces were quickly integrated, giving blacks the opportunity to enter the full range of military jobs and to compete for promotion to noncommissioned and commissioned ranks. The military became a major avenue of educational opportunity and social mobility for blacks.[64]

Truman's work on racial equality had gone well beyond Roosevelt's symbolic gestures. His willingness as president to take a stand and his ability to survive politically were early signals to moderates, black and white, that it was reasonable to support fairness and equality before the law. Truman saw segregation as one of the major evils obstructing progress toward these principles and attacked it with the power of his office. His courageous brand of leadership, which advocated tolerance and understanding, offered a hopeful alternative to the race-baiting ways of mainstream Southern politicians. Truman was deeply disturbed by violence against blacks and other minorities and the destruction of their homes and property immediately after the war. Truman's actions, taken together with the NAACP's string of courtroom victories and efforts of Southern liberals and radicals, laid the groundwork for a frontal assault on the separate-but-equal doctrine. By mid-century the nation was poised for a fundamental change in race relations.

The Dixiecrats and Russell

When Truman made clear his intention to run on a platform that included a civil rights plank, many white Southerners pulled away from the national Democratic Party and created their own States' Rights Democratic Party, better known as the Dixiecrats. The Dixiecrats were dedicated to the perpetuation of states' rights and segregation. They nominated Senator J. Strom Thurmond of South Carolina as their presidential candidate. In the 1948 election the Dixiecrats won in Alabama, Louisiana, Mississippi, and South Carolina. Yet in Georgia only twenty percent of the voters cast ballots for the Dixiecrats. Truman captured Georgia with over 50 percent of the popular vote.[65] But Georgia's most powerful politicians supported Truman in spite of—not because of—his commitment to civil rights. Rather than abandon the powerful Democratic Party in favor of the Dixiecrats, Georgians chose to maintain their positions of influence in the Democratic Party and to fight for the perpetuation of their segregated society from within the existing power structure.

Georgia's choice not to go with the rest of the Deep South was influenced by the actions of Senator Richard B. Russell, who decided to remain a regular Democrat in spite of his vocal opposition to Truman's civil rights policies. In 1948 Russell was perhaps the most influential Senator in the South, if not in the country. At home his opinions were unassailable. Russell, who had started his political career in 1921 in the Georgia General Assembly, went on to become governor of the state in 1930. In 1933 Russell became one of Georgia's two United States Senators and held that elected office until his death in 1971. As late as 1945 Russell had been receptive to President Harry Truman's "Fair Deal," until he realized that the progressive agenda included a call for a permanent Fair Employment Practices Commission (FEPC), which sought to eliminate discrimination in employment on the grounds of race, color, religion and national origin. Russell soon emerged as the Southern congressional spokesman against civil rights, leading the charge against the FEPC and Truman's desegregation of the armed services. In 1947 Russell lashed out against President Truman's Civil Rights actions, calling them "gestapo" and the "most serious affront to the people of [the South] since Reconstruction days."[66]

Yet, in 1948, Russell rejected an invitation to have his name placed in nomination before the Dixiecrat convention. Instead, Russell permitted Charles J. Block to place his name in nomination at the regular Democratic convention. Block, a Macon Attorney and one of Russell's political allies, conceded that Georgia would not bolt the convention but declared that the "South would no longer be the whipping boy of the Democratic Party." Upon losing the nomination to Truman, Russell, who was "emotionally and intellectually" committed to the party of his father, announced that he would vote for Truman, in effect choosing to remain loyal to his party, in spite of his unalterable position on segregation. Russell, as a senior member in the Democratic Party, had a great deal of power through his committee appointments. It was his power within the party that kept him from joining the Dixiecrats in 1948. Moreover, it is likely that Russell's decision to give passive support to the Democratic ticket persuaded other Georgia Democrats, notably Herman Talmadge, to do so.[67]

On the other hand, there is evidence that some Georgians were more moderate on race issues than Russell, Talmadge and the other Southern racist demagogues. At a minimum, many Georgia voters were unwilling to endorse race-extremism when it placed other important interests, such as public schools and universities, at risk. In 1942, Georgia voters had thrown out Governor Eugene Talmadge after he packed the Board of Regents to effect the firing of two professors who advocated racial integration in a laboratory school at the University of Georgia. His actions resulted in the temporary suspension of the university system's accreditation. The threat to the university system became a major issue in the gubernatorial campaign and led to the election of the race-moderate Ellis Arnall.[68] While in office, Arnall pursued a progressive race agenda that allowed for biracial voting and the abolition of the poll tax. Although he remained a segregationist, Arnall favored fair play and economic and political participation for black Georgians. His brief tenure in the governor's mansion demonstrated that Georgia's voters would not sacrifice their university system on the altar of race segregation.

Although many forces were converging to provide a platform for major change in the Jim Crow system, most of the political leadership in the white South still had its "collective head in the sand."[69] In spite of the existence of a growing group of race-moderates, many Georgians, black and white, considered the matter of racial segregation to be settled. Few Southern leaders developed any constructive policies to meet the trend toward acceptance of greater civil rights for blacks.[70] This is not to say that Southern leaders did not develop any policies, rather that the majority of their energies were aimed at perpetuating the apartheid system.

Notes

1. From its inception in 1909 until the Great Depression the NAACP devoted its attention not to schooling but to the struggle against mob rule and lynching, disfranchisement and residential segregation ordinances. In the 1930s the association began to focus its campaign for black equality on schooling. See, Richard Kluger, *Simple Justice: The History of Brown v. Board of Education and Black America's Struggle for Equality* (New York: Knopf, 1977); Mark V. Tushnet, *The NAACP's Legal Strategy against Segregated Education, 1925-1950* (Chapel Hill: University of North Carolina Press, 1987).

2. Dorothy Orr, *A History of Education in Georgia* (Chapel Hill: University of North Carolina Press, 1950), 329. See, generally, J. Morgan Kousser, *Dead End, The Development of Nineteenth-Century Litigation on Racial Discrimination in Schools* (Oxford: Clarendon, 1986); J. Morgan Kousser, "Separate but Not Equal, the Supreme Court's First Decision on Racial Discrimination in Schools" *Journal of Southern History*, 46 (February 1980).

3. Jack Greenberg, *Crusaders in the Court: How a Dedicated Band of Lawyers Fought the Civil Rights Revolution* (New York: Basic Books, 1994), 5.

4. Ernst W. Swanson and John A. Griffin, *Public Education in the South, Today and Tomorrow: A Statistical Survey* (Chapel Hill: University of North Carolina), 53, 59, 63.

5. Mark V. Tushnet, "Thurgood Marshall as a Lawyer: The Campaign against School Desegregation" 40 *Maryland Law Review* (1981), 415.

6. Ibid.

7. Harold Cruse, *Plural but Equal: Blacks and Minorities in America's Plural Society* (New York: William Morrow, 1987), 42-52.

8. Mary G. Hector "Racism, Black Nationalism and W.E.B. DuBois: A Study of a Divided Soul" (Masters thesis: Emory University, 1978), 53, 56-57. See, also Kluger, *Simple Justice*, 165-166; Greenberg, *Crusaders in the Courts*, 59-60.

9. Hector, "Racism, Black Nationalism," 57.

10. Horace Mann Bond, *The Education of the Negro in the American Social Order* (1934, republished with a new introduction by Horace Mann Bond, New York: Octagon Books 1966), x, 436-463.

11. Carter Woodson as quoted in Cruse, *Plural but Equal*, 194.

12. Carter G. Woodson, *The Miseducation of the Negro*, (1933, reprinted with an introduction by Charles H. Nilon, New York: AMS Press, 1977), 17-25.

13. Cruse, *Plural but Equal*, 195.

14. The *Crisis*, October 1935, 300.

15. John Egerton, *Speak Now against the Day, The Generation before the Civil Rights Movement in the South* (New York: Knopf, 1994), 52-55.

16. The *Crisis*, October 1935, 300.

17. Kluger, *Simple Justice*, 133; Mark V. Tushnet, "Organizing Civil Rights Litigation, The NAACP's Experience" in David J. Bodenhamer and James W. Ely, eds., *Ambivalent Legacy: A Legal History of the South* (Jackson: University of Mississippi Press, 1984), 171-184.

18. Tushnet, "Thurgood Marshall as a Lawyer," 415.

19. Ann Short Chirhart, "Torches of Light: African American and White Female Teachers in the Georgia Up Country, 1910-1950" (Ph.D. Diss., Emory University, 1997), 191-201.

20. Joseph Winthrop Holley, *You Can't Build a Chimney from the Top: The South through the Life of a Negro Educator* (New York: William-Frederick, 1949), 87-9; Edward A. Gaston Jr., "A History of the Negro Wage Earner in Georgia, 1890-1940" (Unpublished dissertation, Emory University, 1957), 42; Chirhart "Torches of Light," 83-85.

21. Holley, *Chimney from the Top*, 87.

22. Holley, *Chimney from the Top*, 63.

23. Cruse, *Plural but Equal*, 42, 77.

24. W.E.B. DuBois, quoted in Hector, "Racism, Black Nationalism," 53.

25. See generally, Benjamin E. Mays, *Born to Rebel* (Athens: University of Georgia Press, 1971); Benjamin E. Mays, "Why an Atlanta School Suit?" *New South* 5 (September/October 1950), 1-3.

26. Dewey W. Grantham, *The South in Modern America; A Nation at Odds* (New York: HarperCollins, 1994), 170-193.

27. For a discussion of A. Phillip Randolph and his negotiations with President Roosevelt, see, Paula F. Pfeffer, *A. Phillip Randolph, Pioneer of the Civil Rights Movement* (Baton Rouge: Louisiana State University Press, 1990).

28. Nicholas Lemann, *The Promised Land: The Great Black Migration and How it Changed America* (New York: Knopf, 1991); Diane Ravitch, *The Troubled Crusade: American Education, 1945-1980* (New York: Basic Books, 1983), 118. The Supreme Court stood up for black political participation when it ruled that it was unconstitutional to exclude blacks from primary elections (*Smith v. Allwright*, 1944). The decision legally opened the way for large-scale black voter registration. Numan Bartley, *The Rise of Massive Resistance: Race and Politics in the South During the 1950's* (Baton Rouge: Louisiana State University Press, 1969), 7.

29. David N. Plank and Marcia Turner, "Changing Patterns in Black School Politics, Atlanta, 1872-1973," *American Journal of Education* 95 (August 1987), 584-608.

30. Seventy-Sixth and Seventy-Seventh Annual Reports of the Department of Education to the General Assembly of the State of Georgia (ending June 30, 1948).

31. Paula Fass, *Outside In: Minorities and the Transformation of American Education* (New York: Oxford University Press, 1989), 7, 140-155.

32. Ibid.

33. Theodore Bilbo, as quoted in Fass, *Outside In*, 144.

34. Howard Odum as quoted in Diane Ravitch, *The Troubled Crusade: American Education, 1945-1980* (New York: Basic Books, 1983), 116-118.

35. Gunnar Myrdal, *An American Dilemma: The Negro Problem and American Democracy* 2 vols. (New York: Harper & Row, 1944).

36. See, generally, Lorraine Nelson Spritzer & Jean B. Bergmark, *Grace Hamilton and the Politics of Southern Change* (Athens: University of Georgia Press, 1997).

37. See generally, Cruse, *Plural But Equal*; Tushnet, "Organizing Civil Rights Litigation"; Tushnet, *NAACP's Legal Strategy*.

38. Kluger, *Simple Justice*, 639.

39. John A. Griffin interview, 12 November 1991; Southern Regional Council Papers, Series XVI, Reel 218; Atlanta University Center, Atlanta, GA; Steve Suitts, "The Southern Regional Council and the Roots of Rural Change." *Southern Changes* 13 (September 1991), 5-12.

40. Others participating were: C.H. Gillman, the Georgia Director of the C.I.O.; George Googe, the Southern Director of the A.F.L.; Rabbi David Marx, from The Temple in Atlanta; M. Asby Jones, a Baptist minister from Atlanta; Reverend Gerald P. O'Hara, the Bishop of Savannah and Atlanta; J. McDowell Richards, President of the Columbia Theological Seminary in Decatur; Ryland Knight, a Baptist preacher; Bishop John Moore Walker from the Protestant Episcopal Church in Atlanta; Stuart R. Ogesby, a Presbyterian minister; Bishop Arthur J. Moore from the Methodist Church; and Goodrich C. White, President of Emory University.

41. The incorporators were Methodist Bishop Arthur Moore, Ralph McGill, Rufus E. Clement, President of Atlanta University, Charles Johnson, President of Fisk University, and Howard Odum, from the University of North Carolina. SRC Papers, Series XVI, Reel 218; See also Egerton, *Speak Now against the Day,* 311-316.

42. Steve Suitts argues that the CIC appealed to whites to "act rationally" toward their black neighbors but did not challenge the "region's assumptions of black inferiority." This work, Suitts concluded, left the rural poor—black and white—disfranchised and powerless to improve their own economic conditions. For more on the CIC, see Southern Regional Council Papers at the Atlanta University Center.

43. Griffin interview, 12 November 1991.

44. Frank Adams, *Unearthing Seeds of Fire, The Idea of Highlander* (Winston-Salem: Blair, 1975), 200. Linda Reed, *Simple Decency and Common Sense, the Southern Conference Movement, 1938-1963* (Bloomington: Indiana University, 1991), 159.

45. Anthony P. Dunbar, *Against the Grain, Southern Radicals and Prophets, 1929-1959* (Charlottesville: University Press of Virginia, 1981), viii.

46. Adams, *Unearthing Seeds*, 12.

47. Adams, *Unearthing Seeds*, 17-18; Wayne Urban, *Black Scholar: Horace Mann Bond 1904-1972* (Athens: University of Georgia Press, 1992), 31.

48. Egerton, *Speak Now Against the Day* 154-7.

49. Dunbar, *Against the Grain*, 63.

50. Ibid., 73.

51. Egerton, *Speak Now against the Day*, 197.

52. Grantham, *The South in Modern America*, 164.

53. To a lesser extent two governors in Georgia also played a role softening the center. In the 1930s E.D. Rivers ran his own version the New Deal. Later Ellis Arnall held that progressive course during the war years.

54. Egerton, *Speak Now against the Day*, 91-104.

55. Paula Fass writes that the NYA in Georgia developed a particularly successful program for adults and high school students. Fass, *Outside In*, 131-132. It should be noted, however, that federal aid programs continued to discriminate against blacks.

56. Egerton, *Speak Now against the Day*, 317.

57. "Truman Was a Racist, Scholar Says," *Atlanta Constitution*, 27 October 1991, C9.

58. "Truman Was a Racist, Scholar Says," *Atlanta Constitution*, 27 October 1991, C9.

59. Harry S. Truman as quoted in David McCullough, *Truman* (New York: Touchstone-Simon and Schuster, 1992), 247.

60. Monroe Billington, "Civil Rights, President Truman and the South," *Journal of Negro History* 58 (April 1973), 127.

61. Egerton, *Speak Now against the Day*, 359-75.

62. Lawrence A. Cremin, *American Education: The Metropolitan Experience, 1876-1980* (New York: Harper and Row, 1988), 255.

63. Billington, "Civil Rights," 131; Cremin, *American Education*, 256-7; Steve Perrin, "Before *Brown*: School Segregation and the Truman Administration" (paper presented at the History of Education Society Meeting, Kansas City, MO, October 1991).

64. Cremin, *American Education*, 509-10.

65. This estimate comes from subtracting the percentage of votes received by Republican candidate Thomas Dewey (18%) and the percentage received by Dixiecrat candidate Strom Thurmond (20%) from 100. During the election of 1948 another group broke away from the Democratic Party, and formed the liberal Progressive Party. Their candidate, Henry Wallace, probably received less than 12% of the Georgia vote. Newman V. Bartley, *From Thurmond to Wallace: Political Tendencies in Georgia, 1948-1968* (Baltimore: Johns Hopkins Press, 1970), 6, 32. See, also, Emile B. Ader, "Why the Dixiecrats Failed," *Journal of Politics* 15 (1953), 356-369.

66. *New York Times* 9 May 1950; Gilbert C. Fite, *Richard B. Russell, Jr., Senator from Georgia* (Chapel Hill: University of North Carolina Press, 1991), chapters 11, 12; Merl Elwyn Reed, *Seedtime for the Modern Civil Rights Movement: The President's Committee on Fair Employment Practice, 1941-1946* (Baton Rouge: Louisiana State University Press, 1991) 156-9.

67. Fite, *Richard B. Russell*, 231, 239-41; Harold Clarke Interview, 1991.

68. There are numerous sources that document what came to be known as the "Cocking Affair," so named after Professor Walter B. Cocking, who was fired by Talmadge. See, e.g., Sue Bailes, "Eugene Talmadge and the Board of Regents Controversy" *Georgia Historical Quarterly* 53 (Fall 1969), 409-423; William Anderson, *The Wild Man from Sugar Creek: The Political Career of Eugene Talmadge* (Baton Rouge: Louisiana State Press, 1975);

Harold P. Henderson, *The Politics of Change in Georgia: A Political History of Ellis Arnall* (Athens: University of Georgia Press, 1991).

69. Ravitch, *The Troubled Crusade*, 117.

70. John Egerton, *Speak Now against the Day*, 217-30.

Chapter 3

The Entanglement of Two Movements and the Birth of Massive Resistance in Georgia

There was no serious attempt nor desire in this country to provide Negroes with educational opportunities equal to those for whites. The great surge to equalize educational opportunities for Negroes did not begin until after 1935 when Murray won his suit to enter the University of Maryland. It is also clear that the millions poured into Negro education in the last 20 years were appropriated not so much because it was right but in an endeavor to maintain segregation.

–Benjamin Mays, 1955

We say here in the South that we know the Negro. We believe we have found a place for him a place in our culture. Education and the passing of years may change everything, but I know that there are in my community now many people who will die perpetuating the order as they found it, the scheme of things to which they belong.

–Rollin Chamblis, 1933

The Movement to Equalize Educational Opportunity through Financial Action in the Post-War Period

The end of World War II in 1945 fueled another type of social change in the South. Having endured a depression and a World War, Southerners now had the opportunity to turn their energies and financial resources toward addressing problems in their educational system. As part of the effort to address the educational deficiencies that had been exposed during the war, political and educational leaders across the country called for improvements for public education on a grand scale. In spite of private efforts that focused on inequity of opportunity during the early part of the twentieth century, the quality of public education in the nation was at best uneven and, in many school districts, inadequate.[1] To help bring about fundamental change, school systems would need more money. Although expenditures for public common schooling nationwide had exceeded $2 billion since 1929, Americans were spending less than 3 percent of their income on public schools. By the end of the War expenditures had climbed steadily to $2.6 billion, but this amounted to only 15 percent of the total federal, state and local taxes collected for all public services.[2]

Beyond the problem of this modest outlay for public schooling was the additional complication of inequalities in the amount of money spent on education among and within the states. In 1944 the massive study, *An Inventory of Public School Expenditures*, revealed "shocking variations" in the level of school support across the country. The study, which used 1939 as the base year, found the median classroom yearly expenditures ranged from $400 in Mississippi to ten times that amount ($4,100) in New York. Georgia ranked in a three-way tie for fifth from the bottom, spending a median of $800 per classroom.[3]

The study also discovered that the bottom ten states yielded a fraction of the revenue of the top ten states, in spite of their greater tax effort. The higher taxes paid for by these poorer states raised inadequate amounts of money due to a low tax base. Compounding this inequality was the higher proportion of children in the poorer states. The South in particular stood out as the region bearing the greatest "educational load." If tax effort (and not total revenue generated) were used as a yardstick for evaluating public support for education, the South was far more committed to education than any other region in the nation.[4]

Perhaps more significant than the disparities elaborated upon in *Inventory* was the feeling it aroused in the political and educational communities. In 1945 and 1946, there was a growing consensus that failure to alleviate financial differences would result in educational deficits, which in turn would damage the nation's children and the infrastructure. In 1946, two years after the study, the *Inventory's* chief author, John K. Norton, claimed that children in classrooms which cost $3,000 a year have an "excellent chance" of getting a "first-rate" education while those in classrooms costing less than $1,000 a year "receive a shamefully inadequate schooling."[5] Norton's message was that quality education costs money, and inequality of educational opportunity must be stopped by evenly financing education nationwide. He argued,

> Educational opportunity should cease to be dependent on such factors as the economic and cultural status of the community and family in which the child lives. It should be entirely upon the child's willingness and capacity to learn.

Anything else makes education a creator of artificial and unfair class lines rather than an instrument of equality.[6]

Norton and other educators called on state political and educational leaders to secure adequate financing for educational programs for all children within their states, "with a rock bottom [expenditure of] $2,000 per classroom unit."[7]

By midcentury Norton's call for increased expenditures had been heard and acted upon. In its 1949 report, entitled *The Forty Eight School Systems*, the Council of State Governments endorsed a school finance program that would secure a "reasonably adequate" education for all children supported by state taxes that would distribute the burden of support more equitably. States began enacting bills that reflected the fresh principle that public education was not only a local enterprise but also a state affair. The new partnership between the state and local districts placed major legal and financial responsibilities on the state. By 1952 so-called foundation programs defined as a "basic level of expenditure assured for every child" were operating in over three-quarters of the states.[8]

In 1953 a study conducted by the Office of Education confirmed that financial involvement at the state level was substantial. The comprehensive school finance study, *Expenditures for Education at Mid-century*, reported that the United States was spending over $4 billion on public elementary and secondary education in the 1949-50 school year, nearly doubling what the nation had spent a decade earlier. The report also revealed the median expenditure for each classroom had risen from $1,650 in 1939-40 to $4,391 in 1949-50. Nationwide, state governments were spending approximately 39 percent of the total expenditure. In the South the proportion of state revenue expended was even higher, at 55.4 percent of the total education expense.[9]

Expenditures, like *Inventory*, continued the call for reduction in disparities among school districts. Although differences were less shocking at mid-century than they had been in 1939, they remained large. Classroom expenditures per year ranged from New York's $7,627 to Mississippi's $1,451. Only Mississippi and Kentucky averaged below the "rock bottom" $2,000 minimum set by Norton in 1946.

Public common school equalization efforts were part of the exciting expansion of education in the post-War era. Notwithstanding the large funding disparities still in existence among and within the states at mid-century, the equalization of educational opportunity had revolutionized the way many Americans thought about and provided for their systems of common schools. A group of scholars writing in 1952 referred to this trend as the "most powerful idea of [school] finance in the twentieth century."[10] The scholars should have added that the equalization campaign emphasized the elimination of geographic and class disparities but did not focus on the issue of racial equality. *Expenditures* and *Inventory* chose not to emphasize the vast disparity in expenditures between black and white schools.

The Movement to Equalize Educational Opportunity for Whites across Georgia

The national movement to equalize educational opportunity found early favor in Georgia. On 31 January 1946, Georgia's General Assembly established an education committee to evaluate the public education system and make recommendations based on its findings. One year later the committee, headed by Dr. Omer Clyde Aderhold, Dean of the College of Education at the University of Georgia, completed its investigation and recommended that the state assist local school systems with the burden of financing public education. The survey provided ample evidence that the state's rural white schools and black schools were far below city and national norms. Because schools received most of their funds through local sources, poor counties generally had poor schools. In its extensive, 420-page report the committee identified as critical needs better trained and paid teachers, modern buildings and transportation. The committee recommended a statewide system of common school finance that would provide increased educational spending in each county and improved educational opportunity for all children. Using language that blended the goals of efficiency and democratic equality, the recommendations became the basis for a statewide school reform initiative known as the Minimum Foundation Program of Education (MFPE).[11]

An expensive program proposal, the MFPE would not pass into law without significant statewide backing. The MFPE gained the support of several of the state's key educational leaders and political figures who championed the cause for drastic improvements in the state's inadequate county schools. By the spring of 1948, the powerful and active white teachers' association, the Georgia Education Association (GEA), endorsed the MFPE.[12] The following December, the state's leading educators called on Georgians to wake up and face the major educational "crisis." J.G. Garrison, President of the GEA, in an address to two thousand teachers and principals, acknowledged that funding the MFPE would cost more than any such program ever before conceived in Georgia. But, he went on to assert that $23 million was a reasonable initial demand to fund MFPE. He said far more money would be needed later to provide for critical school needs.[13]

M. D. Collins, State Superintendent of Schools also championed the MFPE.[14]

Collins joined Garrison in arguing for a financing scheme "borne principally by the state" that would equalize educational opportunity in every section of Georgia. Prior to 1937 the school year in Georgia started in the late fall and ended in the early spring, consisting of only four or five months of schooling. Under Collins's leadership, and through the efforts of the teachers associations, the school year was extended to seven months.[15] Collins had long championed legislation that allocated state money based on need and required all children below the age of fourteen to attend school seven months a year. Collins had successfully fought off sporadic movements to divide the state school fund on the basis of taxes paid by each race, and he continued the practice of distributing state funds based on the total number of school-age children in each county.[16]

As he had done all along Collins steered clear of race in his quest to garner support for the MFPE. Having chipped away at the indifference of business-minded elites to gain support for improved schooling for whites, Collins was not interested in entangling his progressive quest with the rights of the Negro. As Collins saw it, the post-war period had already been marred by racial strife and turmoil and the school campaign needed to downplay race in order to succeed. In annual reports to the legislature Collins took care to separate his discussions of equality for all from reports on Negro Education, which were added at the end.

To garner support for the MFPE in the late 1940s, Garrison and Collins lobbied the legislature and found a friend in Roy V. Harris. Harris had served in both houses of the General Assembly and was Speaker of the House from 1937 to 1940, and from 1942 to 1946. Since the 1930s Harris had developed impressive political clout and earned a reputation as the state's political kingpin. By the end of his long career he would be credited as "a man who made five governors" because of his work on winning gubernatorial campaigns. Harris, a self-described racist, shared many of the same progressive beliefs as Collins and supported a greater state role in funding the school enterprise.

At the time that the MFPE was under consideration, Harris wielded enormous political power, even though he no longer held political office. For twenty-one years he had been elected to Georgia's General Assembly, and for six of those years he ran the show as Speaker of the House. Then in 1946 he was defeated in the Democratic primary by fellow Augustan Bill Morris, a bitter foe, who Harris claimed won on account of the Negro vote, brought on by the elimination of the white primary earlier that year. It would turn out to be his last run at political office, but the short, chunky fifty-year-old would manage to keep his hand and much of his power in Georgia politics for at least twenty more years. An addict of the politics of power and a sore loser to boot, the sharp-tongued Harris was unable to step aside gracefully. Years later he recalled that he would not stoop from the two-pronged fight he had been waging: preserving the separation of the races and developing an adequate education system in Georgia.[17]

In 1947 Harris began publishing the *Augusta Courier*. From the start, Harris dedicated nearly half of his weekly print space to the "education crisis" that confronted Georgia. It was through this paper, specifically his editorial column, entitled "Strictly Personal," and his continued presence in the in the state legislative halls as an influential lobbyist, that he would argue for adopting the MFPE.[18]

In 1949 Harris and Collins were the most active and influential education advocates in the state. Both men shared a similar vision of educational reform in Georgia. Their concept, largely consistent with the post-War national equalization movement and the lingering populism in the state, stressed the provision of an adequate public school education for the common people.[19] Collins and Harris, like the famed 19th-century education champion Horace Mann, sought to improve a piecemeal, underfunded system through state-level intervention. Although Harris and Collins leaned toward vocationalism and a practical brand of progressive education, while Mann favored Bible literacy and competency in the three R's, they all shared the belief that only through universal schooling could society be improved.

Mann's vision and his definition of society, however, were larger and more inclusive than either Harris or Collins could imagine. Mann's society consisted of all children no matter where they lived *and* no matter what their ethnic or racial background. Society for Harris—and to a lesser extent Collins—consisted of the state's white population. Where Collins was myopic in his vision on how race would fit into the educational foundation movement, Harris was blind. A staunch segregationist and an enemy of anyone who favored equality for blacks, Harris was ideologically committed to white supremacy and would yield no ground whatsoever toward social justice for non-whites. To Harris, race superseded all other political issues. For example, in 1942 Harris campaigned for "New Dealer" Ellis Arnall against Eugene Talmadge. In 1946, Harris left the Arnall faction to run Eugene Talmadge's campaign for governor, saying "I wouldn't go along with him when he [Arnall] started registering all the niggers so I built up the picture for Gene."[20]

Harris's particular blend of populism and white supremacy was not unique among Georgia politicians. Thomas E. Watson was a well-known Georgian with a comparable ideology; a more recent example is Lester Maddox. Roy Harris, Thomas E. Watson, and Lester Maddox held in tension two contradictory myths. To them America was a land where "all men are created equal;" it was also "a white man's country."[21] Their concept of the "common man" did not include blacks and thus marked the limit of their loyalty to a truly democratic vision of the public school. The school they envisioned would suffer indefinitely from the turmoil of this internal conflict: the paradox of striving for democratic equality while engaging in racial privileging.

The MFPE Gains Legislative Approval but Does Not Take Effect

Members of the Georgia General Assembly traveled from their counties of residence each year for the 90-day legislative session. At the Henry Grady Hotel on Peachtree Street in Atlanta, on the 14th floor, sitting on beds with sandwiches in one hand and a glass of whiskey or a cigar in the other, the lawmakers and political bosses informally considered the MFPE. The major features of the 1949 bill, drafted by Roy Harris, called for increases in teacher salaries and the construction of new buildings. It aimed to improve all public schools by providing every child in the state with a competent teacher, a decent classroom, safe transportation for those living beyond a reasonable walking distance, an adequate supply of textbooks and other learning aids, and a minimum school year of 180 days.[22]

Notably, the bill assumed the preservation of a segregated public school system. At the outset it appeared that the lawmakers had not contemplated what "equalization" would mean for the state's black schools. Most of the initial debate centered around whether the program would give disproportionate financial support to vocational education.[23] Nevertheless, the lawmakers ultimately had to confront the race issue before the bill could be passed. It was Roy Harris who pointed out that if the program were inaugurated without new funds, white schools and white teachers' salaries would be hurt. Equalization without new funds would mean redistributing to black teachers $2 million now going to white teachers, he maintained.[24]

On Monday, 24 January 1949, the House and Senate Education Committees met jointly to consider the bill. The event was witnessed by the largest crowd ever assembled up to that time in the hall of the Georgia House of Representatives. The audience, composed largely of teachers and parents, demonstrated strong support for the bill and for increased funding for the bill. When Speaker of the House Fred Hand asked the crowd if they would support a 3 percent sales tax and increased income taxes to fund the program, every hand went up.[25]

The program was passed, but only after an amendment was added that required new funds to be raised before the program could be put into effect. In January 1949, Georgia's idea of equalizing common school education centered around eliminating geographic and class disparities, as it did elsewhere in the nation. The race issue was not a part of the campaign for equalization. Race only entered into the MFPE debate at the last moment and had the effect of delaying the effective date of the program.

Governor Talmadge Hedges on Funding the MFPE

The issue of raising taxes to fund the MFPE was a sticky one for the newly elected governor, Herman Eugene Talmadge, who favored increased spending on education but had campaigned on a "no new taxes" pledge. Talmadge, born in Telfair County in 1913, started his formal education at age seven in a two-room schoolhouse similar to the one that Harris had attended. Recalling the condition of his first classroom, he remembered, "We could study astronomy through the roof and geology through the floors." As a boy Talmadge preferred "hunting and fishing and playing hooky" to studying—until his ninth-grade teacher got him interested in history, government and debate.[26] During Herman's senior year the Talmadges moved to Atlanta where his father served as a fiery governor of Georgia. His father, Eugene Talmadge, known as ole' Gene and the "Wild Man from Sugar Creek," was a governor who claimed to be the champion of the forgotten man, but who was surreptitiously friendly to industry and business and openly anti-New Deal and anti-Negro.[27] Herman attended Druid Hills High School and the University of Georgia, where he earned a law degree in 1936. He practiced law with his father until he enlisted and served fifty-two months in the Navy. After his honorable discharge in 1945, he returned to Georgia and managed his father's final gubernatorial campaign.

In a 1991 interview Talmadge remembered the 1946 gubernatorial campaign as being one of the first in Georgia to successfully use race as an issue. Eugene Talmadge, with his son as his campaign manager and Harris on his campaign staff, played on the fears and prejudices of white voters, highlighting the fact that the previous governor, Ellis Arnall, had eliminated the poll tax. Eugene Talmadge was quoted as saying, "The people of Georgia must declare whether or not they will continue to run the state or whether they are willing to turn it over to the Moscow-Harlem zoot-suiters." And, he said, "If I get a Negro vote, it will be by accident."[28]

In late 1946 governor-elect Eugene Talmadge died. His son Herman, at the age of thirty-four, was elected to the governorship by the legislature. He served a disputed term as governor for sixty-seven days, but he vacated the office when the Georgia Supreme Court ruled that the way he was elected to the governorship was unconstitutional. Then in a special election in 1948, Herman Talmadge was formally elected governor and served out the remaining portion of his father's unexpired term.[29] Herman Talmadge, eligible to run again for governor, was then re-elected in 1950 to the traditional four-year term. He served until 1955. One year later he successfully ran for U.S. Senator and served in that office until his retirement.

When Talmadge ran for governor in 1948 he had maligned M.E. Thompson, the Arnall faction's candidate, for his "New Deal" policies and pledged he would not support a tax increase without a public referendum. Talmadge appeared on the campaign trail with Ku Klux Klan members and aligned himself against the liberals. As his father, Eugene, had done the previous decade, Talmadge appealed to the extremes, industry and big business and to rural Georgians. He promised not to raise taxes without the support of the common people. Yet Talmadge, with neopopulist Roy Harris on his team, also had campaigned on a platform favoring educational reform, which would eventually require new taxes. Harris, who had directed Talmadge's 1948 campaign and would do the same in 1950, had become known as the spokesman for the teachers in the state.[30] The young governor was in a dilemma.

Perhaps the most important determinant of how Talmadge would escape the trap was his own political instinct. He was aware that no governor who had supported a sales tax package had been reelected to that office except John W. Bricker of Ohio. Supporting a sales tax in 1949 could amount to nothing less than political suicide. Prior to the legislature's consideration of the MFPE, Talmadge had spoken in favor of the program, but when the issue of funding surfaced, he declined vigorously to support the program. Playing election year politics, he suggested that education was good business, but he could not support new taxes at that time. While a referendum on a tax increase was prepared for popular vote, Talmadge stayed out of the crossfire.[31] He would only put his prestige behind the program when and if he was sure it would not cost him critical votes.

For a while, however, it seemed as if Talmadge's choice to wait was more than just election year politics; it reflected his awareness of developments regarding school funding at the federal level, and his hope that Congress might pass a federal aid package in the first few months of 1949. If Uncle Sam might foot the education bill, why rush into an all-out endorsement of the MFPE? Since 1945 there had been a series of drives in Congress to pass a federal aid to education package that would address the regional and district deficiencies that Norton and other schoolmen of the NEA had detailed since the end of the war. Originally sponsored in the Senate by Lister Hill (Alabama) and Elbert Thomas (Utah), and in the House by Georgia's fifth district congressman, Robert Ramspeck, the initial bills were designed to raise teacher salaries nationwide, but particularly in the poverty-ridden South. By the summer of 1948 President Truman called on Congress to pass a $300 million federal aid package that pledged $15 million to Georgia. The proposal gained enthusiastic support from Georgia's teachers and PTAs, and M. D. Collins. As Talmadge marked his time and withheld support for the MFPE, the federal aid to education bill sailed through the Senate, but later stalled in the House. The burden of funding improved schooling was back on the governors and state legislators.[32]

For Talmadge, the problem of funding new school programs involved several other considerations. On the one hand, Talmadge, like other post-War Southern governors, desired economic diversification and sought to attract new industries, some of which were less labor-intensive and required more skilled workers. School improvements would logically lead to a better trained workforce and thus increase social efficiency. As Collins had suggested in his slogan "Education doesn't cost, it pays." School reform might be a sound business investment. On the other hand, a business climate with low taxes and cheap and abundant labor had been the traditional drawing cards for the region. In the post-war period, state development agencies in other Southern states competed with Georgia for new industry. Working through state and local government, some even started offering subsidies, tax exemptions, and free or low cost buildings to interested industrial prospects.[33] If Talmadge was going to support a tax increase for schooling, he would have to be sure it did not interfere with the campaign for new industry or reduce profits of those businesses and industries already operating in the state.[34] It would have to be a tax that raised a significant amount of money but did not burden capitalists and investors with excessive costs.

As he had promised in his campaign for governor in 1948, Herman Talmadge would not raise taxes without a referendum. In the spring of 1949 the issue of financing the MFPE was put to the voters. In addition to the $23 million asked for to start the MFPE, the referendum asked the voters to approve another $23 million for improvements in highways, hospitals, health care, and schools for the handicapped. To pay for these social improvements, the referendum asked for a 42 percent increase in income taxes.[35] The governor still could not bring himself to support the MFPE with anything other than contradictory rhetoric. The GEA, on the other hand, mounted an all-out blitz to promote the MFPE.

The GEA showered the state with an illustrated pamphlet, entitled "It's Our Duty to the Children of Georgia."[36] The pamphlet, by design and tradition, ignored an analysis of the topic of improvements for black schools and teachers entirely, except when combining numbers to make the total statistics appear more powerful. The pupils and teachers pictured in the photographs, of course, were white.[37] The booklet asserted that one-third of Georgia's adults had less than six years of schooling; only a quarter had attended high school; and less than 10 percent attended college. It argued that Georgia was experiencing outmigration of nearly one million people and that schools and teaching corps were substandard. Georgia's teachers, it argued, were teaching forty to sixty children in crude, dark and uncomfortable classrooms in substandard buildings, using worn out textbooks. "Can we blame a teacher," the GEA asked, "for leaving his profession to seek a better paid job in more pleasant surroundings?" The GEA maintained that more than 6,000 teachers had left their jobs in 1948, and 93 percent of the vacancies were filled by those holding emergency certificates, many of whom were only high school graduates. Of the 22,600 teachers in Georgia, many had "little or no professional training." Many of the most qualified teachers had moved to the neighboring states of Alabama, Florida, and North Carolina where annual salaries were between $200 and $850 higher. The GEA pamphlet asked the reader to now picture their child in an "attractive and well-lighted" classroom of thirty children sitting at modern desks, and using current textbooks, "globes, maps, charts and similar learning aids," taught by a "professionally trained, 4-year college, teacher." "Georgia parents," it concluded, "want their children to have the educational opportunities that are comparable with the best given to children in neighboring states." Finally the GEA insisted that the MFPE would meet the needs of the state school program. It asked: "Is $83,4101,720 too much to invest in public schools, University system and teachers' retirement system?"[38]

As could have been expected, the voters did not agree to raise their taxes by 42 percent. To the chagrin of Georgia's education establishment, the referendum was defeated by a vote of 207,777 to 72,088.[39] The day after the referendum nearly 200 teachers from Polk and Haralson Counties quit their classes and urged thousands of other teachers to join them in a statewide walkout. One organizer said that the intent of the "indefinite recess" was to force the governor to call a special session of the legislature and find another way to fund the MFPE program. Ultimately, the teacher walkout situation was resolved by B.E. Thrasher, state auditor, who declared a no-work, no-pay policy, saying teachers' salaries would be docked for the days they remained out. By Saturday the teachers from Polk, Haralson, and 21 other counties had changed their position, agreeing to finish the school year but maintaining that they would not sign new contracts unless the state made some provision to improve facilities and raise their salaries.[40] Former teacher and political foe M.E. Thompson called the governor a "flop" and the defeat of the referendum a repudiation of Talmadge.

Talmadge had not planned on the quick and angry reaction among teachers in the state. Surprised but not flustered, Talmadge refused to call a special session and sought to control the political damage. To silence the opposition and divert attention away from the defeat, he turned to his father's old standby, race. Over the next several weeks he lifted the Confederate flag and called for a return to white supremacy, states' rights, and free enterprise. He spoke out against the bloc voting among "unqualified" blacks in the state, a permanent Fair Employment Practices Commission, other Truman's civil rights initiatives, socialism, commu-nism, "and any of the other 'isms'" from "foreign shores."[41]

His real problem was revenue, or rather lack thereof. Talmadge needed a massive infusion of funds not only to keep the state fiscally operative but also to bolster the push for industry, roads, and vocational training, all of which would help make the state attractive to would-be industrialists. Among other things, money was needed to pave farm-to-market roads and modernize ports in cities like Savannah and Brunswick. The defeat of the referendum meant he would have to go against campaign promises and make unpopular bare-bone cuts of $1.5 million to the existing budget to keep the state solvent. His first targets were two already starved public services: the Georgia Academy for the Blind and the State Hospital for the Insane. By the middle of the summer Talmadge realized that he could not continue to slash the state budget and eliminate state employees and remain politically viable.

The answer might be found in federal aid, but as Talmadge saw it federal aid could only be accepted without federal "interference." Specifically, he would accept no racial stipulations. Unmistakable signs that the political safeguards for white supremacy were slowly but surely eroding were most disconcerting to Talmadge. *Smith v. Alwright* had dismantled the white primary in Texas in 1944 and put in place federal jurisprudence that led to its demise in Georgia two years later. In 1945 Governor Ellis Arnall abolished the poll tax and thus cracked open the ballot box to blacks and poor whites alike. Post-war Georgia was edging along a long continuum from oligarchy toward democracy, which for traditionalists was regress. Talmadge's disdain for Truman over issues relating to black civil rights, federal employment regulation, and other shifts toward more federal authority led him to oppose "federal interference" and funding stipulations.

Another roadblock to federal aid was the lack of funds to meet federal matching requirements. Federal legislation had offered states matching programs for vocational education, technical training, paving roads, building hospitals and schools, and revenue for infrastructure—but in most programs states were required to match the contribution.

That spring and early summer Talmadge was in a bind. He realized he needed several million dollars of match federal categorical aid to pay for vocational education, vocational rehabilitation, the school lunches, roads, hospital construction, and old-age pensions for the upcoming fiscal year. He needed to continue to attract industry to the region and could not turn to capitalists to fund reform. His plan to let the people vote for a tax increase had yielded nothing, and now he faced the prospect of letting the state government go bankrupt and missing the opportunity to qualify for federal aid if he did not raise revenue internally. His father's conservative political legacy told him defy the federal government and forgo the revenue, but Herman was not a clone of Eugene, and his business-pragmatism and self-pride led him to find a way to raise the money.

For Talmadge there was no real problem in finding a way to get legislative support for a tax increase. At the time he had the political support of about 70 percent of the legislators. He also had the power to appoint the Speaker of the House and the floor leader, who controlled the legislative sessions. He sensed that whatever he asked the legislature for—"within reason"—they would vote into law.[42] Instead, Talmadge's difficulty was in finding a way to win public support for a tax increase. Talmadge would eventually gain popular support for a tax increase by harnessing the white public's anxiety about the black civil rights movement.

The Black Campaign for Equal Schooling in the Post-War Period

The last few months in 1948 marked a period of considerable legal activism in the black struggle for educational opportunity across the South. In higher education, a petition strategy led to the acceptance of the first black at the University of Arkansas Law School; and in Oklahoma a federal district court ruled it was unconstitutional to deny a black applicant admission to the state's flagship institution on the basis of race. Another law school challenge was also playing out in a federal court in Texas. The Oklahoma and Texas cases would ultimately be decided by U.S. Supreme Court in the summer of 1950.[43]

Within Georgia, leaders of black and biracial organizations continued to work toward school equalization. In public schools across the South there were signs that black and biracial activism to equalize school expenditures were beginning to bear fruit. Georgia and five other Southern states had increased the average per pupil expenditure for blacks from $16.70 to $74.85 in 1948, raising it from 37 percent to 62 percent of the white average. Atlanta, through the efforts of Grace Hamilton and others, had taken the lead in the state with a petition campaign demanding parity in facilities, per pupil expenditures, and teacher salaries.[44]

Since 1944, Hamilton's Atlanta Urban League had compiled reams of evidence documenting white educational advantage in the city's system. In an impressive effort, Hamilton organized the biracial Citizens' Committee for Public Education (CCPE). The CCPE, shared the Urban League's careful analysis of the conditions of Atlanta's black public schools with many of the city's middle-class whites, who had somehow remained ignorant of the plight of the black schools.

The League and the CCPE disseminated more that 250,000 pamphlets and brochures, complete with charts and photographs, documenting the conditions. The work involved sixty white and black organizations in the city, including PTAs, church clubs, voters leagues, and organized labor.[45] Working in cooperation with A.T. Walden and the local NAACP, the Atlanta Urban League pressed the recalcitrant board to begin construction of new buildings and building additions.[46] The effort succeeded in winning for Atlanta blacks a proportionate share of a local school construction bond, demonstrating that the biracial movement at least in Atlanta, was a force to reckoned with.

At the state level, Charles L. Harper, head of the Georgia's black teachers association, the Georgia Teachers and Education Association (GTEA), worked with William Boyd, the head of the state chapter of the NAACP, to file petitions with state, city, and county boards demanding parity in school expenditures. To shield local black teachers from firing or reprimand, only Harper's name and signature appeared on the petitions. He also enclosed a resolution passed at the 1949 GTEA conference in Augusta that recommended a leveling-up approach to equalization. The GTEA petitions did not seek admission to white schools but rather demanded comparable accommodations for black children. Georgia blacks were determined to force the state to pay a high price for the right to segregate.[47] If ignored, the petition strategy would lead to demands for access to the white public universities and the white public schools. Harper warned that if the petitions were ignored or denied, the next stop would be federal court.

The petition strategy gained energy and dove-tailed nicely with the invigoration of regional liberal biracialism and a nationwide campaign to improve public schooling. By the late 1940s, National Urban League and the Southern Regional Council had affiliates at state and local levels and were investigating a number of problems that plagued the region. In January 1949 the Southern Regional Council released a study that estimated there was a $545 million disparity between black school plants and white school plants across the South. The study, released only months in advance of the more widely publicized Strayer Report, found remarkably similar comparisons; it estimated that the mean value of school property for each black child enrolled was $36, compared with $221 for each white pupil.[48] In Georgia in 1949 the Department of Health, Education and Welfare (HEW) estimated white public school property was worth $136 million, while black school property was valued at $22-million. Georgians spent an average of $80 per year on each black pupil and $145 per year on each white pupil. In that same year black teachers, who averaged $646 per year in pay, taught an average of 34 pupils, while white teachers, who averaged $843 annually, taught an average of 27 pupils.[49]

The U.S. Supreme Court decisions stating that the Constitution required "substantially equal" facilities had not caused the white community to equalize education for blacks.[50] Throughout the existence of the separate-but-equal doctrine, whites had failed to provide equal school facilities for black children. In spite of hard evidence of lopsidedness, white local elites were resolved to maintain their funding advantage to the end. In one instance, as a consequence of a NAACP suit, a superintendent and three board members in Gloster, Gwinnett County, were found in contempt and fined $250 each for slighting their black schools. The judge, Sterling Hucheson, also issued an injunction against the board and decreed the court would continue to monitor the situation.[51] But continued monitoring of the unequal system would no longer satisfy the NAACP. Lawsuits seeking school desegregation were publicly announced as the next step.[52]

Georgia Leaders React to the Black Movement

The public position of the national office of the NAACP did not go unnoticed by Georgia's white state leaders. On 3 January 1949, Harris, observant of the successful erosion of segregation in higher education, had no doubt that efforts would soon be made to desegregate the common schools.[53] Harris contended that Southern blacks would follow the policy set by the national chapter to "unsegregate" society. "The national association," he argued "sets the pace and negroes follow in a solid bloc." Writing in the *Courier*, he claimed that "negroes were determined to destroy the pattern of segregation in the public schools and everywhere else." Harris threatened to use all his power to fight for the maintenance of the pattern of segregation. "The lines have been drawn. The issue has been made. And the battle will continue as long as the negroes keep the destruction of segregation as their goal and object."[54]

Until 1949 Governor Herman Talmadge refrained from commenting directly about the actions of the NAACP, focusing most of his anti-integration energies toward the federal government in Washington.[55] But in 1949, as pressure mounted to find an innovative way to gain popular support for a 3 percent sales tax, Talmadge realized he could get some political mileage out of the school/race issue. In search of a solution, he held meetings with the State Auditor B.E. Thrasher, Speaker of the House Fred Hand, floor leader Frank Twitty, and his advisors, Roy Harris, Burkett Dean ("Buck") Murphy, and Walter B. ("Bee") Brooks.[56] Ultimately, Talmadge seized on white fear of court-ordered school desegregation to gain support for a tax increase. On 22 October 1949 Talmadge made a radio address, persuading the people that they would have to fund improvements in their schools or face the prospect of court-ordered desegrega-tion.[57]

His fiery speech was fueled by a lawsuit that had been initiated in Irwin County. In August 1949 the NAACP, representing eighteen black parents in Irwin County, filed a suit in federal court against the local school board. The suit demanded full parity of facilities as required under the 14th amendment. The suit alleged that white schools in the county were worth $344,723, while black schools were valued at only $13,175. The suit also pointed out disparities in the allocation of transportation, books, teacher pay and average number of teaching days.[58]

In his radio address Talmadge placed the blame for the Irwin County controversy squarely on the shoulders of "northern agitators," who he claimed were trying to move "Negro children into the nearest most convenient white schools." Linking school funding to the race issue, Talmadge said, "These agitators . . . know we cannot furnish either white or Negro schools with identical facilities overnight." He bitterly denounced the Irwin County suit and promised that "Georgia would fight this dastardly effort with all the strength and resources we have."[59] Although the suit did not connect school equalization with black access to white schools, Talmadge did. By making this connection, Talmadge had found what he considered to be a politically sound reason for revising the tax system and working vigorously toward improving the state's system of public education. He would do it to preserve the "Southern Way of Life."

MFPE Inextricably Linked to Race Issue

Talmadge's race-baiting paid off. Three days after his radio address the *Atlanta Constitution* editorialized that funding the MFPE was the only answer to the Irwin County suit. Within one week the State Department of Commerce came out in favor of the MFPE.[60] Georgians began to think about improving the state's system of education in order to preserve their system of segregation. The issue now was not whether the legislature would fund the plan, but rather whether they would provide for a sales tax to finance it in the 1950 legislative session or in the 1951 session. By 1950, therefore, the race issue had become tightly linked to the MFPE. Georgians were convinced by Talmadge that they must spend money on public schools, and specifically on equalizing education for blacks, to avoid the threat of forced desegregation.

Although Talmadge had successfully linked race to increasing state expenditures on public education and had navigated successfully through politically treacherous waters, there were still a few dangerous rocks that threatened to sink his vessel. Ahead of him was the gubernatorial election in November. Even with race linked to funding the MFPE, Talmadge feared that pushing for a tax increase would cost him votes. During the winter and spring of 1950, his strategy was to refrain from publicly acting on a sales tax and an increase in income tax, thus avoiding a potential drop in voter support in November. Talmadge said he wanted to help the schools "when possible," but he also said he opposed new taxes for education at that time.[61]

Perhaps the biggest rock in Talmadge's channel was time. The governor had a full nine months until election day. School advocates were already accusing him of playing election year politics and urging him to call a special session of the General Assembly to deal what the *New York Times* was now calling the "school crisis." In June 1950, Talmadge again used the fear of forced desegregation to argue for support of the MFPE. It was two U.S. Supreme Court decisions, *Sweatt v. Painter* and *McLaurin v. Oklahoma*, that gave him an excuse to reinject race into politics. The Court had ruled that Heman Sweatt must be admitted to the University of Texas law school since no comparable law school for blacks existed in the state. In *McLaurin* the Court declared that physically separating a black graduate student in class, the library and in the cafeteria was also a denial of equal protection under the 14th amendment.

Talmadge was the first Southern governor to react to the high court's rulings. Talmadge said, "As long as I am Governor, Negroes will not be admitted to white schools." Then, picking up on Roy Harris's words from January 1949—17 months earlier—he declared that "the line is drawn. The threats that have been held over the head of the South are now pointed like a dagger ready to be plunged into the very heart of the Southern tradition."[62]

Other reactions in the state were less politically charged. Superintendent Collins immediately saw that *Sweatt* and *McLaurin* represented critical steps toward a challenge to racial segregation in the common schools. Collins estimated it would cost 100 million dollars to equalize Georgia's black schools. Charles Harper, of the GTEA, was more explicit about relationship between the Supreme Court decisions, equalization and segregation. "The state will have to provide equality or integrate Negroes into the white schools." George Mitchell, director of the Atlanta-based Southern Regional Council (SRC), declared that it was "the South's duty to provide equality" and urged universities to welcome qualified blacks who sought admission.[63] But in Georgia, where political power was in the hands of the rural county elites, remarks like those coming from the SRC and the black community had limited influence.[64]

The Crystallization of Defiance

Following the *Sweatt* and *McLaurin* decisions, state leaders in Georgia rallied around the race issue in an early crystallization of official resistance to desegregation. The policy of resistance born during the 1950 state Democratic convention would suffuse state politics for the next decade.

The convention was held in August in the City Auditorium in Macon. Five thousand delegates from every county attended the convention and heard several different state leaders speak on the issues that confronted Georgians. The convention was dominated by those who supported Governor Talmadge. Speakers lauded the Governor's two years in office and spoke of the "remarkable progress" the state had made under his leadership. Other orators used the occasion to condemn the U.S. Supreme Court and Georgia's "carpetbag" daily newspapers. The delegates went on to endorse the Governor's official platform that included a pledge to maintain segregation and full financing of the MFPE. Delegates unanimously approved a resolution that pledged all state officials "to preserve racial segregation in the schools and colleges, [court] decisions to the contrary notwithstanding." Their move got front page coverage in the *New York Times*, the *Atlanta Constitution* and other papers.[65]

The resolution also declared that the *Sweatt* and *McLaurin* rulings were not binding in Georgia. Roy Harris, who served as the floor leader at the convention, took the segregation resolution one step further when he announced that even if the decisions were binding, state leaders in Georgia "will go to jail before [they] will let Negroes and whites go to school together."[66] Four years before *Brown,* Georgia's leaders knew where the Supreme Court was heading on the issue of segregation and vigorously expressed their disapproval.

Georgia's state representatives were not the only lawmakers deploring the erosion of segregation. Fifth District Congressman James C. Davis lauded Talmadge and the state's Democrats for standing up to the federal government at their 1950 convention. Georgia Senator Richard B. Russell was also adamant in his refusal to allow the segregation barriers to fall. Russell, working from within the Democratic Party rather than defecting to the Dixiecrats, emerged in the late 1940s as the South's leader against Truman's civil rights policies. In 1949 Russell introduced a bill that would redistribute the South's black population across the United States.[67] Although the U.S. Senate refused to give serious consideration to the bill, Russell was highly respected in Georgia, and his outspoken opposition to black civil rights gave encouragement to white defiance within the state.

While Georgia's most powerful politicians embraced the democratic convention platform, some leaders responded negatively to the resolution to defy the law of the land. Former governor M. E. Thompson, who was preparing to run against Talmadge for governor, called the action "regrettable" and ill-advised. The sharpest criticism came from federal district court judge Abraham Conger from the middle district of Georgia. Conger, a native Georgian, was inflamed by the delegates' audacity in defying the highest court in the land. Conger declared that such actions by a small group of men "willed by prejudice, inebriated by power, and blinded by egotism" would lead to anarchy.[68] Obviously incensed, Conger, though a segregationist, called the resolution "a sputum of a negligible, vicious, vociferous, selfish few who thrive and prosper upon turmoil, strife, confusion, hate, prejudice and intolerance."[69]

Notes

1. David Tyack and Elisabeth Hanscott, *Managers of Virtue* (New York: Basic Books, 1982), 163-164.

2. The steady increase in expenditures was interrupted in 1933-34, during the low point of the Great Depression. Harl R. Douglass and Calvin Grieder, *American Public Education: An Introduction* (New York: Ronald Press, 1948), 413-414.

3. John K. Norton and Eugene S. Lawler, *An Inventory of Public School Expenditures in the United States: A Report of the Cooperative Study of Public School Expenditures* 2 vols. (Washington, DC: American Council on Education, 1944). For a summary, see John K. Norton, "The Myth of Educational Equality," *American Mercury* 62 (1946), 16-23.

4. Ibid.; see also, M.E. Thompson, "Problems of Public Education in Georgia," *Emory University Quarterly* 3 (October 1947), 129-33; Norton and Lawler, *An Inventory of Public School Expenditures*, 87.

5. In 1946 Norton was the chair of the Department of Education Administration at Teachers College Columbia, past president of the American Educational Research Association (AERA), chairman of the National Conference on Financing of Education, and director of research for National Education Association (NEA).

6. Norton, "The Myth of Educational Equality," 18, 23.

7. Ibid.

8. Department of Health, Education and Welfare, *Expenditures for Education at Mid-century* (Washington, DC: Government Printing Office, 1953), 86; Calvin Grieder and William Everett Rosenstengel, *Public School Administration* (New York: Ronald Press, 1954), 423-4; John T. Walhquist et al. *The Administration of Public Education* (New York: Ronald Press, 1952), 377.

9. Department of Health, Education and Welfare, *Expenditures for Education at Mid-century*, 86.

10. Walhquist, *The Administration of Public Education*, 377.

11. Special Committee on Education, *A Survey of Public Education of Less Than College Grade in Georgia: A Report to the General Assembly of Georgia by Its Special Committee on Education* (Atlanta, 1 January 1947); 1949 Georgia Laws 1407-23; James Hilliard Broughton, "A Historical Study of Selected Aspects of the Equalization of Educational Opportunity in Georgia, 1937-1968" (dissertation: University of Georgia, 1969), 129; *Augusta Courier,* 29 August 1949, 1.

12. In the 1930s the GEA had established itself as the chief white professional organization in the expanding educational hierarchy. The GEA was run by the state's cadre of progressive schoolmen, education professors and change-oriented local superintendents. GEA members included the Chancellor of the university system, a future president of the University of Georgia in Athens (UGA), and a host of others from education departments at UGA, Mercer, Emory, and Oglethorpe Universities. The association's officers viewed themselves as agents of change. See, generally, *Georgia Education Journal,* 1930-1960.

13. "Legislators Warned on Fund Needs for Georgia Schools," *Augusta Courier,* 6 December 1948, 2; Roy V. Harris, "Strictly Personal: Education Essential for Prosperity, Happiness of People of Georgia," *Augusta Courier,* 10 January 1949, 2. See also *Augusta Courier* 19 September 1949, 1; *Augusta Courier,* 14 October 1949, 1.

14. *Augusta Courier,* 21 March 1949, 4-5; *Augusta Courier,* 19 September 1949, 1; Talmadge interview, 30 July 1991. For more on Collins, see Georgia Department of Education, M. D. Collins Collection, Georgia Department of Archives and History, Atlanta, GA.

15. *Augusta Courier,* 19 September 1949, 1; Broughton, "Selected Aspects of the Equalization," 130.

16. *Augusta Courier,* 19 September 1949; *Augusta Courier,* 21 March 1949, 1; Talmadge interview, 30 July 1991.

17. Roy V. Harris Collection, AVA1:6, "History of Education in Georgia," transcript of 1982 interview, Richard B. Russell Memorial Library, University of Georgia, Athens, Georgia.

18. Harris Collection, Series I, Box 1, folder 4, Richard B. Russell Memorial Library, University of Georgia, Athens, GA; William Anderson, *The Wild Man from Sugar Creek: The Political Career of Eugene Talmadge* (Baton Rouge: Louisiana State Press, 1975), 216; Clarke interview, 8 April 1991; Talmadge interview, 30 July 1991; Also see *Augusta Courier* between 1947-1951.

19. "Populism," as it is used here, refers to political philosophy in support of the common people. The term comes from the agrarian movement, organized in 1892, that sought to improve farmers' conditions. Georgia's Thomas E. Watson surfaced as a national populist leader in 1896, and fought Northern industrialists and big business who controlled what came known as the "New South." For a while Watson believed that the poor, both black and white, could join political forces to forge governmental policies that would meet their pressing social needs. Later in his life he began to see blacks as an albatross around his neck. He forsook the agrarian-industrial struggle and, to the dismay of many of his supporters, directed his energies against Catholics, Blacks, Jews and Socialists. See C. Vann Woodward, *Tom Watson, Agrarian Rebel* (New York: Oxford University Press, 1938).

20. Roy V. Harris, as quoted in "Georgia, Pick the Winning Side," *Time* (26 June 1950), 18; Roy V. Harris, "Reaction," *Richmond County History* 7 (Fall, 1975), 76.

21. Marilyn Gale Hector, "Racism, Black Nationalism, and W.E.B. DuBois," (master's thesis, Emory University, 1978), 43.

22. *Augusta Courier*, 3 October 1949, 1; *Augusta Courier*, 10 October 1949, 1; Broughton, "Selected Aspects of the Equalization," 126; 1949 Georgia Laws 1406-1422.

23. *Statesman*, 3 February 1949, 1; *Augusta Courier*, 10 January 1949, 1.

24. *Atlanta Constitution*, 25 January 1949, 1; *Atlanta Journal*, 25 January 1949, 7.

25. *Atlanta Constitution*, 25 January 1949, 1.

26. Transcribed Talmadge interview, "Early Years and Depression," Georgia's Political Heritage Project, Special Collections, State University of West Georgia, Carrollton, GA; 1985; Herman E. Talmadge, *Talmadge: A Political Legacy, A Politician's Life—A Memoir*, edited by Mark Royden Winchell (Atlanta: Peachtree Publishers, 1987), 19-21. See also Talmadge folders, Atlanta Historical Society Archives, Atlanta History Center.

27. See, generally, Anderson, *Wild Man from Sugar Creek*.

28. William L. Belvin Jr. "The Georgia Gubernatorial Primary of 1946" *Georgia Historical Quarterly* 50 (Spring 1966) 43; Talmadge interview, 30 July 1991; Transcribed Talmadge interview, "Race Relations and Segregation," Georgia Political Heritage Project, State University at West Georgia.

29. Belvin, "The Georgia Gubernatorial Primary of 1946"; Roger N. Pajari, "Herman E. Talmadge and the Politics of Power," in *Georgia Governors in An Age of Change: From Ellis Arnall to George Busbee*, eds., Harold P. Henderson & Gary L. Roberts (Athens: University of Georgia Press, 1988), 78; Herman E. Talmadge, *Talmadge: A Political Legacy, A Politician's Life—A Memoir*.

30. Roy V. Harris Collection, Series I, Box 1, folder 4, Richard B. Russell Jr. Memorial Library, University of Georgia, Athens, GA; *Richmond County News*, 19 July 1978; Roy V. Harris "Georgia, Pick," 18; Talmadge, *A Political Legacy*, 98.

31. *Statesman*, 20 January 1949, 4; Talmadge interview, 30 July 1991.

32. *Atlanta Journal*, 27 November 1945, 3, 22; *Atlanta Journal*, 1 May 1949, 10-A; *Atlanta Journal*, 6 May 1949, 10; See generally, Diane Ravitch, *The Troubled Crusade: American Education, 1945-1980* (New York: Basic Books, 1983), 26-42.

33. James C. Cobb, *The Selling of the South: The Southern Crusade for Industrial Development (Baton Rouge: Louisiana State University Press, 1982)*, 44-45.

34. *Atlanta Journal*, 26 August 1949, 3.

35. *Atlanta Constitution*, 26 February 1949, 1; *New York Times*, 6 April 1949, 24.

36. Georgia Education Association, *It's Our Duty to the Children of Georgia to Support the Minimum Foundation Program of Eduction*, Atlanta: May 1948.

37. Ibid. One enrollment and attendance chart, however, made distinctions based on race, the effect of which provided abundant evidence that racial disparities remained the rule and not the exception. The chart documented in no uncertain terms white privilege; white teachers earned an average of $700 more than their black peers, had six less pupils in their classrooms; white schools used 2,724 buses to transport 189,670 pupils, while black schools utilized 147 buses to transport 10,509 pupils. While 38% of the school-age population was black, only 32% of the teachers were black, and one of every 180 school buses were used

to transport black pupils. One indicator of the scarcity of black high school opportunity was that only 22% of all high school pupils were black.

38. Ibid.

39. Broughton, "Selected Aspects of the Equalization," 122; *Atlanta Journal*, 9 April 1949, 1.

40. *New York Times*, 8 April 1949, 27; 67; *New York Times* 10 April 1949, 67; *Atlanta Journal*, 9 April 1949, 1.

41. *Atlanta Journal*, 2 April 1949, 4; *Atlanta Journal*, 16 April 1949, 1; *Atlanta Journal*, 12 June 1949, 1A.

42. Talmadge interview, 30 July 1991.

43. *Sipuel v. Board of Regents*, 332 US 631 (1948); *McLaurin v. Oklahoma*, 339 US 637 (1950); *Sweatt v. Painter*, 339 US 629 (1950); *Atlanta Journal*, 3 September 1948, 41; *Atlanta Journal*, 16 September 1948, 13; *Atlanta Journal*, 15 September 1948, 39.

44. *Atlanta Journal*, 11 April 1948, 5.

45. Citizens Committee on Public Education, "The Negro School Child in Atlanta, A Report in Pictures," (Atlanta, no date, available at Emory University Library); Lorraine Nelson Spritzer and Jean B. Bergmark, *Grace Hamilton and the Politics of Southern Change* (Athens: University of Georgia Press, 1997), 103-109.

46. Petitions dated December 1945, September 1948, February 1948 and April 1949 were sent to the Atlanta board. The supporting evidence for the petitions is documented in Atlanta Urban League, "A Report of Public School Facilities for Negroes in Atlanta, Georgia," (Atlanta: Atlanta Urban League, 1944); and Atlanta Urban League, "A Supplemental Report on the Public School Facilities for Negroes, 1948," (Atlanta: Atlanta Urban League, 1948). During the time period, the board held at least one meeting per month but refused to take any action with regard to the petitions. Grace Hamilton papers, Atlanta Historical Society, MSS #597, box 4, folder 8.

47. *Atlanta Journal*, 27 April 1949, 13.

48. *Augusta Courier*, 29 September 1949, 2; *New York Times*, 26 January 1949, 9; "What Will It Cost to Equalize School Buildings in the South?" *New South* (January 1949), 6-8.

49. Department of Health, Education and Welfare, *Expenditures for Education at Mid-century* (Washington, DC: Government Printing Office, 1953); Department of Health, Education and Welfare, *Preliminary Statistics of State School Systems, 1961-62*, (Washington, DC: Government Printing Office, 1963).

50. Louis R. Harlan, *Separate and Unequal: Public School Campaigns and Racism in the Southern Seaboard States, 1901-1915* (New York: Atheneum, 1969).

51. Ernst W. Swanson and John A. Griffin, *Public Education in the South, Today and Tomorrow: A Statistical Survey* (Chapel Hill: University of North Carolina Press, 1955), 63; *Atlanta Journal*, 5 May 1949, 51.

52. Although the removal of all racial barriers was the NAACP's goal from the outset, it had chosen to begin its battle by litigating for equal facilities, not integrated facilities. The NAACP did not publicly announce that it would challenge the constitutionality of the separate-but-equal doctrine until 1948, when the national office of the NAACP declared that educational equity was "unattainable within the framework of a segregated system." *Atlanta*

Daily World, 15 December 1948, 2.

Although the inequalities in school facilities were obvious, as long as the separate-but-equal doctrine remained in place, the NAACP would have to mount a separate challenge to the operation of each school system, compare the white facilities to the black facilities, and prove in court that the system did not offer an equal education to blacks. The problems of such a litigation strategy were daunting. Although there was considerable initial debate within the NAACP as to what litigation path to follow, Thurgood Marshall started in 1945 to reconcile internal differences within the organization and by 1949 had gained support for a direct attack on segregated public school education.

As part of his effort, Marshall advised the presidents of seventeen black land grant colleges that it was in the best interests of blacks to oppose racial segregation in education. At a meeting in Washington, DC, Marshall expressed opposition to the concept of regional black universities. It was at this meeting that Rufus Clement, President of Atlanta University, was accused of "running away from the segregation issue," a charge he denied. Clement allegedly was discussing with Georgia schoolmen and state officials the idea of a regional, segregated system in higher education. He asserted that he did not support a regional system for the South, but was accused by his colleagues of missing Marshall's talk in order to "duck" the segregation question. *Atlanta Journal*, 21 October 1948, 19; Mark V. Tushnet, "Thurgood Marshall as a Lawyer and the Campaign Against School Segregation, 1945-1950," *Maryland Law Review* 40 (1981).

53. *Gaines v. Canada*, 305 US 337 (1939); *Sipuel v. Board of Regents*, 332 US 631 (1948).

54. *Augusta Courier*, 3 January 1949, 1.

55. At the Southern Governors Conference in Savannah in December 1948, Talmadge introduced a resolution condemning Truman's civil rights proposals and pledging to support Southern members of Congress in opposing such "unconstitutional legislation." Talmadge's resolution, which also denounced the centralization of power in Washington, DC, was adopted by the governors, as was another resolution that set up a "Southern Foundation" for the purpose of telling the nation the South's side of the segregation issue. See *The Statesman*, 23 December 1948, 2.

56. During the summer of 1949, Talmadge called a special session of the legislature and succeeded in getting a $20 million emergency tax package through the General Assembly. The package fell $63 million below what would be needed to fund state programs.

57. *New York Times*, 23 October 1949, 5.

58. *Atlanta Journal*, 8 August 1949, 6; *New York Times*, 10 September 1949, 56.

59. *New York Times*, 23 October 1949, 5.

60. *Atlanta Constitution*, 25 October 1949, 1; *Augusta Courier*, 31 October 1949, 4.

61. *New York Times*, 10 March 1950, IV:6.

62. *New York Times*, 6 June 1950, 19.

63. *New York Times*, 6 June 1950, 19.

64. V. O. Key, Jr., *Southern Politics in State and Nation* (New York: Knopf, 1949), chapter 6; Joseph L. Bernd, *Grass Roots Politics in Georgia: The County Unit System and the Importance of the Individual Voting Community in Bi-factional Elections, 1942-1954* (Atlanta: Emory University Research Committee, 1960).

65. *New York Times*, 9 August 1950, 1; *Atlanta Constitution*, 10 August 1950, 1; *The Statesman*, 17 August 1950, 1, 4. For his part, Talmadge reveled in the glory of defiance. In a symbolic gesture he removed two blacks he had mistakenly appointed to the State's White House Committee to represent Georgia at the White House Conference on Children and Youth. The national committee later voted not to seat the Georgia delegation. *New Republic*, 9 October 1950.

66. Roy Harris, as quoted in *Atlanta Constitution*, 10 August 1950, 1, 4; *New York Times*, 9 August 1950, 1.

67. *Atlanta Journal*, 23 September 1950, 1; *New York Times*, 9 May 1950, 1; Gilbert C. Fite, *Richard B. Russell, Jr., Senator from Georgia*, (Chapel Hill: University of North Carolina Press, 1991), 225, 245. (Also see Fite, chapters 11, 12); Richard Kluger, *Simple Justice* (New York: Vintage, 1977), 334.

68. *Atlanta Constitution*, 20 September 1950, 2; *Atlanta Constitution*, 7 September 1950, 18; *Augusta Courier*, 2 October 1950, 2; *Augusta Courier*, 9 October, 1950, 2.

69. There is no doubt that Conger was a segregationist and was thus sympathetic to the segregationist argument. Still, he believed in the authority of law, which in his view required unfettered compliance. Editorially, the *Atlanta Constitution* agreed with this approach and referred to him as "a man of integrity and of belief in life and government by law." *Atlanta Constitution*, 7 September 1950. Conger, who died in early 1954, did not live to see the *Brown* decision handed down. He was replaced on the federal bench on 18 May 1954, one day after *Brown*, by W. A. Bootle, who would play a major role in the implementation of *Brown* in Georgia. *Atlanta Journal*, 18 May 1954, 7.

Chapter 4

Determination and Defiance

Since our laws plainly say that there must be separation, but equality under separation, it should never have been necessary to file suits anywhere in the South to get what the law provides. The law should have been obeyed from the beginning. Now our own laws and, speaking as a minister, our own sins are catching up with us.

            –Benjamin Mays, 1950

White Defiance Catalyzes Black Desegregation Movement

William Boyd, the state president of the NAACP, and NAACP attorney A.T. Walden responded immediately to the State Democrats' resolution to defy the Supreme Court. Boyd pointed out that the recent *Sweatt* and *McLaurin* decisions were binding. "Georgia is still part of the United States. We had hoped for state leadership that would make litigation in Georgia unnecessary." Boyd, who also chaired the political science department at Atlanta University, declared that such actions "may be good politics, but it is not sound policy." Then he said "They have thrown down the gauntlet. We will have to meet the challenge or break the faith with the Negro people."[1]

Within a month of the Macon convention, Austin T. Walden, Atlanta's black political boss, and Thurgood Marshall, the NAACP's litigation chief, filed a suit in federal court in Atlanta against the Atlanta School Board.[2] Widely reported, *Aaron v. Cook* was filed on 19 September 1950, by 200 black school children and their parents. The suit alleged that the educational opportunities offered black students were not comparable to those offered to the white students. It further alleged that the black children could only secure educational advantages, opportunities and facilities equal to those afforded white children by being allowed to attend the elementary and secondary schools "which defendants are now unlaw-fully and illegally maintaining and operating exclusively for white children."[3] The action made an alternative plea for parity between white and black elementary and secondary school facilities, or admission for blacks to the white schools.

The two-pronged suit reflected the national NAACP's new school strategy. The primary goal of the suit was to break the race barrier in common school education. But, if the courts would not order that blacks be admitted to the white schools, then plaintiffs wanted at least equal facilities. The suit was the first two-pronged suit filed in a major Southern city.

For a variety of complex reasons, however, not all of Georgia's black leaders had been eager to fully endorse Marshall's edict to pursue the integration prong. A core of black leaders in Atlanta, including Walden, Grace Hamilton, and Charles L. Harper, though open to the idea of using desegregation as a distant rhetorical threat, privately cringed at the thought of mounting a local challenge to *Plessy*. They were well aware of the strong opposition to "racial mixing" in the Deep South in both its most ruthless forms such as lynching and Ku Klux Klanery and its more subtle manifestations. Moreover, there had been significant progress for blacks within the separate-but-equal restriction in the second half of the 1940s, particularly in Atlanta. Under Harper's leadership, the GTEA reorganized in 1941 and became a statewide driving force for teacher-pay equalization, and per-pupil spending equalization, abolition of one teacher schools and replacement with consolidated schools and provision of black graduate and professional school opportunities.[4] Hamilton's Urban League had been working with Walden and others to improve the conditions for Atlanta blacks.[5]

For his part Walden had experienced some successes in dealing with William B. Hartsfield, the mayor of Atlanta, to win concessions for Atlanta's black community. As one of the city's first black political strategists, Walden, starting in the 1920s, helped organize the black vote, which in some municipal elections held a balance of power in city politics. In 1935, when blacks were assured a larger school appropriation they supported a bond issue that carried the vote. Afterwards, however, the Atlanta school board improved white schools, but reported that revenue had run out for black schools. Not to be double-crossed again, Walden and others, in 1938 and 1940, organized the black vote and defeated both school bond issues. In the 1940s, managing the black vote in the mayoral race, he was also able to deliver a bloc vote in exchange for getting street lights installed in black neighborhoods.[6] Like a powerful ward boss in late 19th century New York City, Walden could not be ignored by city officials. He was an acknowledged leader with the political savvy to get what he wanted from the white political structure. "He knows how to get along with our people," remarked Mayor Hartsfield in 1961, "and they know how to get along with him."[7]

While not afraid to fight city hall, Walden had grown accustomed to working within the separate-but-equal system. Over the years "Colonel" Walden had developed a good relationship with the NAACP's national office and had won Marshall's loyalty. Born in 1885, the son of former slaves, Walden began practicing in Macon, Georgia, in 1911 and was the only black lawyer in Atlanta in 1919. Between 1911 and the 1950s he was one of only a handful of attorneys in Georgia with the credentials and the courage to litigate on the Negroes' behalf. By 1949, however, there was some concern among Atlanta's younger black intelligencia that the 64-year-old Walden was not up to the task of coordinating the legal campaign. William T. Boyd and Grace Hamilton wrote Marshall about this concern. "The stakes are high and [Governor Talmadge and his staff] will throw their big guns at us," wrote Boyd. "In light of the above I am requesting of you that you have Walden keep you informed of every move and that you lend us all possible aid."[8]

The Genesis of the Private School Plan

The general white reaction to the Atlanta suit was highly critical. The *Atlanta Constitution* declared that the suit had even offended "a majority of liberal leaders known to be sincerely concerned with improving race relations and equalizing educational opportunity." Ralph McGill, editor of the moderate newspaper which had supported school equalization efforts, wrote, "The Negroes have succeeded in alienating the support of a great many who worked continuously through the years for equal school opportunities." Atlanta's black press also expressed reservations about the suit. C.A. Scott, editor of the *Atlanta Daily World*, questioned the "wisdom, desirability or necessity of seeking entrance into the white public schools."[9]

Less surprising was Governor Talmadge's response, reported in Atlanta papers on 20 September. He predicted that any attempt by blacks to enter all-white public schools "would result in more confusion, disorder, riots, and anything [sic] since the War Between the States." Talmadge offered the Atlanta School Board all of the state's resources to fight the suit. Pointing to the record-breaking mail he had been receiving since the suit was filed, the governor asserted that white Georgians would never accept a court order to desegregate. He pulled from his pocket and read a quote from one letter that was extremely inflammatory "Our rifles are ready," it said. In closing, the governor claimed that there were "not enough troops or police in the United States to enforce such an order."[10]

Roy Harris's reaction may have been the most vehement registered in the state. On 2 October 1950, Harris lambasted the "liberals in Atlanta, especially the Atlanta newspapers," for encouraging and promoting social justice for blacks. "Atlanta liberals have gotten themselves and the rest of Georgia into a hell of a fix. One of the laws of nature is that you reap what you sow." Writing in the *Augusta Courier*, Harris made two predictions about what would happen if the Atlanta public schools desegregated: (1) whites and industry would leave the city and the state to avoid intermingling; and (2) whites in Georgia would stop taxing themselves for public education and place their children in private schools. Harris wrote:

> Why should we pay 40 to 50 million dollars[11] every year to destroy the white race in Georgia? The [MFPE] is designed to furnish adequate and proper educational facilities and opportunities for both the whites and the blacks in Georgia. It was designed in part to guarantee to the negroes eventually equal school facilities and equal opportunities for education and training. Why should the white people . . . pay exorbitant millions every year in taxes for the sole purpose of destroying the white race in Georgia? That's what financing the Minimum Foundations Program would mean. The negroes pay less that 3 percent of the cost of public schools. the whites pay more than 97 percent. If the public school system is to mean the destruction of the pattern of segregation then we ought to do away with the public school system and devise another to take its place. We could establish some type of private school system in this state whereby the white people . . . could pay in accordance with their ability for the education of their children. We could take 97 percent and create a real system of education for all the white people of this state. . . . If the negroes have sense enough to work with us in the construction of separate but equal school facilities then we should go ahead with rapid progress to finance a real system of education for both [races]. . . . [W]ere it not for the efforts of white people . . . . the negro would still be a naked savage in the jungles of Africa.[12] If the negro is not willing to live with us under the pattern of segregation then we should change our plans for levying millions of dollars of taxes on our necks as [sic] to be used . . . for destroying everything on the earth the white man holds sacred in race relations.[13]

Harris's inflammatory editorial marked the emergence of the idea of a private school plan and proved to be a significant step in the further crystallization of white resistance to non-segregated public schooling. Harris, who had for so long championed the improvement of public schools, now suggested that they be abolished. But, his editorial was not inconsistent with his principles. As had been demonstrated in his relationship with Ellis Arnall and by his delaying the effective date of the MFPE, Harris considered white supremacy more important than any other cause.

The White Response to Harris's Private School Plan

Harris's novel idea attracted considerable attention. On 3 October 1950 the *New York Times* mentioned the political boss's anti-segregation plan, which was the first of its kind in the nation.[14] By January 1951 Harris's idea had crossed the state border into Virginia, where lawmakers of that state would consider—but ultimately reject—a resolution to convert their schools into a private system. By March 1951 the private school concept had also hopped across the Savannah River from Harris's home city of Augusta into South Carolina. There Governor James F. Byrnes began to use it as a threat to end the public school system if the federal courts banned segregation.

In October 1950, however, most state leaders in Georgia, although sympathetic with Harris's position, would not comment on the issue. Governor Talmadge publicly avoided it, choosing instead to concentrate on streamlining his monumental sales-income tax package bill with legislative leaders.[15] Behind closed doors he decided that his best option was to push for a sales tax. A sales tax, it seemed, would not only satisfy teachers, schoolmen, and other progressives who sought to expand the state role, but also assuage the New South business leadership, who would tolerate a regressive tax imposed at the retail level. The tax, would be borne in large part by the masses, would improve state services available to white elites and would improve schooling for whites and blacks. Talmadge hoped that, by providing enough revenue to equalize schools, the sales tax would preserve the institution of segregation, the key symbol of white supremacy. Talmadge knew he could play the race card and gain support for a tax increase. His was a scheme that blended progressive innovation with conservative tradition. He would posture defiance, protect white business interests, and generate wide support for a regressive sales tax. The governor had been well-schooled in how the politics of race could serve his ambitions. His major concern at the moment was his uncertainty about how open defiance to segregation would affect the campaign for industry and modernization. Keeping the state ever attactive to relocating industry was among his foremost priorities.[16]

Yet Harris, who participated in the tax revision meetings, felt no discomfort speaking for the governor and others in the state legislature about the prospect of abandoning the schools. "Everyone I have seen is standing right with me. They are ready to do anything on earth to preserve segregation."[17] Harris then suggested that the General Assembly was likely to refrain from funding the MFPE until *Aaron v. Cook* was settled.

Harris framed the issue for Georgians as he saw it. If the blacks were unwilling to live with segregation, then the state's whites would be unwilling to support public schools. In Harris's model the blacks would be responsible for the closure of public schools. In a state and region that had long scape-goated blacks, Harris's messages did not fall on deaf ears.

By threatening to close the schools, Harris had raised for the first time the issue of Georgia's loyalty to public education. Ralph McGill, editor of the *Atlanta Constitution*, was quick to see the issue as a crucial one. McGill, who had supported equalization and segregation, cringed at the thought of abandoning public education. In response to Harris's editorial, McGill pointed out that "Southerners of Scottish blood" were "predestined to a passionate belief and trust in education. The public school is the foundation of America and of the country we have built. It could not have been built save by the secular public school."[18]

M.L. St. John, the political editor for the *Constitution*, was also disturbed with Harris's tactics. State leadership is simply "hustling out its old standby—the racial issue," wrote St. John on 11 October. He chided the administration for using race to "color up" the issues. The people of Georgia deserve a "peaceful solution to the racial problem, not an aggravation of it," he asserted.[19]

Yet, except for McGill, the significance of Harris's remarks about the private school plan escaped St. John and many others in the state, who perhaps viewed the political boss as a loose cannon. The private school plan would soon find its way into governors' offices and state legislative halls in every Southern state. By the time of the *Brown* decision every deep South state, except Louisiana, had taken steps toward abandoning their public system and shifting to a private school alternative. Southern resistance to common school desegregation had started in earnest already in 1950, not in May of 1954.

The Black Response to Harris's Private School Plan

In the face of Harris's vehement response to *Aaron v. Cook*, black leaders spoke up to confirm the necessity of the suit. On 4 October 1950 Benjamin E. Mays, Morehouse College President and soon to be member of the board of directors of the national chapter of the NAACP, maintained that the court action started by 200 black Atlantans was "timely and democratic." As a young man growing up in the South, Mays knew that the white public schools were incomparable to the black public schools.[20] It was his personal conviction that equality of educational opportunity could not be obtained in a separate-but-equal system. Alluding to Harris's claims that blacks wanted only to mingle with whites, Mays countered that George McLaurin and Heman Sweatt sued to enter traditionally white graduate programs "not to be with whites, but because they wanted the same education that whites were getting. . . . The burden of proof is upon the South to prove that it can have two separate but equal school systems."[21] Speaking at the Hungry Club Mays expanded on this theme:

> To argue that [the initiaters of the suit] want Negro children to go to school with white children is to miss the point entirely. Mixed schools are not at the heart of the suit. . . . The motive behind the Atlanta suit represents the growing conviction, rightly nor wrongly, among Negroes everywhere that there can be no equality under segregation . . . the "separate but equal" theory is a myth. . . . There is a growing conviction among Negroes that if one racial group makes all the laws and administers them, holds all the power and administers it, and has all the public money and distributes it, it is too much to expect that group to deal as fairly with the weak, minority, non-participating group as it deals with its own. . . .The stress [of desegregation] is not on mixed schools, but on the inequality that results from the dual educational systems.[22]

For Benjamin Mays and probably for many other blacks advocating desegregation, securing an adequate education at public expense for children of color was at the heart and soul of integration. It was based, in the words of one scholar, on a determined "belief in learning and self-improvement as a means to individual and collective dignity."[23] The belief had its roots in the Antebellum era and had survived in spite of the fact that efforts to gain a fair share of schooling in the segregated system had been thrwarted at every turn. The goal of the early struggle was neither to make society color-blind, or for that matter color-conscious, but rather to gain freedom and justice. At midcentury Mays thought that if the schooling of blacks could be tied in time and place to that of whites, it would be virtually impossible to isolate and disciminate along the color line with regard to the distribution of public money. Integration would tether black to white children together; black children would receive the same kinds of inputs that the local and state governments had awarded to white children. It was noble and clever idea for an out-of-power people. It was an idea destined to spark conflict, chaos and backlash.

By 12 October several other black leaders from Atlanta convened to reaffirm their support for the Atlanta lawsuit. The meeting was held at the Friendship Baptist Church. The Reverend D.V. Kyle, pastor of the Big Bethel AME Church, spoke first—in words echoing the research of black psychologist Kenneth Clark.[24]

Emphasizing his own understanding of the psychological dangers of segregation, Kyle declared that "the personality of the segregated black child is warped and distorted long before he reaches graduate level and the time [to end apartheid] is past ripe." Mr. D.A. Dobbs, Grand Master of the Georgia Masons, spoke next. Dobbs, perhaps feeling more challenged and agitated by Harris's well-publicized threats than the previous speaker, referred to the Atlanta suit as a "showdown," and announced that there must be "no turning back, no compromising."[25]

Despite this challenge to Georgia's white power structure, there was not solidarity at the meeting. C.A. Scott, editor of the *Atlanta Daily World*, explained to the group that he was in "full accord with the objective of the suit seeking immediate equalization," but he expressed his doubts about the objective of attacking segregation.[26]

Scott was not the only black Georgian who felt this way. The all-black Board of Trustees of the Meriwether Colored Training School, a black elementary and secondary public school in Manchester, Georgia, unanimously approved the principle of racial segregation and voted to "repudiate and condemn" the Atlanta anti-segregation suit.[27]

The Legislature Moves to Make the Private School Plan Law

By January 1951 the leaders in state government began taking steps that would leave no doubt about their commitment to the previous summer's resolution to maintain "the Southern way of life." Lawmakers, led by Governor Talmadge, who had become known as the South's leading advocate of white supremacy, approved a measure that would deny funds to public schools that admitted blacks. The measure began as a part of a larger, more serious proposal from the governor's office and took the form of a provision inserted into the state appropriations bill. The original proposal, which the Talmadge administration thought initially would require amending the state constitution, contained three major points. The first would cut off state funds from any unit of the university system or any school system if the courts voided segregation in that unit. The second would give the General Assembly the power to provide "individual grants to individual persons for educational purposes, and for the use of sums so granted at private schools, colleges and universities chosen by the grantee." The third would give the General Assembly the power to deliver "any property now owned by the state ... to private individuals for educational purposes." By the middle of February, however, it became clear to Talmadge that no constitutional amendment would be needed if he dropped the second and third points of the provision. Acting on Talmadge's advice, the senate approved the first point of the plan, and amended its "unit clause," a move that made the fund-withholding action applicable to all units of the university system even if only one school had to admit one black.[28]

On 16 February 1951, the General Assembly approved a record-breaking $207,505,708 state appropriations bill that contained the Senate's version of the fund denial provision. Nearly half of the appropriations would go toward financing the MFPE as long as the schools remained segregated. The law required the state to cut off funds to all public schools in the event of the admission of one black to one public school. Cutting off state funds would most likely result in statewide school closings. Likewise, the admission of one black to any one of the colleges in the university system would result in denying funds to all units of the university system and probably cause statewide closings at that level.[29]

The *Atlanta Journal* reported on 10 February 1951 that "critics" of the legislation, who had fought unsuccessfully to dismantle the fund-cutting measure, pointed out that the plan "unnecessarily endanger[ed] the state's entire education program." The *Christian Century* criticized the governor for engineering such drastic measures. John Popham, the Southern correspondent for the *New York Times*, pointed out that while there was a "prevailing sentiment" in Georgia in favor of racial segregation in the common schools, there was also "a willingness to go along with the admission of Negroes to graduate school[s]." The most common position taken by advocates of the legislation was that it would be better to close the schools than to allow for "chaos and confusion." Others suggested that the move reflected an astute understanding of the politics of state government. Political observers noted that Talmadge's supporters framed the issue sharply to boost their faction's political appeal.[30] Although the wisdom of the plan to close the schools would continue to be debated over the next ten years, it now had the force of law.

Equalization Program Finally Begins

On 1 April 1951 Georgia's newly approved sales tax went into effect. The long-awaited financing of the MFPE took four years, two months, and twelve days. The $81,649,380 appropriated for the program would increase each teacher's salary by $350 per year. The program also set up a state salary schedule for public teachers and called for the hiring of an additional 800 teachers to instruct Georgia's 775,000 students.[31]

The MFPE also provided for equal teacher and pupil expenditures for both races. This was a major step forward for black schools in Georgia. But, because existing black schools had been so seriously underfunded for many years, even equal funding would not actually equalize the schools. In 1945 black students, constituting nearly 35 percent of the school population, received on average 14 percent of the disbursement of local school boards. Five years later at 33 percent of the school population, blacks received 15 percent of the allotment. At the time of the *Brown* decision, the allocation stood at 19 percent of the total; and 1958, during reign of massive resistance, the allocation had climbed to 25 percent of the total allocation while the black student popluation had declined slightly to 32 percent.[32]

While the gap was closing gradually, parity within the separate-but-equal doctrine was still myth. Further, the black children of Georgia could not receive the full benefit of the MFPE until a large-scale building project could be carried out. The 1951 legislature therefore set up the State Building Authority (SBA). The Authority, a public corporation, would generate revenue by selling bonds, which in turn would be retired by renting school buildings to the local districts. By 1954, the program called for $200 million of state money, $50 million provided by the local school systems and an additional $24 million provided by the federal government.[33] By setting up an efficient system for building new schools and equalizing funding, state leadership hoped to improve the system of common schools in the state as well as convince the federal courts that Georgia was living up to the letter of the separate-but-equal doctrine mandated by *Plessy*.

During the 1951, 1952, and 1953 school years, Herman Talmadge spoke at several school building dedications and commencement exercises, touting his greatly expanded education program. Nearly half of added state revenue for fiscal 1951 went to public schools. By 1952, he boasted that the state was spending $110 million on education, or 53 percent of its annual state budget and that MFPE money was reaching 143 of the state's 209 school systems, resulting in a per pupil expenditure of $152, a thirty dollar increase over the 1949-50 school year figure. Talmadge claimed that he was doing more for his state's system of education than any governor in the union.[34]

Indeed, under Talmadge's administration the state was paying a higher percentage of the total expenditure on public education than all but five other states. Between 1949 and 1951 the average teacher salary increased $623 per year and the per pupil expenditure increased from $123 to $166 per year (see Tables 4.1 and 4.2). Yet, in spite of these gains, Georgia was still paying its teachers $864 less than the national average and spending $78 less on each of its school-age children than the rest of the country. Talmadge was making significant improvements to the public schools, but Georgia, being one of the poorest states, ranked only forty-first in per pupil expenditure out of the forty-eight states.

Table 4.1 - Per-Pupil Expenditure in Georgia 1933-1955
(Public Elementary and Secondary Schools)

1933	1937	1939	1941	1943	1945	1947*	1949*	1951*	1953*	1955*
$28	$38	$42	$46	$56	$65	$104	$123	$166	$177	$194

Table 4.2 - Percent of state funds used to finance public common school education in Georgia, New York, and the U.S., 1929-1954

	1929-30	1939-40	1949-50*	1951-52*	1953-54*
Georgia	36.5	58.2	71.9	64.7	69.1
New York	28.6	33.9	41.4	40.5	35.7
U.S. (mean)	16.7	30.7	42.4	38.6	37.4

Source: Department of Health Education and Welfare, "Statistics In State School Systems," in *Biennial Survey of Education, 1948-56* (Washington DC, Government Printing Office: n.d.).

* Years that Talmadge served as governor

Talmadge Emerges as South's Spokesman for Separate-But-Equal

By the spring of 1951 it was still not clear whether *Aaron v. Cook*, the Atlanta suit, would be the test case for the constitutionality of the separate-but-equal doctrine. One and a half years had passed since A.T. Walden and Thurgood Marshall had filed the case. It was still pending in federal court, but it lay dormant on the docket.[35] Four similar cases challenging segregated common schools—in Delaware, Virginia, Kansas, and Washington, D.C.—were filed soon after the *Aaron v. Cook* case and consolidated with a suit in South Carolina as *Brown v. Board of Education. Brown* was heard by the United States Supreme Court before the Atlanta case was ultimately dismissed for lack of prosecution in 1956.

In 1951 politicians from other states rallied behind the Talmadge's call for continued segregation. Governor James F. Byrnes of South Carolina and Governor Fielding Wright of Mississippi adopted the position that public schools would be discontinued if segregation was abolished. Virginia Senator Harry F. Byrd, who would coin the term "massive resistance" some five years later, spoke in Georgia twice during 1951, lauding Talmadge's state leadership on both occasions and criticizing President Truman's leadership at the national level.[36]

Meanwhile, Talmadge received support from another unexpected source. In June 1951 a special panel of federal court judges in Charleston handed down a 2-1 decision upholding segregation in the common schools of Clarendon County, South Carolina. Judge John J. Parker, with Judge George Bell Timmerman concurring, wrote that "educational facilities and opportunities must be made equal, but how this is done is a matter for school authorities and not the courts so long as it is done in good faith . . . but it must be done promptly." In a sharp twenty-page dissent Judge Waties J. Waring wrote "the whole thing is unreasonable, unscientific and based on unadulterated prejudices. Segregation is per se inequality." Talmadge, who was entertaining Senator Byrd that week in Atlanta, was "delighted" with the decision and expressed his confidence that upon appeal the high court would "follow the precedent of more than one-hundred years and uphold the [lower court's] decision."[37]

Meanwhile the NAACP reported that they would immediately appeal the decision to the U.S. Supreme Court. Outspoken NAACP executive secretary Walter White, who had just arrived in Atlanta and was staying within walking distance of Talmadge's office and Byrd's Hotel, predicted that in spite of the ruling, segregation in all forms would be abolished in the next ten years. White scoffed at the threats by state leadership in Georgia, South Carolina, and Mississippi to move to a private school system. "The courts would undoubtedly consider such moves as calculated and obvious violations."[38]

The next day forty NAACP lawyers met in Atlanta at their annual convention and called for an immediate attack on all racial segregation practices at the state and municipal levels. Publicly clarifying the evolving plan, Chief Counsel Thurgood Marshall announced that the strategy of the Legal Defense Fund would hinge entirely on the theme that segregation at any level creates "psychological roadblocks" that prevent blacks from attaining equal status. To carry this message forward, Marshall said that his staff had already put together a panel of over 100 experts in psychology, education, and anthropology.[39]

By June 1951 Herman Talmadge was discussing with his advisers the possibility of resurrecting the 119-year-old interposition doctrine, which declared that a state had the right to interpose its sovereignty between the federal government and its people. By October, Georgia Attorney General Eugene Cook, a segregationist and strict constructionist, argued that challenges to segregation should stay out of court and go instead to the state legislature.[40]

Plan to Equalize Facilities Stalls at Critical Moment

As in 1951 the school situation was one of the most important concerns at the 1952 January legislative session. During the 1951 session lawmakers had adopted the MFPE to finance segregated public education and had created the State Building Authority (SBA). Through the leadership of Fred Hand, Speaker of the House and SBA chief, the General Assembly had also appropriated five-million dollars per year for a total of 20 years to the SBA so they, as an agency of the state, could mastermind the massive public school construction program.[41] Yet since the end of the 1951 session several studies had revealed that an additional five million dollars each year for 20 years would be required to construct the needed school houses in the state. Georgia, now committed to an equalization strategy, would only need to appropriate the additional funds to allow construction to begin. This could be accomplished simply by appropriating the necessary funds to the SBA and letting them get on with the equalization campaign.[42]

Simplicity, however, was not the order of the day. Talmadge, acting on Fred Hand's advice, asked the legislature to approve a referendum that the state's constitution be amended giving the SBA complete control of the school building program.[43] The collectively powerful rural county lawmakers, ever suspicious of the concentration of power, whether in Washington or Atlanta, resisted authorizing new legislation that would expedite the building campaign. During the session, rural lawmakers became increasingly louder in their demands that the additional revenue required to equalize public schools be distributed to the individual counties so they could control the construction process at the local level. In a state that prided itself on local control at the county level and referred to local government as "the bulwark of Democracy," the challenge to a centralized, city-based authority was serious.[44]

Determining how the new money for school construction would be distributed to the localities became the most important school issue of the 1952 session. There was also some disagreement as to who had the authority to set state educational policy, the state superintendent of schools or the state board of education. State Superintendent M.D. Collins, who had held the post since 1932, claimed that as a constitutional officer of the state elected by the people, his office had more authority than the governor-appointed State Board of Education. Siding with the State Board were influential leaders in the House, Fred Hand and Speaker Pro Tem,

George L. Smith, who proposed to introduce legislation that would give the State Board the power to appoint the state superintendent. The power struggles over construction funds and policy authority stalled the building program at a critical moment. At the eleventh hour, only months before the United States Supreme Court would consider if it had jurisdiction in the school segregation cases, Georgia solons found they could not agree on a swift plan to equalize. Meanwhile, in a highly publicized show of resistance just across the Savannah River, the South Carolina General Assembly took the first tangible step toward abandoning public schools by agreeing to give the voters a referendum on whether the state constitution could be amended to allow such action. The recalcitrance of the two deep South seaboard states was undeniable and the combined effect of the stall and threat in early 1952 did little to encourage a divided and reluctant high court to duck the school-segregation issue. In June the nine Supreme Court justices agreed to grant certiorari on the Clarendon County case.[45]

The row in Georgia over how money would be distributed to local authorities would result in a deadlock that would go unresolved (and perhaps not unnoticed by the Supreme Court) through the 1953 legislative session. Talmadge, committed to equalization, overrode the deadlock with an executive order that gave to the SBA temporary control of all the funds for one year. Yet by the summer of 1952, while plans for construction were plentiful, there had been virtually no ground-breaking ceremonies.

The Private School Plan Is Exported for Development

In 1952 the private school plan in Georgia was no further along than it had been in May 1951. Although the 1951 fund denial provision for any school that attempted desegregation remained intact, state leaders were preoccupied with the details of how equalization would be achieved. The lawmakers, perhaps confident that the South Carolina ruling in favor of the separate-but-equal principle would be upheld upon appeal, were further encouraged by the Supreme Court's decision to defer ruling on the appeal in January 1952.

Meanwhile, legislatures in other Southern states were moving faster. The legislature in South Carolina, through the leadership of Governor Byrnes, had picked up on the private school plan and was in the process of drafting a referendum for a popular vote. The referendum called for a constitutional amendment to convert the public school system to a private one. On 4 November 1952 the citizens approved the amendment by a 3-to-1 margin. The amendment struck from the South Carolina constitution the phrase that the legislature must provide "a liberal system of free public education for all children between the ages of six and twenty-one years." Mississippi and Virginia were also studying the merits of such a maneuver.[46] The private school plan, the brainchild of Roy V. Harris and the political clincher for Herman Talmadge, had been exported for development.

Talmadge Reinforces the Legislative Backbone
of His Stick and Carrot Policy

In his 13 January 1953 "State of the State" address to a joint session of the General Assembly, Talmadge sketched out his policies on public education and race. He discussed the increased outlay for common schools, the increase in teachers' salaries and the provision of "adequate but equal" facilities (as opposed to "separate but equal" facilities) for both races, claiming that Georgia for the first time was living up to the Constitution.[47]

Later that week Talmadge addressed the legislators in joint session twice more, once to refine his budget philosophy and another time to submit his budget to them as the law required. Clearly articulating his goals for education, he called on the lawmakers to sustain educational spending, continue equalizing salaries for teachers, and continue equalizing facilities between the races. Commenting on race relations in the state, the chief executive claimed that things were "good" and that if Georgians were left alone, the school issue could be worked out equitably. But he added, Georgians were in "grave danger" and "must be prepared with a plan in the event of a calamitous [Supreme Court desegregation] decision." The "plan" would be one of defense of the tradition of segregation and would serve as a "spotlight for other states to follow."[48] In spite of Talmadge's pioneer rhetoric, Georgia in 1953 was following the trail that James Byrnes, governor of South Carolina, had already forged in his state.

On 10 November 1953, only six months before *Brown*, Talmadge's lieutenants went to work. Anticipating a decision that would require desegregation, Talmadge insiders began to formulate legal devices designed to resist. On the advice from his legal and political counselors—Buck Murphy, Durwood Pye, and Bee Brooks—and with the help of his lieutenants in the legislature—Frank Twitty, Fred Hand, Jack Ray, and George L. Smith—Talmadge proposed a resolution for a constitutional amendment that would give the General Assembly the authority to provide public funds for private education and "discharge [itself] from all obligation ... to provide adequate education for its citizens."[49] The idea was to channel state, county, and local funds into tuition grants for students who would use the money to pay for segregated private schooling. Since private schools were thought to be beyond the reach of the federal courts, the Talmadge administration maintained that such an arrangement would provide a legal mechanism to avert any court decision favoring desegregation.[50] To take effect, the amendment would have to be approved by a two-thirds majority in both houses of the General Assembly before it could be submitted to the voting public for ratification or rejection.

During the same session Speaker Hand and floor leader Twitty also proposed legislation to establish the Georgia Commission on Education (GCE). The proposed commission would study "legal" ways to maintain segregated schools in the state, submit findings to the legislature, and draft bills to be considered by the legislature. Both proposals—the grants for educational purposes and the establishment of the Georgia Commission on Education—were written into Georgia law by December 1953.[51]

Herman Talmadge and his advisors had hoped that the U.S. Supreme Court would uphold the *Plessy* doctrine. Talmadge knew, however, that hope was not enough. His 1953 proposals to the General Assembly were far-reaching steps that had two sequential purposes, both of which aimed ultimately to maintain racial segregation in Georgia. First, the private school plan sought to influence the way in which the school segregation cases were decided. But in the event of what Pye later described as "an untoward ruling," they set up the private school plan as a second line of defense. The proposals were designed to circumvent the *Brown* decision even before it was handed down.

John Griffin and the Ashmore Project

In 1953 Talmadge and his advisors were not the only people in Georgia attempting to influence the outcome of *Brown*, although because of their political ambitions and strong belief in white supremacy they may have been the most committed to maintaining segregation. One native Georgian who was against racial segregation in education, and who viewed it as a harmful barrier in the way of racial equality, was John A. Griffin, a sociologist at Emory University. Griffin, who had earned his doctorate at the University of Wisconsin in 1939, returned to the South in 1951 to study the problems of the region's rural poverty. In addition to rural poverty, Griffin had a consuming interest in issues of education in the South, and he had been watching the drama of the school desegregation cases closely as they unfolded in the federal courts. By 1952 Griffin, well aware of the NAACP campaign against segregated schools, thought a major court decision on segregated schools was imminent. Griffin believed that there was a need for a current, definitive, statistical study to discern level of inequality between black and white elementary and secondary schools. With the *Brown* cases pending in five different federal district courts, Griffin and several Atlantans began talking with several of the region's universities about "the need for sufficient data on the extent to which the separate school systems in the South were equal." Yet, due to the political sensitivity of the issue, no Southern university would take on the project or even supply any researchers to participate in the study.[52]

Consequently, Griffin and Harold Fleming, assistant director of the Southern Regional Council, contacted The Fund for the Advancement of Education (FAE), a branch of the New York-based Ford Foundation. After convincing the FAE of the immediate need for this timely study, the Ford Foundation decided to underwrite the project.

With the help of the Southern Regional Council (SRC), the FAE persuaded Harry S. Ashmore, executive editor of the *Arkansas Gazette*, to head the project.[53] Ashmore, who had a daily newspaper to run, had only limited time to devote to the study, but finally agreed to head the project and write the final report. A team of researchers from the fields of law, education, and social science would be assembled to conduct the field research and write monographs on various aspects of the dual systems. At Ashmore's request, the Fund then recruited Phillip G. Hammer, executive officer of the National Planning Association of the South in Atlanta, to chair the central committee for what became known as the "Ashmore Project."[54] During the summer of 1953 the central committee, composed of Hammer, Griffin, Fleming, Mozell Hill from Atlanta University, and Ruth Morton from the American Friends Service Committee, administered the collection and organization of the data. In a 1991 interview Griffin recalled that:

> The motivation was to get the study done fast so that the Court would take it into account before handing down *Brown*. Data was expeditiously collected . . . in the summer and fall of 1953, and the timely study was written in the early winter of 1954 by Harry Ashmore. The book was published on May 16, 1954, one day before the Court handed down the *Brown* decision. Advanced reports of the research findings had been in the hands of the court prior to the decision. The study may have influenced the decision.[55]

Predictably, the Ashmore Project concluded that separate-but-equal schools in the South were still a myth. Ashmore did, however, point out that the South was spending a larger percentage of its income on education than did other states, and that the gap between black schools and white schools by 1953 had narrowed. In spite of this trend across the South, only seven dollars were being spent on black schools for every ten dollars spent on white schools; black schools had fewer books in their libraries; and black teachers, on the average, were still being paid less.

Notes

1. *Atlanta Journal*, 10 August 1950, 22.

2. *Aaron v. Cook*, No. 3923 (1950) National Archives, East Point, GA. 1950; Benjamin E. Mays, "Why an Atlanta School Suit?" *New South* 5 (September/October 1950), 1-3; *New York Times*, 24 September 1950, 77; *New York Times*, 26 September 1950, 22; *The Statesman*, 28 September 1950, 1, 4.

3. *Aaron v. Cook*, 7.

4. Interview with Horace E. Tate, August 1995; Also see Samuel E. Hubbard, et al., *Rising in the Sun, A History of the Georgia Teachers and Education Association, a Half-Century of Progress* (Atlanta, no date), 112.

5. Since her appointment as executive secretary to the Urban League in 1943, Hamilton succeeded in getting $4 million of $9 million bond issue allocated to Atlanta's black schools and had helped narrow the gap between black and white teacher salaries. Letters between Hamilton and Marshall between 1944 and 1950 provide evidence that Hamilton worked tirelessly documenting and publicizing inequalities between black and white schools, and her efforts received the direct support of Marshall. Hamilton to Marshall, 19 December 1944 and 11 December 1945; Marshall to Hamilton, 26 March 1944, Library of Congress, NAACP Files, Group II Series B Box 137, File: Schools, Georgia, Atlanta General, 1944-49.

6. David Plank and Marcia Turner, "Changing Patterns in Black School Politics, Atlanta, 1872-1973," *American Journal of Education* 60 (August 1987), 590-595; Also see *Atlanta Journal*, 30 March 1961; More influence came about with the demise of the "White Primary" in 1946, which allowed Atlanta blacks to register as Democrats and trade votes for city services. See Grace Hamilton Papers, Atlanta Historical Society, Manuscript Series 597, box 4, folder 4.

7. S. Ernest Vandiver Papers, Box 11, Richard B. Russell Memorial Library, University of Georgia, Athens, GA.

8. Boyd to Marshall, 19 August 1949; Carter to Walden, 5 May 1949 and 5 July 1949, Library of Congress, Manuscripts Collections, NAACP Files, Group II Series B box 137, file: Schools, Georgia, Irwin County, 1949-50.

9. Quote from *Atlanta Daily World*, 21 September 1950, 9; *New York Times*, 24 September 1950, 77; *Atlanta Constitution*, 20 September 1950, 1, 4.

10. *Atlanta Constitution*, 20 September 1950, 1; *Atlanta Journal*, 20 September 1950, 2; *New York Times*, 26 September 1950, 22.

11. As was often the case, Harris's statistics were not completely accurate. In this instance he underestimated the amount of state aid for public common school education. According to HEW numbers, in the 1949-50 school year the state of Georgia was providing 71.9% of the money used to finance the operation of the public elementary and secondary schools. This amounted to $123.37 x .719 per pupil for 718,037 full-time pupils, or

approximately $63.7 million.

12. See Neil R. McMillen, *The Citizens' Council: A History of Organized Resistance to the Second Reconstruction, 1954-1964* (Urbana: University of Illinois Press, 1971), 180. McMillen's study of organized white resistance to racial desegregation, suggests that white segregationists, like Harris, often depicted blacks as less evolved than whites. Moreover, McMillen argues, this train of white thought assumed that any black gains were a result of white efforts. McMillen's contention is supported by the above quote.

13. Roy Harris, "Strictly Personal," *Augusta Courier*, 2 October 1950, 1; Also in same issue see "Schools Are Used As Part of Plan to Force Complete Social Equality."

14. "Private School System Urged in Georgia to 'Foil' Negro Anti-Segregation Plan," *New York Times*, 3 October 1950, 24.

15. *Atlanta Constitution*, 3 October 1950, 1, 5; Talmadge interview, 30 July 1991.

16. James C. Cobb, *The Selling of the South: The Southern Crusade for Industrial Development* (Baton Rouge: Louisiana State University Press, 1982), 76; Numan V. Bartley, "Politics and Government in the Postwar Era," in Kenneth Coleman, ed., *A History of Georgia*, 2ⁿᵈ ed. (Athens: University of Georgia Press, 1991), 225-38.

17. *Atlanta Constitution*, 5 October 1950, 22.

18. *Atlanta Constitution*, 12 October 1950, 1.

19. *Atlanta Constitution*, 11 October 1950, 10.

20. Benjamin E. Mays, *Born to Rebel* (Athens: University of Georgia Press, 1971), chapter 3.

21. Benjamin E. Mays, "Why an Atlanta School Suit?" *New South* 5 (September/October 1950), 1-3; *Atlanta Daily World*, 5 October 1950, 1.

22. Mays, "Why an Atlanta School Suit?" 2

23. James D. Anderson, *The Education of Blacks in the South, 1860-1935* (University of North Carolina Press, 1988), 285.

24. Kenneth Clark conducted research on the psychological effects of segregated schooling for black children. Some of his work was cited in the *Brown* decision. See Richard Kluger, *Simple Justice* (New York: Vintage, 1977), 315-366.

25. *Atlanta Daily World*, 12 October 1950, 1.

26. *Atlanta Daily World*, 12 October 1950, 1.

27. *Atlanta Journal*, 23 September 1950, 1.

28. "The Georgia Approach," *Time*, 26 February 1951, 47; *New York Times*, 1 February 1951, 27; *New York Times*, 15 February 1951, 33; *Georgia Laws*, 1951: 421-422.

29. *New York Times*, 16 February 1951, 48; *New York Times*, 18 February 1951, 48; *Augusta Courier*, 26 February 1951, 2; *Georgia Laws*, 1951: 360-385, 417-444.

30. *Atlanta Journal* 10 February 1951, 1; James P. Wesberry, "Georgia Politicos Are Desperate," *Christian Century*, 14 February 1951: 195; *New York Times*, 18 February 1951, 48.

31. *Atlanta Constitution*, 22 February 1951, 1; *Southern School News*, 3 September 1954, 5; *Georgia Laws*, 1951, 1407-1423.

32. Payments and expenditures by local school boards included instruction, building operation and maintenance and captial outlay. See Annual Report of the Georgia Department of Education for 1946, 55; Annual Report for 1950, 322; Annual Reprot for 1954, 329;

Annual Report for 1958, 391; Annual Report for 1964, 315.

33. *Southern School News*, 3 September 1954, 5; *Georgia Laws*, 1951, 240-261; *The Statesman*, 10 May 1951, 2; R. O. Johnson, "Desegregation of Public Education in Georgia: One Year Afterward"; *Journal of Negro Education* 24 (Summer 1955), 228-246; Talmadge interview, 30 July 1991.

34. *The Statesman*, 20 September 1951, 2; *The Statesman*, 8 October 1951; Herman E. Talmadge, "Highlights of Governor Talmadge's Address" *County Commissioners Comments*, 3 (1952), 5.

35. *Aaron v. Cook*, 1950; Donald Hollowell interview, 25 July 1991.

36. *The Statesman*, 19 January 1951, 2-3; *New York Times*, 22 July 1951, 45; *Statesman*, 28 June 1951, 1, 3; *The Statesman*, 15 November 1951, 1.

37. *New York Times*, 24 June 1951, 72; *The Statesman*, 28 June 1951, 1.

38. *New York Times*, 24 June 1951, 72.

39. *New York Times*, 26 July 1951, 25; *New York Times*, 27 June 1951, 24.

40. *New York Times*, 28 May 1951, 16; *New York Times*, 17 October 1951, 24; Herbert O. Reid. "The Supreme Court Decision and Interposition." *Journal of Negro Education*, 25 (Spring 1956), 109-117. "Strict constructionists" refers to a philosophy of Constitutional interpretation that favors strict adherence to the text of the Constitution and the original intent of its framers.

41. Talmadge interview, 30 July 1991.

42. *The Statesman*, 17 January 1952, 1; Talmadge interview, 1991. Also see, *Georgia House Journal*, 1952.

43. Ibid.

44. Joseph L. Bernd, *Grass Roots Politics in Georgia: The County Unit System and the Importance of the Individual Voting Community in Bi-factional Elections, 1942-1954* (Atlanta: Emory University Research Committee, 1960), 4-6; V. O. Key, Jr., *Southern Politics in State and Nation* (New York: Knopf, 1949), 115-119.

45. *New York Times*, 9 January 1952, 18; *New York Times*, 6 January 1952; *New York Times*, 29 January 1952, 16; Kluger, *Simple Justice*, 538.

46. *New York Times*, 29 January 1952, 31; *Southern School News*, 3 October 1954, 12; H. G. McClain, "South Carolina's School Amendment." *New South* (February 1953), 2.

47. *Georgia House Journal*, 1953, 29.

48. *Georgia House Journal*, 1953, 30.

49. *Georgia House Journal*, 1953, 1000; George McMillan, "Talmadge, The Best Southern Governor?" *Harpers Magazine* 209 (1954), 40; Pye interview, 27 July 1991; Talmadge interview, 30 July 1991; *Georgia Senate Journal*, 1953, 982-893.

50. Durwood T. Pye, *Report to the Members of the General Assembly by the Georgia Commission on Education, December 1954*, (Atlanta, 1954); Herman E. Talmadge, "School Systems, Segregation and the Supreme Court" *Mercer Law Review* 6 (Spring 1955), 189-201.

51. *Georgia House Journal*, 1952, 1000; *Georgia Senate Journal*, 1952, 982; *Georgia Laws*, 1953, 64-6, 240-242; Paul D. Bolster, "Civil Rights Movements in Twentieth Century Georgia" (Ph.D. diss., University of Georgia, 1972), chapter 4.

52. Griffin interview, 12 November 1991; Also see John Egerton, *Speak Now against the Day, The Generations before the Civil Rights Movement in the South* (New York: Knopf, 1994), 484-487.

53. Ashmore later received a Pulitzer Prize for his coverage of the desegregation of Central High School in Little Rock, Arkansas.

54. Peter H. Rossi, Book review of *The Negro and the Schools*, by Harry S. Ashmore, *Harvard Law Review* 68 (1955), 1108-1110; Rossi, 1955, p. 1108; John A. Griffin, "The Harmful Impact of Segregation." *Southern Changes*, 13 (November 1991), 17.

55. Also see Griffin, "The Harmful Impact of Segregation," 17-19. Because the Ashmore Project at the time of publication did not know for sure whether segregation would be struck down, the book was outdated after only one day. As one observer noted "Never did a book become so obsolete so quickly." Within a month Ashmore penned a second edition of *The Negro and the Schools*, which took into account the Supreme Court's decision. Rossi, Review of *The Negro and the Schools, Harvard Law Review* 68 (1955), 1108-1110; Harry S. Ashmore, *The Negro and the Schools*, 2nd ed. (Chapel Hill: University of North Carolina Press, 1954).

Chapter 5

The Brown Decision and the Private School Plan of 1954

In these days it is doubtful that any child may reasonably be expected to succeed in life if he is denied the opportunity of an education. Such an opportunity, where the state has undertaken to provide it, is a right which must be made available to all on equal terms.

–*Brown v. Board of Education*, 1954

The School Desegregation Decision

In 1952 NAACP Legal Defense Fund chief Thurgood Marshall won an appeal to the U.S. Supreme Court on five school segregation cases, grouped as a class action suit, that became known as *Brown v. Board of Education*. The Court required numerous briefs from plaintiffs and defendants on the issue of segregated education as well as an implementation strategy for a unitary school system if the Court decided to nullify the *Plessy* doctrine. After hearing several series of arguments by plaintiffs and defendants, the Court unanimously declared in 1954 "that in the field of public education the doctrine of 'separate but equal' has no place. Separate educational facilities are inherently unequal."[1]

But the Court had refrained from granting immediate relief to the plaintiffs. The Court restored the cases to the docket and put the victorious Marshall team and the defense counsel to the task of preparing and presenting further argument on implementation.[2]

The Immediate Reaction

As Chief Justice Earl Warren read the *Brown* decision in a calm, almost monotonous voice, the event was picked up immediately by the media all over the world. The national black press was exuberant, but in the words of one observer, "there was no dancing in the streets."[3] The *New York Times*, *London Times*, Paris's *Le Monde*, and Zurich's *Neue Zeitung* praised the decision as just and as an impressive example of a vigorous democracy. George Mitchell, the executive director of the Southern Regional Council, stated that the decision would now give every child in the South an equal opportunity to get an education. Ruby Hurley, NAACP regional secretary, said the decision "knocked the props from under Russian propaganda." Lillian Smith, an outspoken writer and one of only a handful of white Southerners who had been steadfast in her denounciation of Jim Crow (which she had publicly opposed since the 1930s), called the decision "every child's Magna Charta."[4] Most newspapers in the South refrained from hostile editorials and urged calm, constructive approaches to the "problem." Many of the region's editors noted that the decision did not demand immediate compliance; one headline predicted: "Change Not Immediate."[5] This headline would prove to be the understatement of the decade.

Ralph McGill, the editor and columnist of the *Atlanta Constitution*, was on assignment in London when he learned about the decision. The fifty-six-year-old editor had for some time been aware that the *Plessy* decision he had lived with comfortably, was going to fall, and as if to mourn its death, he refrained from sending back any mention of the historic decision.[6] A few weeks prior to *Brown* McGill had hoped that the high Court would leave *Plessy* intact but realized that "world sentiment" was so strong against segregation that it would soon fall. When a young United Press reporter asked for his reaction, McGill commented, "I am surprised that the vote was unanimous," and ended with, "I think that is all I want to say at this time." In spite of his liberal reputation, McGill clung to his white Southern identity and did not speak out in favor of *Brown*.

The new White House leadership was, at best, lukewarm about the termination of the separate-but-equal doctrine. Shortly after the decision was handed down, President Dwight Eisenhower distanced himself from the high Court's ruling. When asked to comment on the decision, Eisenhower responded publicly that it was not desirable for a President to support or disapprove of any Supreme Court decision. Privately, Ike was bitter. In the early spring of 1954 at a White House dinner he had encouraged Warren to go easy on the white South. The warhorse was comfortable with Southern mores and worried that the Court might not show sympathy for the segregationists. Although years later he would acknowledge that the decision was correct, in the aftermath of the decision he remarked privately that his appointment of Warren ranked as one of his biggest mistakes. Although Eisenhower effectively enforced the desegregation of the armed forces and encouraged the prompt desegregation of public schools in the nation's capital, his conservative, pro-states' rights administration put little effort into inspiring compliance with *Brown* at the state level.[7]

The seventeen states in the greater South, as could be expected, did not embrace the decision either. Nevertheless, they were not solid in their opposition to *Brown*. The border states—Delaware, Kentucky, Maryland, Missouri, West Virginia, as well as the District of Columbia—swiftly began drawing up desegregation plans.[8] Most of the peripheral South by the start of the 1954-55 school year had no plans to comply with or defy the ruling.[9] Only the Deep South and Virginia indicated they would move to a position of "legal" defiance.

The Brown Decision and Talmadge

The most aggressive immediate reaction in the United States came from Talmadge.[10] Talmadge, who had hoped the *Plessy* ruling of 1896 would stand, was dedicating an airport in Cedartown, Georgia, when he learned of the decision. Years later, in a 1985 interview at West Georgia College, Talmadge recalled being surprised by the ruling:

> About the time I concluded my speech someone reported to me that the Supreme Court had ... outlaw[ed] segregation in our public schools. Well, I got away from Cedartown just as quick as I could and went back to Atlanta. The news media were calling on me for statements from all over the country. I along with I think every Southern governor ... took a very strong position ... [and declared] that the Supreme Court of the United States had gone too far.[11]

Talmadge returned to Atlanta and led the charge to defy *Brown*. He declared at his news conference that the Justices had reduced the Georgia Constitution to a "mere scrap of paper" and that they "had blatantly ignored all law and precedent and usurped from the Congress and the people the power to amend the Constitution and the power of Congress to make the laws of the land."[12] Leaving no doubt about his choice between non-segregated public schools and private schools, he said "Georgians . . . will not tolerate the mixing of the races in the public schools, or any other public tax-supported institutions. The Georgia Constitution provides for separation of the races. It will be upheld."[13]

Six days later, speaking on CBS's *World Today*, Talmadge's rhetoric had not softened. On the Sunday morning national telecast Talmadge declared that blacks and whites would not attend the same schools "even if troops were sent in," and he warned that while Georgia would not secede from the Union, her "people w[ould] not comply." Although he conducted no surveys, he turned to the power of statistics and asserted that "98 percent of the white people and 98 percent of the colored people in Georgia wanted their schools left alone." In fact, had Talmadge bothered to consult with the people, as the American Institute of Public Opinion (AIPO) did two months later, he might have found that 20 percent of the South approved of the high Court's decision, while another 7 percent were undecided. He also would have found that even under the threat of violence and economic reprisal during the height of resistance in 1956, 53 percent of Southern blacks registered their approval of *Brown*.[14]

Talmadge, who was a lame-duck governor in 1954, privately aspired to the Senate. Rather than come forth with constructive leadership, he decided to appeal to the overwhelming majority (perhaps as many as 75 percent) of Georgia voters who opposed school desegregation. With the race issue again in the middle of the now familiar state-federal disagreement, Talmadge, predictably and regrettably, chose to adhere to segregation at any cost. Talmadge publicly challenged the Supreme Court to enforce the decision, and in doing so he missed an opportunity to be a champion of the schools.

Brown and School Equalization

The U.S. Supreme Court had ruled that the only way to equalize schools was to remove the race barrier. Yet, in the wake of *Brown*, Georgia's political and educational leaders never deviated from the school equalization program. Instead Georgia continued its equalization program and accelerated the building of an officially segregated system.

Georgia's press and school leaders were quick to adopt a position that the *Brown* ruling only directly affected those six schools systems that were part of the class action suit. Moreover, because the Court had postponed a decree to implement *Brown*, Georgia would continue working within the separate-but-equal philosophy, which meant proceeding with its three-year-old equalization policy. Many school leaders asserted that the best thing that they could do to improve education for both races would be to ignore *Brown* and get on with the equalization campaign. Jim Cherry, school superintendent in Dekalb County schools, and Harold Early, superintendent of the Savannah public schools system, joined State Superintendent M.D. Collins in predicting that school desegregation in Georgia was a long way off and that separate white and black schools would continue to be built. Unlike South Carolina, which on the suggestion of Governor James F. Byrnes temporarily halted its equalization campaign pending the second *Brown* decree, Georgia's State Building Authority went right on building schools as if *Brown* had never happened.[15]

For years after *Brown*, the state maintained its separate "Division of Negro Education" and continued to keep separate statistics for "white" and "Negro" schools. Moreover, the state's own reports demonstrate not only that the schools continued to be officially separate but also that they continued to be unequally funded. Reports of the Department of Education document beyond question its own discrimination against Negro schools. For example, enrollment during the 1957-58 school year was 654,592 (white) and 305,819 (Negro), or 68.2 percent and 31.8 percent, respectively. Total counties' expenditures reported for care of grounds was $48,680 (white) and $10,998 (Negro), or 81.6 percent and 18.4 percent respectively. Amounts disbursed by boards of education for textbooks, $140,333 (white), $41,192 (Negro), or 90.8 percent and 9.2 percent, respectively; library books, $515,792 (white), $77,522(Negro), or 86.9 percent and 13.1 percent, respectively; instructional equipment, $411,893 (white), $96,602 (Negro); capital outlay, $149,350,672 (white), $57,467,409 (Negro), or 72.2 percent and 28.8 percent, respectively. During the same year there were 21,147 (77 percent) white and 6,443 (23 percent) Negro graduates from four-year high schools.[16]

Neither integration nor equalization were a reality. State officials maintained the unlawful system with a sense of arrogant self-righteousness.

The Immediate Response in the Black Community

Atlanta's black community was, in general, cautiously optimistic about the *Brown* decision. Among the leaders, it was Benjamin E. Mays who perhaps showed the most enthusiasm. Mays, appearing on the same national television broadcast shortly after Talmadge had finished, declared that "the back of segregation had been broken." John Wesley Dobbs, the city's black Republican leader and one time a political rival of Walden, characterized the decision in economic terms. "It's not that we want to push ourselves on the white people," Dobbs reasoned, but "[y]ou can't hold a high paying job unless you have an education."[17] *The Atlanta Daily World*, the conservative daily that reflected the views of "old guard" blacks, editorialized that Monday had been "one of the most important days in the history of the country for freedom for all citizens of the nation"[18]

C.A. Scott, editor of the *World*, however, steered clear of the implications that the desegregation decision would have on the Atlanta Public school system, which presently was a defendant in federal court in *Aaron v. Cook*. Recalling the episode thirty-seven years later in a 1991 interview, Scott said that he "favored desegregation as much as anyone else but was being practical. The situation required moderation."[19] Dr. Rufus E. Clement, the president of Atlanta University, who in 1953 had been the first black to be elected to the Atlanta School Board, also expressed a preference for moderation when he said, "It is now important for all the courageous and honest people of both races . . . to approach the situation with calmness, with good will and with intelligence."[20] When questioned by the white Atlanta newspapers, "Colonel" A.T. Walden, who represented the Atlanta plaintiffs in *Aaron v. Cook*, assured them that he would not press the suit until the Court further clarified its decision. Walden was no doubt cognizant of his governor's defiant tone. Walden, in effect, was trying to avoid dropping the hot ash that might set the state ablaze. Walden said, "We don't want to rush precipitously with the present suit until we have time to consider the whole situation." He even suggested that it might be unnecessary to pursue the suit.[21]

If Atlanta's local black leadership was "walking on ice" in the days following *Brown*, there was more of a marching parade at the national level. Shortly after praising the language and unanimity of the decision, Thurgood Marshall called for a regional meeting in the South to discuss a strategy for desegregation. That weekend leaders from the seventeen states that had segregation laws met in Atlanta and wrote what became known as the "Atlanta Declaration." The Declaration, reprinted in 1979 in *The Crisis*, was a bold strategy statement for the abolition of the segregation of "America's children on the irrelevant basis of race and color." It left no doubt in reiterating that the NAACP had prevailed in *Brown* and now had the sanction of federal law and the federal government. Addressing the issue of defiance, the statement warned that the NAACP would "resist the use of any tactics contrived for the sole purpose of delaying desegregation." Although it called for integration on all levels of education, the manifesto followed *Brown* in setting no time limit. The NAACP recognized the practical problems inherent in moving from a segregated system to a unitary system, but it nevertheless instructed all of its branches to petition their local school boards to abolish segregation without delay. The NAACP also offered assistance to "law-abiding citizens who were anxious to translate this decision" into a "speedy" desegregation program.

The manifesto was a call for unity, stating that *Brown* was a victory for all Americans, not just blacks. It linked its purpose to democracy by reminding its audience that segregation in public education was not only unlawful, but also un-American.[22] Speaking at a news conference on 23 May, Marshall elaborated on the petition strategy, indicating that it was chosen to circumvent the politicians.

Marshall, however, as well as the many moderate commentators in the South, underestimated the extent to which Georgia's politicians and local school officials would cling to the dying body of Jim Crow.[23]

Private School Plan Is an Issue in Gubernatorial Primary

The combination of *Brown* and Talmadge's rhetoric reignited race as a political issue in Georgia as no other federally sponsored action had done since Reconstruction. All of those aspiring to be governor in January 1955 were using the decision, coupled with the private school plan, to distinguish themselves from each other. Significantly, five of the six candidates made campaign pledges to continue public education in the state. Three of the five candidates opposed the private school plan, with one, Mrs. Grace W. Thomas, arguing for compliance with *Brown*. The other four candidates who opposed the private school plan—Fred Hand, Charles Gowen, M.E. Thompson, and Thomas Linder—opposed compliance with *Brown* but criticized the plan. Gowen suggested that county superintendents be given definite authority to say which schools children of the two races should attend. Hand, in a much more vague statement, urged Georgians to remain calm and called for "a solution . . . within the bounds of . . . Southern tradition that does not disrupt public education . . . a solution which maintains segregation arrived at in a legal and peaceful manner." Former governor M.E. Thompson sought to short-circuit the decision with a head-in-the-sand suggestion that called for a U.S. Constitutional Amendment to nullify the decision.[24] Agriculture Commissioner Tom Linder initially chose segregation over public education. The aging Linder commented "We are going to have segregation in Georgia. No ruling they can make will stop it." But within a month Linder would temper his position and favor letting parents decide on whether to send their children to mixed or segregated schools. Lieutenant Governor S. Marvin Griffin, who would win the office, campaigned using the strongest statements against desegregation. He was the only candidate who favored the private school plan. Griffin declared, "I will maintain segregation in the schools of this state and the races will not be mixed, come hell or high water."[25]

The gubernatorial candidates were not the only ones offering public comment on the private school plan. M. D. Collins, who had come out strongly against the plan, urged Georgians to remain calm. He predicted that it would be a half a century before segregation ended in Georgia. Attorney General Eugene Cook, who had been excluded from the group of Talmadge's closest legal advisors because of the things he had said in public when he was, as Harris put it, "splificated," used opposition to the *Brown* decision to unite himself with state leadership.[26] Originally opposed to abolishing the public schools, Cook denied that blacks suffered from an inferiority complex due to segregation and joined Talmadge in calling for a private system as a last resort measure.[27]

Constitutional Amendment for the Private School Plan Supported by GCE, but Not Harris

On 28 September 1954 Governor Talmadge called a meeting of the Georgia Commission on Education (GCE) to discuss the upcoming private school plan amendment. At the meeting the commission voted 13-3 in favor of the amendment. They recommended that the public school remain open as long as possible, but in the event of forced desegregation, state funding would automatically stop. Voting against endorsement out of a variety of motives were M.D. Collins, Fred Hand, and Roy Harris. Collins, who had now served twenty-two years as the state's school superintendent, simply could not be party to abandoning the public school system he had worked so hard to improve. At the meeting Collins paraphrased Winston Churchill, saying, "I was not elected to liquidate the public schools of Georgia." He pledged that he would begin a statewide speaking tour to crusade against the amendment. Hand, whose political influence was quickly fading in the aftermath of the 1954 gubernatorial primary, opposed the private school amendment because he believed that it would place his coveted School Building Authority (SBA) in jeopardy.[28]

Roy Harris had at least two reasons for voting against endorsing the amendment, neither of which reflected a softening of his racist views. First, he was reluctant to support any measure endorsed by Griffin or Talmadge.[29] Second, he foresaw serious legal problems with the private school plan. Harris questioned whether a private school supported by public funds would legally constitute a private school.[30] Disagreeing with Pye, Murphy, Brooks, and Talmadge, Harris felt that the U.S. Supreme Court would not distinguish between a public school system and a private school system funded with public money. In a vintage "Harrisism" he reasoned, "I don't believe you can change the sex of a baby girl by calling her John, Sam or Bill. It will still be a girl. The [schools] will be private ... in name only." Praising an episode in West Virginia where white community members bodily removed black children from a previously all-white public school, he suggested that the only way to guarantee segregation was to physically intimidate blacks who tried to attend school with whites.[31]

Talmadge, Governor-elect Griffin, GCE secretary Durwood Pye, and

Attorney General Eugene Cook, however, persuaded the other GCE members that the plan was the best defense of segregation.[32] Two days after the GCE meeting, at the state Democratic convention, the party put its stamp of approval on the private school plan and called for its ratification. Party leaders also put through resolutions denouncing *Brown* and condemning President Dwight David Eisenhower for his appointment of U.S. Supreme Court Chief Justice Earl Warren.[33]

Private School Plan Is Put to the Voters

With the *Brown* decision only five months old, Georgians gave themselves one month to debate the merits of approving or rejecting a constitutional amendment that would give the General Assembly the power to "discharge" themselves "of all obligation" of providing "adequate education for the state's citizens. The proposed amendment would provide citizens with "grants from state, county and municipal funds ... for educational purposes."[34] The amendment made no provision for the conversion of public schools to private schools, and it did not detail to whom and how the funds would be distributed. It did not attempt to untangle whether the grants could be used at parochial schools,[35] nor did it anticipate the impact that such a measure would have on the state's public school teachers.

The private school "plan" was, in fact, not an alternative educational plan at all. There was not any blueprint, no design arrangement, and no formulated scheme for educating the state's 800,000 public school children. In essence, Georgia's state leadership was asking the state's citizens for a permit to do anything they saw fit to the public school system, including abolish it.

Because there was, as yet, no real plan, critics—such as Superintendent Collins, State Representatives Hamilton Lokey and James Mackay, *Atlanta Daily World* editor C.A. Scott, and *Atlanta Constitution* political editor M.L. St. John—labeled the constitutional amendment a "pig in a poke." Lokey appealed to voters not to "commit educational hari kari."[36] Opposition also came from the United Church Women, the Business and Professional Women's Club, The Daughters of the King, the Georgia Federation of Labor and the CIO.

The most organized and vocal opposition to the plan came from the state's school organizations and voter leagues. These associations stressed that the amendment was unwise, unnecessary, illegal, and that it would hurt large numbers of children in the state. The GTEA and its white counterpart, the GEA, and the state Parent-Teacher Association were all critical of the proposed amendment. J. Harold Saxon, executive secretary of the GEA, declared that teachers across the state would march to the polls to defeat the amendment. Echoing Superintendent Collins, Saxon explained that "the matter would be kept in the courts for a long time." Saxon also questioned the legality of the private school amendment and pointed out that a move to a private system would place in jeopardy the public school retirement system, from which 40,000 people drew benefits.[37]

Leaders of the state's two most powerful black political organizations, the Georgia Negro Voters League and the Atlanta Negro Voters League, mobilized the black vote to defeat the amendment.[38] The Georgia League of Women Voters (GLWV), perhaps the most persistent critic of the private school plan, also urged defeat of the amendment. As early as February 1954, the GLWV had urged the state's citizens to "study and discuss" the amendment "thoroughly and objectively." The GLWV reasoned that Georgians had made "steady and continuous progress" for "nearly one hundred years" toward improving public schools and had "unshaken confidence" that this institution would continue to "produce intelligent and problem-solving citizens."[39] As the vote neared, the GLWV sponsored public forums on the school/race issue and initiated efforts to solicit opinions from the state Attorney General on whether the private school plan would guarantee segregated education, and whether it was legal for the Georgia Commission on Education (GCE) to spend state funds publishing materials favoring the amendment.[40] Continuous efforts by the voters leagues, the school associations, and public school enthusiasts, persuaded two out of every three Georgia dailies to come out against the amendment.[41] Typical of the newspaper editorials that opposed the amendment was a column in the *Savannah Tribune* that noted that "aside from being of doubtful legality and a threat to the education of boys and girls, the private school plan is unnecessary . . . [and] should be defeated." The *Atlanta Daily World* reprinted the column on 20 October. Taking a different approach, the *Atlanta Journal/Constitution* published an article on 17 October entitled "Georgia's Education System Stands at Fork in Road." Rather than reviewing the legal pitfalls and pointlessness of the amendment, the column traced the origins and development of the state's "221 year-old" public school tradition.[42]   Meanwhile, powerful supporters of the amendment campaigned vigorously in favor of ratification. The State Democratic Party and its chairman, Jim Peters, threw all of their weight behind "Amendment No. 4."[43] Right up to the vote Talmadge, Griffin and their supporters countered the anti-amendment campaign with their own tours of statewide speaking engagements. Talmadge appeared several times on television to argue for the adoption of the amendment.[44] To strengthen their case still more, the Talmadge faction sought to answer the critics who argued there was no plan. For example, the Georgia Commission on Education (GCE) endorsed the "Pye Plan," drafted by GCE executive secretary Durwood Pye. The Pye Plan sketched out some of the conversion details, including procedures for leasing public schools to private groups for educational purposes.[45] By the end of October the GCE had spent nearly $10,000 of their state-appropriated budget campaigning for approval of the amendment. Most of the money was spend on 60,000 mailings.[46] The advertising campaign for the amendment used inflammatory slogans like, "Your child's education is in peril. Vote for Amendment #4."

Two weeks before the vote, the debate was hot. Pro and anti-amendment advocates debated in churches, schools and on radio and television on almost a nightly basis. No one could predict which side would win. On 2 November 1954, Georgia voters went to the polls and approved the private school amendment by a vote of 210,488 to 181,148. A thin majority of 54 percent voted for the amendment; a large minority—46 percent—voted against it. Election returns, amply reported in the press, indicated that most of the support for the amendment came from the rural counties across the state, while the urban areas and the black community voted against it.[47] Thus, in spite of vigorous efforts to persuade voters to reject the amendment, the anti forces lost to the power of the Talmadge faction. One journalist editorialized that Talmadge's and Griffin's use of the race issue, coupled "with the aura of their primary success still around them, carried an effectiveness that the other side could not muster."[48] There is little doubt that the voters were encouraged by the Talmadge machine to vote along the race line. The plan was promoted to the voters as the only way to maintain a system of common schools and segregation. The vote in favor of the amendment effectively reestablished and reinforced the state's four-year policy of defiance of the Supreme Court in the name of maintaining segregated education. The value of white privilege was above the law.

In the wake of the vote Governor-elect Griffin deflected criticism that the schools would soon be abolished and said that the state would only use its new power as a last resort measure. Griffin went on to promise that there would be no enabling legislation in the 1955 legislative session.[49] With the exception of one bill that made it a felony for any official to spend money on mixed schools, Griffin proved true to his word.

Notes

1. *Brown v. Board of Education*, 347 US 483 (1954). To appreciate the drama in Washington, DC, see Richard Kluger, *Simple Justice* (New York: Vintage, 1977), 700-736, and Benjamin Muse, *Ten Years of Prelude: The Story of Integration Since the Supreme Court's 1954 Decision* (New York: Viking, 1964), chapter 2. For an earlier interpretive account, see J. Harvey Wilkinson III, *From Brown to Bakke: The Supreme Court and School*

Integration (New York: Oxford University Press, 1979). Wilkinson interpreted the Court's decision as "the most important political, social and legal event in America's twentieth century. "Its greatness," he wrote, "lay in the enormity of injustice it condemned, in the entrenched sentiment it challenged and in the immensity of law it created and overthrew." Wilkinson asserted that *Brown* "was a beginning point of American introspection, and a crossroads, not only for an outcast race, but for an outcast region, a testing ground for liberal values and theory, a challenge for the rule of law and the authority of the Court." Wilkinson, quoted in C. Vann Woodward, book review *From Brown to Bakke, The New Republic* 23 June (1979), 27.

2. Muse, *Ten Years of Prelude*, 80.

3. Muse, *Ten Years of Prelude*, 19.

4. The fifty-seven-year-old Georgian submitted her letter first to the *Atlanta Constitution*, which did not publish it. It was eventually published in the *New York Times*. Clayton, 78 *Georgia Historical Quarterly*, (Spring 1994), 93.

5. *Atlanta Constitution*, 24 May 1954, 9; Muse, *Ten Years of Prelude*, 17, 20.

6. Harold H. Martin, *Ralph McGill, Reporter* (Boston: Little Brown, 1973), 134.

7. By March 1953, Eisenhower had ended segregation in the schools on army bases in Georgia. This move prompted Herman Talmadge to comment that Eisenhower had made a "great mistake," and that "Truman's advocacy of such measures contributed greatly to Eisenhower's [Presidential] victory." *New York Times*, 26 March 1953, 21; Griffin interview, 1991. For more on Eisenhower see Francis M. Wilhoit, *The Politics of Massive Resistance* (New York: Braziller, 1973), 43-44; Numan V. Bartley, *The Rise of Massive Resistance: Race and Politics in the South During the 1950's* (Baton Rouge: Louisiana State University Press, 1969), 61-63; Kluger, *Simple Justice*, 753. For an apologetic account on Eisenhower and his views on race, see James C. Duram, *A Moderate among Extremists: Dwight D. Eisenhower and the School Desegregation Crisis* (Chicago: Nelson-Hall, 1981).

8. Bartley, *The Rise of Massive Resistance*, 68; Richard Lewis, "The South Isn't Solid," *New Republic*, 28 June 1954, 16; R. Ray McCain, "Reactions to the U.S. Supreme Court Segregation Decision of 1954," *Georgia Historical Quarterly*, 52 (1968), 373.

9. James W. Ely, *Crisis in Conservative Virginia: The Byrd Organization and the Politics of Massive Resistance* (Knoxville: University of Tennessee Press, 1976); Benjamin Muse, *Virginia's Massive Resistance* (Bloomington: Indiana University Press, 1961). But see, Kathleen Murphy Dierenfield, "One 'Desegregated Heart': Sarah Patton Boyle and the Crusade for Civil Rights in Virginia," 104 *The Virginia Magazine of History and Biography* (Spring 1996) 251-284.

10. Muse, *Ten Years of Prelude*, 21; Wilhoit, *The Politics of Massive Resistance*, 33.

11. Transcription of 1985 Talmadge interview with Professor Steely, "Race Relations and Segregation," 13, Georgia's Political Heritage Project, Special Collections, State University of West Georgia (formally West Georgia College), Carrollton.

12. Kluger, *Simple Justice*, 710, erred in interpreting Talmadge's statement at this news conference. The meaning of Talmadge's first statement was that the Georgia Constitution (which required separation of the races), not the United States Constitution (as Kluger suggests), had been reduced to a "mere scrap of paper."

13. *Atlanta Journal*, 18 May 1954, 7; *New York Times*, 18 May 1954, 1.

14. *Atlanta Constitution*, 24 May 1954; American Institute of Public Opinion Survey, "AIPO's Summary of Reactions to Supreme Court Decision" 16 July 1954, 106-107; American Institute of Public Opinion Survey, "White Attitudes to Supreme Court and ICC Decisions" 28 February 1956, 108-109.

15. *Atlanta Journal*, 18 May 1954, 9; *Atlanta Journal*, 23 May 1954, 16; *Dekalb News Era*, 20 May 1954, 1; *New York Times*, 18 May 1954, 14; *New York Times*, 22 May, 1954, 15.

16. Annual Reports of the Department of Education to the General Assembly of the State of Georgia: 1954, 1955, 1956, 1957, 1958.

17. *Atlanta Journal*, 18 May 1954, 9.

18. Quote from Muse, *Ten Years of Prelude*, 19; See *Atlanta Daily World*, 18 May, 19 May, 20 May 1954; *Atlanta Constitution*, 24 May 1954, 9.

19. C.A. Scott interview, 13 November 1991.

20. *Atlanta Journal*, 18 May 1954, 1; Also see Muse, *Ten Years of Prelude*, 20.

21. *Atlanta Journal*, 18 May 1954, 1; *Atlanta Journal*, 23 May 1954, 16; *New York Times*, 22 May 1954, 15.

22. *Atlanta Journal*, 18 May 1954, 7; 24 May, 1954 16; "Atlanta Declaration," *The Crisis* (June/July 1979), 198.

23. See for example, Bernard Raymond, "The South Moves Toward Desegregation," *Christian Century* (2 October 1954), 9-11; Sarah P. Boyle, "A Voice from the South," *Christian Century* (17 December 1952), 1471-1473; Harold C. Fleming, "The South Will Go Along," *New Republic* (31 May 1954), 6-7.

24. Thompson was elected Georgia's first lieutenant governor in 1946. He served a shortened term as governor in 1947-1948 following governor-elect Eugene Talmadge's death. See Harold P. Henderson, *Georgia Governors in an Age of Change: From Ellis Arnall to George Busbee*, eds. Harold P. Henderson & Gary L. Roberts (Athens: University of Georgia Press, 1988), 49-60; William L. Belvin Jr. "The Georgia Gubernatorial Primary of 1946" *Georgia Historical Quarterly* 50 (Spring 1966), 37-53; Roger N. Pajari, "Herman E. Talmadge and the Politics of Power," in *Georgia Governors in an Age of Change*, 75-92.

25. *Atlanta Journal*, 18 May 1954, 9; *New York Times*, 30 May 1954, 1; *New York Times*, 30 June 1954, 19; *New York Times*, 5 September 1954, 1.

26. Talmadge instead relied on Buck Murphy for legal advice. Murphy, who served as Talmadge's chief of staff, and later as Griffin's chief of staff, is most likely the architect of the school closing bills of 1956. See James A. Mackay, "Crisis in the Public Schools, An Address," 3 November 1958, HOPE papers, Atlanta Historical Society, Atlanta; *Atlanta Constitution*, 2 September 1981, 17.

27. *Atlanta Journal*, 18 May 1954, 9; *Augusta Courier*, 9 September 1949, 2; *New York Times*, 19 May 1954, 1; *New York Times*, 24 May 1954, 19; *New York Times*, 25 May 1954, 16. In another move that must have appealed to his pro-states' rights governor, Cook, who was also serving as president of the National Association of Attorney Generals, attempted to ban U.S. Attorney Herbert Brownwell from speaking at their annual conference because of his integrationist position and role in *Brown. New York Times*, 23 July 1954, 4; *New York Times*, 4 August 1954, 23; *New York Times*, 18 September 1954, 10.

28. *Atlanta Daily World*, 29 September 1954, 1; *Southern School News*, 4 November 1954, 10; *Atlanta Daily World*, 1 October 1954, 4.

29. By the summer of 1954 Harris was bitter about his waning influence in state politics, particularly his failure to be kingmaker for a sixth time. He had managed Fred Hand's 1954 gubernatorial bid, in which Hand finished a disappointing fourth behind Griffin, Thompson, and Linder. After Griffin won the primary, Harris began to disparage nearly every Talmadge or Griffin idea. During August and September 1954, Harris publicly criticized Talmadge for his private support of Griffin in the 1954 gubernatorial race, *Atlanta Journal/Constitution*, 29 August 1954, 6A; *Atlanta Journal*, 13 September 1954, 8; *Atlanta Journal/Constitution*, 19 September 1954, 3C; *Atlanta Journal/Constitution*, 26 September 1954, 5B.

30. *Brown* had made clear that a state could not discriminate in the administration of public programs on the basis of race. However, *Brown* had not constrained private parties from discriminating on the basis of race. If the schools set up under the private school plan could be determined to be truly "private" schools, constitutional constraints would not apply. However, if the "private" schools were revealed as a sham and adjudicated to be de facto public schools, they could not escape constitutionally required desegregation. *Brown v. Board of Education*, 1954; Robert A. Leflar and Wylie H. Davis, "Segregation in the Public Schools," *Harvard Law Review* 67 (January 1954), 377-435.

31. *Augusta Courier*, 4 October 1954; *Atlanta Daily World*, 29 September 1954, 1; *Atlanta Daily World*, 1 October 1954, 4; *Atlanta Journal*, 26 October 1954, 1; *Southern School News*, 4 November 1954, 10.

32. Eugene Cook, attorney general of Georgia, *The Georgia Constitution and Mixed Public Schools: An Official Opinion from the Attorney General* (Atlanta, 1954). Durwood Pye interview, 27 July 1991.

33. *Southern School News*, 4 November 1954, 10.

34. *Georgia Laws*, 1953, 24.

35. It was unclear whether state funds could be spent at parochial schools because the First Amendment to the U.S. Constitution and the Georgia Constitution require separation of church and state.

36. *Atlanta Daily World*, 6 October 1954, 1; *Atlanta Constitution*, 28 October 1954, 10; *Atlanta Journal*, 21 October 1954, 2; *Atlanta Constitution* 30 October 1954, 1.

37. *Atlanta Daily World*, 8 October 1954, 1; *Atlanta Journal*, 21 October 1954, 2.

38. *Atlanta Daily World*, 6 October 1954, 1; *Atlanta Daily World*, 9 October 1954, 1; *Atlanta Daily World*, 14 October 1954, 1.

39. Paul D. Bolster, "Civil Rights Movements in Twentieth Century Georgia" (Ph.D. diss., University of Georgia, 1972), 150; Mrs. Philip J. Hammer (ed.) League of Women Voters, *Georgia Voter* 24 (February-revised 1954), 1-6.

40. *Atlanta Journal*, 21 October 1954, 1; Interview with Frances Pauley, 15 October 1991.

41. *Atlanta Journal*, 20 October 1954, 2; *Atlanta Journal*, 21 October 1954, 1; *Atlanta Journal*, 31 October 1954, 1.

42. *Atlanta Journal/Constitution*, 17 October 1954, 1E.

43. *Atlanta Journal*, 25 October 1954, 1; *New York Times*, 14 September 1954, 23; *Atlanta Daily World*, 27 October 1954, 1.

44. *Atlanta Journal*, 13 October 1954, 35; *Atlanta Journal*, 14 October 1954, 6; *Atlanta Journal*, 27 October 1954, 1.

45. *Atlanta Constitution*, 28 October 1954, 7; Durwood T. Pye, *Report to the Members of the General Assembly by the Georgia Commission on Education, December 1954* (Atlanta, GA, 1954).

46. *Atlanta Daily World*, 27 October 1954, 1; Pye interview, 27 July 1991.

47. For more election analysis, see Numan V. Bartley, *From Thurmond to Wallace: Political Tendencies in Georgia, 1948-1968* (Baltimore: Johns Hopkins Press, 1970), 29-30; *Atlanta Constitution*, 31 October 1954, 1; *Atlanta Journal*, 25 October 1; Pye interview, 27 July 1991; Lokey interview, 19 April 1991; *Atlanta Constitution*, 3 November 1954, 1; *Southern School News*, 1 December 1954, 6.

48. M. L. St. John, *Atlanta Journal*, 2 November 1954, 2.

49. Mackay, "Crisis in the Public Schools," HOPE papers, Atlanta Historical Society, Atlanta, 2.

Chapter 6

Massive Resistance Reaches Maturity

> All over the South the lights of reason and tolerance and moderation began to go out under the resistance demand for conformity. . . . A fever of rebellion and a malaise of fear spread over the region. . . . Words began to shift their significance and lose their common meaning. A "moderate" became a man who dared open his mouth, an "extremist" one who favored eventual compliance with the law, and "compliance" took on the connotations of treason. Politicians who once had spoken for moderation began to vie with each other in defiance of the [federal] government.
>
> – C. Vann Woodward, 1966

By May of 1955 Georgia and the rest of the Deep South were braced for the U.S. Supreme Court's postponed decree on the implementation of *Brown*. The Court might order immediate desegregation, as the NAACP Legal Defense Fund had requested, or it could allow for gradual compliance, as the lawyers for the defense had argued, and as the Eisenhower administration had encouraged. In choosing the latter, the Court reasoned that local school systems differ enormously and that an immediate order to desegregate all schools would be unfair. The Court required only a "prompt and reasonable start" toward compliance. The decision, known as *Brown II*, set no fixed date for desegregation, stating only that schools must desegregate "with all deliberate speed."[1] The decision placed the practical task of devising remedies and enforcing the decision on the judges of the federal district courts and the U.S. courts of appeals. White leadership in the Deep South breathed a sigh of relief, noting among other things, that many of the judges, who would later be called "fifty-eight lonely men," were natives of states in which they sat.[2]

The Black Response

The black leadership in Georgia sanctioned *Brown II*, although with less optimism than that with which they had greeted *Brown I*. Rufus E. Clement, the conservative President of Atlanta University and the only black on Atlanta's Board of Education, noted that the order "offered the South an opportunity to work together constructively." Two of the more liberal black leaders cautiously endorsed the decision. Benjamin E. Mays, president of Morehouse College, hoped that the Atlanta School Board would assume the responsibility of effecting desegregation and "not try to shirk it."[3]

One outspoken black leader, Joseph Winthrop Holley, the eighty-one-year-old founder and President Emeritus of Albany State College, continued his support of segregation. Since his publication in 1948 of *You Can't Build a Chimney from the Top*, Holley had grown even more reactionary (although today some might argue he was postmodern) in his views on race and education and no less vocal in his opposition to the NAACP's effort to dismantle segregation. In 1953 he published a sequel to *Chimney* entitled *What If the Shoe Was on the Other Foot?* in which he argued that race was the "great hallmark of distinction," and that it must be preserved via segregation. In 1955 Holley published *Education and Segregation*, in which he made a distinction between desegregation at the graduate level, which he favored so long as it was done very slowly, and desegregation at the common school level, which he linked to communism. A believer in white cultural superiority, Holley warned that unless blacks put aside plans of a liberal education and learned "to work with our hands as well as with our heads, we shall remain the economic bondsmen we were in our father's time." "There is, truly, a place for the arts, a time for equality, a season for the trappings and embellishments that many of us love so well," he wrote. "But equality must come from within, and the time is *not* (italics his) now ripe. Until a child has grown to manhood's stature, he makes himself ludicrous in a man's attire." In a discussion that must have delighted reactionary segregationists who were working overtime to link pro-black with pro-red, Holley asserted that desegregation at the common school level was part of a communist plot.[4] For Holley even the *Brown II* decree to desegregate all public education "with all deliberate speed" was simply too much too fast.[5]

Mainstream black leaders rejected or ignored Holley and continued to work for desegregation. William Boyd, Georgia's NAACP president and political science professor at Atlanta University, remarked that *Brown II* had taken the middle of the road by "not reaffirming . . . segregation, but [also] by giv[ing] even the most recalcitrant southern state an honorable way to conform to the decision." Despite this conciliatory statement, Boyd went on to call for a reinvigoration of the

NAACP petition strategy, instructing Georgia's thirty-five local chapters to petition their local school boards immediately. Boyd also instructed the local chapters to follow up with periodic inquiries until they received a response and, if no response was forthcoming, to be ready to go to Court in September 1955. As part of the Georgia campaign, Boyd's state chapter offered to help those cities with no branches.[6]

The 1954 NAACP strategy statement, the Atlanta Declaration, had called for local branches to file petitions with school boards seeking compliance with *Brown*. But, because of the vehement white reaction to *Brown*, local branches of the NAACP moved cautiously. Before *Brown II*, only the Bibb County (Macon) and Muscogee (Columbus) chapters had submitted petitions. During the five months after *Brown II* only eight chapters submitted petitions, and those met white resistance. The Chatham Board of Education in Savannah, one of the eight to receive a petition, flatly rejected the NAACP demand for integration, citing that state law and the state constitution prohibited it. The Bibb County Board was no less defiant. It responded to the petitions by amending the annual budget to include a requirement that no local funds be spent on any mixed school. The board also approved a plan to build another all-girls high school to keep black boys from sitting next to white girls in the event that its resistance plans failed.

The Atlanta branch initially delayed any action on advice of counsel of A. T. Walden, who ordered "an exhaustive study" of the now four-year-old Atlanta suit, *Aaron v. Cook*. Walden, well aware of the ratification of the private school amendment, was concerned that a desegregation order in *Aaron* might cause the closing of the Atlanta schools. Ultimately he recommended that the local branch continue to pursue the petition strategy rather than push for action in the pending suit.

The Atlanta Board of Education, perhaps relieved that Walden did not press the *Aaron v. Cook* suit, was more diplomatic when it received a petition for desegregation in June of 1955. The board quickly appointed a committee to "study" the desegregation issue. In August, while the climate of defiance intensified, the Atlanta board acted on the advice of State Attorney General Eugene Cook and approved the study committee's resolution. The resolution pointed out that the board was subject to the mandates of all laws and authorities, and it would have to do its best to preserve the system until federal and state authorities could resolve legal differences. The resolution also contained a foot-dragging technique: It directed Ira Jarrell, Atlanta's superintendent, to make studies on such issues as the relationship between race and I.Q., race and achievement, race and average educational training, the impact of integration on the preservation of safety and order, the ability of blacks to teach whites, and the impact of integration on extracurricular activities. Jarrell quickly launched the studies, hiring an educational researcher from Princeton University to direct the project. Jarrell would not say, however, how long the project would take, although she did make it clear that it would not be completed by the first of the year.[7]

White State Leadership and the Reinforcement of Defiance

While the NAACP cautiously proceeded with a petition strategy, and the school boards rejected petitions or resorted to subterfuge, the political forces in Georgia that rallied behind Talmadge got more serious in their language and actions to resist the two *Brown* decisions. Talmadge himself, no longer in state government, was eyeing the U.S. Senate seat occupied by the aging Walter George. To stay in the public eye and to capitalize perhaps on the political support he had harnessed in the aftermath of *Brown*, Talmadge appeared on his new weekly television show, which he devoted to political discussions, and spoke repeatedly of maintaining segregation. Talmadge also continued to get his views to Georgians through his writing. He published a weekly newspaper, *The Statesman*, and published his first book in October 1955, *Segregation and You*, a strongly worded collection of his states' rights, pro-segregation arguments.[8]

Roy Harris returned to Augusta and continued to write fiery articles and editorials in his *Augusta Courier* that excoriated the federal government, the NAACP and the "liberals" for ending legal segregation. Paradoxically, he continued to encourage Georgians to support the equalization of their public schools. While in Augusta during November 1954, he also began to discuss with other segregationists the possibility of establishing a private organization committed to using "legal means to preserve the social, political and economic institutions of our Beloved Southland"—meaning, of course, racial segregation and the county-unit system. From these discussions the States' Rights Council of Georgia emerged in December 1955. In the summer and fall of 1955 Harris, the originator of the private school plan concept, shouted defiance loudly from the sidelines, encouraging resistance to the end.[9]

At the receiving end of many of Harris's cheers was State Attorney General Eugene Cook. Cook, whom Harris had once tried to run out of state government because of his drinking problem, was now, according to Harris, the best man to lead the fight against integration. Cook accepted the challenge to be Georgia's segregation point man.

Shortly after *Brown II*, a public exchange on the pages of the *Macon Telegraph* confirmed Cook was up to the task. That summer *Telegraph* editor Bert

Struby wrote a series of editorials calling for a "summit meeting" between the Georgia Attorney General, Georgia's schoolmen, and Legal Defense Fund Chief, Thurgood Marshall. When Struby's editorials continued into the fall, Cook ripped off a heated reply. "I cannot express my concern over recent insistence from certain quarters that our education officials hold 'summit conferences' with representatives of the NAACP looking toward voluntary settlement of the public school segregation problem," Cook wrote. "There is no middle ground for a compromise . . . . The rabid representatives of the left-wing, socialist inspired NAACP have frankly admitted they are not interested in securing the best possible education for Negro children, but rather their ultimate goal is an enforced mixing of the races which inevitably will lead to intermarriage."[10]

In the fall of 1955, Cook began a state-financed campaign that George Mitchell, executive director of the Southern Regional Council (SRC), claimed was launched to stamp out all "independent thought, and stifle all dissent with respect to school segregation."[11] On 19 October 1955, speaking to the Peace Officers Association, Cook lambasted the NAACP, the SRC, and its affiliate, the Georgia Committee on Interracial Cooperation (GCIC). Cook declared that the NAACP, SRC, and GCIC were "dominated by individuals, who . . . have long records of affinity and participation in Communist, Communist-front, fellow-traveling, left-wing, and subversive organizations and activities." Cook published the speech later that year in a pamphlet entitled *The Ugly Truth about the NAACP.*[12]

Over the next decade, but particularly during the next three years, Cook, armed with his interpretation of state and federal law, would keep these organizations "on the defensive and battling for their own survival."[13] One scholar who reviewed the Southern legal attack on the NAACP, noted that the Georgia Attorney General refined and tightened common law offenses of barratry (habitual stirring up of quarrels and suits), champerty (assisting in litigation with money or service in exchange for some of the proceeds of a case) and maintenance (officious intermeddling in a suit which in no way belongs to one, by maintaining or assisting a party) in a deliberate attempt to weaken the NAACP.[14] This scholar also described how the state revenue service harassed the Atlanta NAACP chapter in a purported investigation of income tax evasion.

Another scholar noted that Attorney General Cook specifically attacked black teachers who were well-represented in the NAACP. Cook advised local superintendents to check the records and to fire teachers who were NAACP members. Cook's activities, aimed at derailing the NAACP, had a major impact on that organization's ability to effect change.[15]

In addition to the State Attorney General's Office, other administrative agents of state government participated in what Virginia Senator, Harry Byrd, would soon officially label "massive resistance." In August 1955 the Georgia Board of Education adopted a resolution to revoke "forever" the license of any teacher who advocated desegregation. The Board later revised its policy, opting to require teachers to sign a pledge to "uphold, support and defend the constitution and the laws" of Georgia.[16]

Marvin Griffin, who had won the governor's office on the issue of segregation, showed no signs whatsoever that he would soften his rhetoric on the maintenance of segregated schools. In response to *Brown II*, Griffin proclaimed that Georgians would not accept desegregation "no matter how much the court seeks to sugar coat its bitter pill of Tyranny. . . . We know it is the Supreme Court that has departed from the Constitution and the law, not us."[17] Shortly after moving to the capitol, Griffin declared that people and organizations that favored complying with federal law "should be chased out of town with a brushy top sapling."[18] Although Griffin did not mention any names, it is likely that he was directing this statement at people such as Phillip Hammer, organizer of the Ashmore Project; Jane Hammer and Frances Pauley, active members in the Georgia League of Women Voters; Morris Abram, a Jewish attorney who challenged the county-unit system; William B. Hartsfield, the moderate mayor of Atlanta; and Ralph McGill, editor of the *Atlanta Constitution*. It is also likely that Griffin's statement was aimed at voter leagues, the Southern Regional Council, and the NAACP.

Governor Griffin's bite turned out to be as bad as his bark. On 5 February 1956, the same day that the University of Alabama exploded in violence when a black student named Autherine Lucy attempted to attend classes, Griffin addressed a joint session of the Georgia General Assembly. He asked the legislature to declare the *Brown* decision null and void. Griffin went on to declare that the private school plan was Georgia's "first, last and only absolute remedy" for providing segregated schools within the terms of the U.S. Supreme Court decision.[19]

The Georgia legislature, save for a small group of moderates, "followed the leader." Legislators enthusiastically added the Confederate "Stars and Bars" to the Georgia state flag and renamed it, "The Battle Flag of the Confederacy."[20] In both houses, Griffin's lieutenants had already introduced, read three times (as is required), and pushed through committee, the private school plan legislation. The 1956 session of the General Assembly interrupted Griffin's call for a resolution for "interposition," which would declare the 13th and 14th amendments to the U.S. Constitution null and void, with several minutes of rousing applause. The legislature then adopted Griffin's proposed resolution for interposition and formally approved the private school plan bills.[21]

Later that afternoon Griffin signed six bills into law that "set up the machinery for conversion of public schools to private schools."²² These bills breathed life into the Private School Plan of 1954, which emerged as the new "Private School Plan of 1956." James A. Mackay, a member of the General Assembly in 1956, recalled in a 1991 interview that Buck Murphy, special counsel to Governor Griffin and member of Durwood Pye's Georgia Commission on Education, was the chief architect of these and other Georgia massive resistance laws. One law authorized the leasing of public school buildings for private educational purposes; another authorized the School Building Authority to lease buildings; another made it a misdemeanor for anyone to enter a closed school; another extended retirement benefits to teachers in non-public schools; and still another required fire inspections of private schools.²³

Act 11 of the enabling legislation was, by far, the most important of the six bills. It required the closing of public schools in the event of a decree ordering desegregation and provided for tuition grants for individual students in an amount to be determined by the governor. It also directed that state and local taxes be collected "as may be necessary" to accomplish a transition to a private school system. Finally, in a move that sought to avoid entangling use of state money with the church, Act 11 made it a misdemeanor for any parent to use their child's tuition grant to send the child to a sectarian school.

Resistance to *Brown* was nearly unanimous in the legislature. There were, however, seven moderate members of the General Assembly who opposed the private school plan and massive resistance. This group, known as the "Sinister Seven," was led by James A. Mackay and Hamilton Lokey, two outspoken critics of the private school amendment of 1954. Lokey recalled casting the lonely vote against what became known as Georgia's "Interposition Resolution":

[Dekalb Representative] Jamie [Mackay] got us, the Sinister Seven, together and said "Let's let these guys have their way, interposition doesn't mean a damn thing. Let's all go to the men's room when they vote on it in the morning." Well, they did. My trouble was that I came in late that morning and took my seat just before they called for the vote. And so [we voted]. "All those in favor." The green lights went on. "All those opposed." One red light went on, and it was mine. Jack Ray and [floor leader] Frank Twitty—they were all personal friends—came up and said, "Ham, come on, let's one time show the people of the United States that we're unanimous on this subject." I said "I'm afraid I can't do it, it's a matter of principle. I can't do it." It was the one vote against the Interposition Resolution. Well, I got an editorial in the Washington Post and the New York Times about "that courageous man who stood against the Georgia Legislature." Hell, if I'd been there on time I would've been in the men's room with the rest of them. That's the only time I was ever mentioned in a national newspaper.²⁴

The legislators had become a frenzied and unified mob by early 1956. Considerable pressures were placed on any politician who opposed their actions. Moderates believed they had to weigh their options and pick their fights. "You can't fight everything and win," Mackay later commented. To sit out the vote, as the Sinister Seven did was a calculated political move, which they believed would maintain their positions of influence during a time when no dissent was tolerated. As Mackay later pointed out, the interposition issue had been decided by the "War-Between-the-States," and to fight about it with the 179 legislators who vigorously supported it would be time and energy poorly spent."[25]

The Public School Declaration

Whatever the level of wisdom for hiding out during the interposition vote, the group of seven in the General Assembly, known collectively as the "Sinister Seven," did exit the men's room on that cold February morning and stand up to be counted when the time came to vote on the private school bills. After casting their votes in opposition to the plan, the Sinister Seven[26] issued the "Public School Declaration." Coauthored by Lokey and Mackay, the Declaration stated:

> We believe in the public schools of Georgia. They are our greatest asset. The work of Georgians for seventy-five years and the expenditure of hundreds and millions of dollars in public funds have made our schools what they are today. Our children now have educational opportunities comparable to those of children in other parts of the United States. We believe that every boy and girl and every parent and every Georgian has a stake in the preservation and strengthening of our public school. We believe that anything that harms the public schools does irreparable harm to the future of our children and our state. Believing these things, we cannot support legislation which would: 1. Destroy our public schools. 2. Place in the hands of one man, whoever he might be, unlimited power to shut down our public schools and dole out our school money. 3. Provide for the lease, sale, transfer or other disposition of public school properties without statutory safeguards to protect the public interest or provide who will get our schools and on what terms, and without any provisions whatsoever for the welfare or future of our teachers other than retirement pay. 4. Substitute for our present accredited public schools a grant of money to be applied toward an education of unknown quality in unspecified locations, for an uncertain school year, with no required academic standards and with no provision for building maintenance other than fire safety. 5. Deny the right of peaceful assembly, petition, or open discussion relative to the school problem. We believe in our traditional way of life, but we must find a solution to our present school crisis consistent with this declaration of principles.[27]

The Public School Declaration was an unequivocal statement against the private school plan and represented the first clear articulation in Georgia of the moderate position on the issue of school closings. And as time would tell, the school closing provision of the private school plan would rally moderates and bring about the collapse of massive resistance. The Declaration's endorsement of public education would prove to be compelling to moderates. Still, it did not mention segregation and thus failed to enunciate or reach for the more fundamental goal of providing equal educational opportunity and open access for black children.

During the snowballing of defiance in the mid-1950s, black and biracial organizations weighed in support of public education. At its meeting in 1956, the GTEA passed a resolution calling for "fair play and good will" and desegregation of the state's public schools. The GTEA also went on record opposing the state's private school plan. Although the GTEA did little else to support *Brown* beyond passing these organizational resolutions, its stance on the school-race issue was particularly effective in countering white assertions that blacks did not desire desegregation.[28] This display of black solidarity was particularly courageous. Black teachers, perhaps, would lose the most if public schools desegregated.[29] The chances were great that white teachers would be hired before black teachers in a biracial system. Also, the black teacher's influence and leadership role in the black community would be diminished in an biracial system.

The GCIC, headed by Guy H. Wells,[30] President Emeritus of Georgia State College for Women in Milledgeville, included some of the state's most liberal clergy and civic leaders. Many of those who served as members of the GCIC were also members of the SRC. Wells was no friend of segregation. In 1948 he hosted several biracial meetings of Georgia educators at his home in Milledgeville to exchange facts and ideas about the educational problems in Georgia. One such meeting prompted a cross-burning in his front yard, an event that did not alter Well's conviction that biracial action was necessary in solving the state's educational problems.

As executive director of the GCIC, Wells bypassed the recalcitrant state politicians and went directly to the people of the state, urging local communities to comply with *Brown*. He focused his efforts, for the most part on middle-class moderates and liberals of both races and devoted his energies to a simple, admittedly incremental, but, as he saw it, a *critical* goal: the peaceful transition to desegregated schools. In the SRC tradition, Wells and other members of the GCIC urged the "white and black members of each community [to] come together and plan the wisest way to proceed" in accommodating the ruling that separate school facilities were inherently unequal. In June 1954, before public opinion had hardened on the school-race issue, the state board of the PTA, perhaps influenced by Well's initiative, decided to support the desegregation of the public schools.[31]

Wells's actions, however, did not go unnoticed by the powers that adopted and implemented the state's official policy of massive resistance. In 1956 the State Board of Education and the Board of Regents urged the Teachers Retirement Fund, who paid Wells a monthly retirement pension of $519, to terminate his benefits. The request was supported by Governor Marvin Griffin, who said that Wells was acting "a little ugly" for someone who was on the state payroll.[32]

The trustees, who were the only ones empowered to terminate employee benefits, courageously resisted the Boards and the Governor. However, the State Board of Regents, led by member Roy Harris, had the final say in the matter. The Board of Regents removed his title as the President Emeritus of Georgia State College, thus canceling his position and his pension.[33]

The SRC, now under the direction of George Mitchell, also urged yielding to *Brown*, and now advanced an economic argument that equated compliance with the realization of the "New South" vision of prosperity, or what some had once called the "Atlanta Spirit."[34] Mitchell, an economist, who had also chaired the board of the Highlander Folk School and served on the board of the Southern Conference of Human Welfare, had worked with Myles Horton in 1952 to develop a program at Monteagle in adult education geared at preparing the South for integration.[35] Mitchell framed his argument in favor of racial integration in a manner designed to appeal to moderates and business leaders. His strategy was to discuss the effects of resistance on social stability. Mitchell argued that instability, and the national unpopularity of Jim Crow would deter new industry from relocating to Deep South. If moral suasion and calls for "fair play" had failed, he reasoned, perhaps the capitalist free-market argument might prevail.

The influential newspaper editor, Ralph McGill, had little difficulty embracing what one scholar called a "pocketbook ethics" rationale.[36] In one of his classic front page columns called "Once a Biscuit Is Opened," McGill wrote:

> [Southern politicians have] opened the biscuit for industry, labor unions, larger city populations and less rural, but spend much of their time and emotions continually trying to put the biscuit back together just like it was. They can't. No matter how much molasses of tradition and recrimination they pour on it, it will never go back, "just like it was."[37]

In spite of the efforts of the NAACP, liberals and moderates, power in 1956 rested in the hands of the Talmadge-Griffin forces, who led the mob that chanted "segregation forever." Only eight members of the General Assembly signed the Public School Declaration. The General Assembly continued in its defiance, passing more massive resistance measures including a law forfeiting the retirement benefits of peace officers if they failed to enforce segregation, a law defining the duties of state law officers regarding school segregation laws, and a resolution urging Congress to reject a federal aid for education bill. The Georgia House also passed a resolution that called for a return to segregation in the armed forces.[38]

By the early winter of 1956 Georgia's congressional leaders had officially joined the chorus crying for continued segregation, in spite of its unconstitutionality. On 12 March 1956, Senator Walter George introduced in the U.S. Senate the "Declaration of Constitutional Principles," better known as the "Southern Manifesto," a document drafted by a committee chaired by George. The manifesto, which was signed by all but three Southern Congressmen, formally denounced *Brown* and resolved to reverse the decision and to resist its implementation. Senator Harry Byrd was the chief architect of the resolution, and Senator Richard B. Russell wrote the final draft of the Southern Manifesto.[39]

Massive resistance in Georgia, a policy that had been born some six years earlier, had reached maturity. And as long as there was no suit filed in federal court challenging the status quo in the schools, the resisters could continue rallying behind the rhetoric of defiance and continue stockpiling their anti-integration ammunition without fear of destroying two cherished traditions—public schools and segregation. But as James Mackay would write in the Emory University student newspaper in 1956, the private school plan was something more than ammunition; it was a "ticking time bomb" that, if allowed to go off, would "damage the good name of Georgia . . . disrupt the school system [and] . . . do injury to the children involved."[40]

Private Organized Resistance

The Citizens' Council. While the Deep South's public resistance to *Brown* strengthened during the second half of the 1950s, it only accounted for a portion of the white resistance. The decision sparked a revival of the Ku Klux Klan across the South and gave rise to alternative resistance organizations known as the Citizens' Councils. Reaching their zenith in the last half of 1955 and the first half of 1956, the Councils maintained the primary and unchanging goal of resisting the implementation of the *Brown* decision.[41] Unlike the Klan, the Citizens' Councils "sought identification with the 'better class' of whites . . . and were [in theory, if not in practice] ostensibly committed to strictly 'legal' avenues of circumvention and defiance of the federal mandate."[42]

In the fall of 1955 the States' Rights Council of Georgia (SRCG) sponsored its first meeting in Atlanta. At meeting's end, R. Carter Pittman from Dalton had been chosen to be president, and William T. Bodenhamer, a Baptist minister and member of the State Board of Education, had been appointed as the executive director. Although both men were "firebrand" white supremacists, neither did much to further the organization that they headed.[43]

In 1971 Neil R. McMillen wrote what is considered the definitive history of the White Citizens' Council Movement in the South. He cited Georgia as the only state in the Deep South that did not develop a vibrant Council. While Mississippi, Alabama and Louisiana boasted a combined membership of well over 100,000 collectively, Georgia, at its peak, had fewer than 10,000 members. In spite of having an all-star cast of seemingly dedicated segregationists, including ex-Governor Herman Talmadge, Governor Marvin Griffin, political boss Roy Harris, and Attorney General Eugene Cook, popular support for the States' Rights Council of Georgia (SRCG) was weak.[44] The lack of popular support for the Citizens Councils in Georgia was due, perhaps, to the existence of the county unit system, which enhanced the influence and power of local leaders and county organizations and therefore rendered the Citizens' Councils less important to the segregationist cause.[45]

The States Rights Council of Georgia and its national affiliate, the States Rights Council of America, in retrospect, ultimately contributed to the demise of Roy V. Harris. Since the 1930s Harris had been one of the powerful men in Georgia politics. Even after leaving public office in 1946, Harris remained a power broker, working behind the scenes to influence and intimidate legislators, the governor and others in state government. Sometime after *Brown II*, however, Harris gradually began to fade as a political boss. He had become obsessed with segregation and the preservation of white supremacy and purity. Not a week would pass in which Harris would not use his newspaper to race-bait, red-bait, slash, burn and cut anyone or any development that publicly or privately "compromised" the racial status quo. The state and national Citizens' Councils came to rely on Harris as a speaker and ardent defender of the separation of the races. From 1956 on Harris put a great deal of his time and energy into the Citizens Council movement, and pushed relentlessly for a unified South to win the fight against integration. Recruited by Councils, he spoke at numerous rallies and events in the region—in places like Pointe-A-La Hauche, Louisiana, New Orleans (where he predicted a race war), Kilgore, Texas, and Yazoo City, Mississippi. Yet the more Harris left the state to speak on his only issue, the less influential he became at home. By 1960, the one-time Kingpin of Georgia politics, was just a reactionary, right-wing, bigoted extremist without much clout.[46]

The Ku Klux Klan. Endeavoring to be heard as a legitimate, reasoned voice against desegregation, the Citizens' Council launched a deliberately class-conscious resistance campaign. Councils in various states sought support from those in politics, business, and the professional fields, and thus disassociated themselves from working-class whites. The Citizen's Councils rejected lower-status white resisters who sometimes joined the Ku Klux Klan.[47] Unlike the Citizens' Council, the Klan was not very active in the rural, Black belt of the South where their numbers were few and where county elites controlled local politics and economics.[48] The Klan drew its strength from fast-growing industrial centers located in the foothills of the Southeast. Although the *Brown* decision created a sense of urgency among the "hooded segregationists," the Klan was slow to organize, not reaching its peak until late 1956, 1957, and early 1958.[49]

By late 1956 the anti-Semitic, anti-Catholic, anti-black Klan reorganized under the leadership of Atlanta spray-painter Lee Edwards. Edwards claimed that his group, the U.S. Klans, was the legitimate successor of the Invisible Empire. Edwards established active organizations in all the states surrounding Georgia and in Arkansas. In spite of this interstate revival, incompetent leadership and lack of unity kept the Klan politically weak. Splinter organizations became common across the South. Estimates of Klan membership in the post-*Brown* period ranged from 10,000 to over 100,000.[50]

While the Klan remained disorganized in the mid- and late 1950s—splintered by rivalries and without reliable leadership—the strength of the Klan lay in its capacity for violence and intimidation. The Klan was responsible for many notorious bombings, beatings, murders, cross burnings and hooded marches during the post-*Brown* period. Although these acts terrified minority groups, they did not attract support from the white majority. The news media, politicians, and local community leaders kept a running attack on the Klan.[51] Most status-conscious politicians and community elites, many of whom were quite comfortable with the Jim Crow system, distanced themselves from the violent, predominately working-class Klan. As a result, Klansmen were often denied charters and the use of public facilities.[52]

Massive Resistance Grows More Strident, Extreme, and Defensive

The state legislators in the 1957 session of the General Assembly continued to work to circumvent the Supreme Court's rulings against school segregation by race. Having reinforced the private school plan in the 1956 session, the pro-segregation legislators turned their energies toward setting up processes to win more approval of their one-year-old resistance measures and to silence objection to them. In 1957 the General Assembly expanded the authority of the governor, empowering him to abolish compulsory school attendance laws and to suppress violence at his discretion. Legislators also passed a bill that protected the retirement benefits of teachers in the event of a transition from public integrated schools to private segregated schools. The lawmakers then passed yet another resolution calling for the impeachment of six U.S. Supreme Court Justices.[53]

In the same session the legislators extended the powers of the Georgia Commission on Education (GCE) by authorizing the agency to express pro-segregation views through the distribution of pamphlets, advertisement campaigns, and media briefs. Legislators also approved a measure that permitted the GCE to hold hearings, subpoena witnesses, and investigate any instances that compromised the state's position on segregation.[54]

By the summer of 1957 the GCE had been allocated $376,000 to achieve these goals. The GCE was now a well-funded, pro-segregation, state propaganda machine with investigatory powers designed to intimidate opposition. T.V. Williams Jr., who replaced Durwood Pye as executive director in 1956, now hired private detective agencies to investigate possible violations of the state's segregation laws. During one well-publicized investigation on Labor Day weekend in 1957, an agent "infiltrated" a biracial civil rights conference in Monteagle, Tennessee, at the Highlander Folk School just over the north Georgia border. The agent took photographs of integrated social functions that were later published in a GCE pamphlet entitled *Communist Training School*. In the text which accompanied the photos, the GCE, perhaps aware of the lingering McCarthyism in the state,[55] "attempted to prove conclusively that there existed a master plot against segregation and the civil rights movement had direct connections with Communists."[56] The fact that the conference took place in a neighboring state, and was thus beyond the jurisdiction of the GCE, did not seem to matter. By the end of the year the agency had purchased, with Governor Griffin's consent, $3,200 worth of wiretapping equipment, recording devices and a long-range camera. The governor-sponsored actions were so extreme that even Lieutenant Governor Ernest Vandiver, a faithful segregationist, criticized it as a "gestapo action."[57]

The operations of the GCE were not the most extreme manifestations of pro-segregationist sentiment. State Representative A. A. Fowler from Douglasville sponsored a plan that would move black families from Georgia into predominantly white neighborhoods in other sections of the country. The absurd plan, reminiscent of Senator Richard Russell's 1949 redistribution proposal, sought to literally export the "race problem," giving the non-South a sample of the "Southern Way of Life," while at the same time reducing the number of blacks in the South. Although the plan could not be implemented by the state, due to state constitutional and legislative obstacles, it was taken up by Roy Harris's States' Rights Council, which chartered it as the "American Resettlement Foundation."[58]

Durwood Pye, the former executive secretary of the GCE, also continued his brutal assault on the forces that favored desegregation. In 1956 Governor Griffin named him to a Fulton County Superior Court judgeship. Within a year of his appointment he presided over a contempt-of-court proceeding against the NAACP. The proceeding resulted from an investigation by Revenue Commissioner T.V. "Red" Williams[59] into the financial records of the Atlanta chapter of the NAACP.[60] When the NAACP refused to turn over the records, Pye signed a court order of contempt against the organization and its president John H. Calhoun and fined the organization $25,000. NAACP attorneys, who were aware of Pye's recent segregationist activities, had demanded Pye disqualify himself because of personal prejudice against blacks. But Pye had refused, saying he had no strong racial views other than being against "mongrelization of the races."[61]

By 1956 massive resistance in Georgia had reached maturity, and by the summer of 1957 it had reached a cantankerous and defensive old age. The private school plan had been reinforced by the legislature. The legislature, led by Governor Griffin, had also approved measures to suppress and intimidate black opposition and to gag white moderates and liberals. The total effect was a climate where any diversity of opinion was unacceptable. Although massive resistance leaders had spurned the Ku Klux Klan as extremists, their own activities had become increasingly more excessive. Perhaps they sensed that the foundation of their massive resistance wall was beginning to erode.

Notes

1. *Brown v. Board of Education*, 349 US 294 (1955).

2. C. Vann Woodward, *The Strange Career of Jim Crow*, 3rd ed. (New York: Oxford, 1974), 153; Jack W. Peltason, *Fifty-Eight Lonely Men: Southern Federal Judges and School Desegregation* (New York: Harcourt, Brace and World, 1961); See also, Jack Bass, *Unlikely Heroes: The Unlikely Story of Southern Judges of the Fifth Circuit Who Translated the Supreme Court's Brown Decision into a Revolution for Equality* (New York: Simon and Schuster, 1981).

3. James P. Wesberry, "Georgia Politicos Are Desperate," *Christian Century* (6 July 1955), 798; *Southern School News*, 6 July 1955, 11; Paul D. Bolster, "Civil Rights Movements in Twentieth Century Georgia" (Ph.D. diss., University of Georgia, 1972), 159.

4. Joseph Winthrop Holley, *Education and the Segregation Issue* (New York: William-Frederick Press, 1955), 22.

5. One could argue here that Holley was an intellect and politician ahead of his time. His public positions and arguments showed a sensitivity and determination to preserve black culture that few of his contemporaries dared air. On the other hand, Holley, as a college

president in the Jim Crow Era, must have understood the political and economic obstacles facing blacks in the Deep South. Still, he openly supported a system of segregation in public education that financially shortchanged blacks at all levels. Notably, segregationists in power used his support of cultural distinctiveness as a justification for segregation. One has to question whether Holley was advancing the social and cultural interests of blacks (or what might be termed the "black public good") or his private interests within the segregated (and heretofore unequal) system.

6. James P. Wesberry, "Georgia Politicos Are Desperate," *Christian Century* (6 July 1955), 798; *Southern School News*, 6 July 1955, 11; Bolster, "Civil Rights Movements in Twentieth Century Georgia," 159.

7. Bolster, "Civil Rights Movements in Twentieth Century Georgia," 159; *Southern School News*, September 1955, 16; October, 1955, 13. *The Statesman*, 14 July 1955, 1; 8 September 8, 1955, 1; *Southern School News*, August, 1955, 4; H. Mark Huie,Sr., "Factors Influencing the Desegregation Process in the Atlanta School System, 1954-1967" (Ph.D. diss. University of Georgia, 1967), 77-78.

8. See *The Statesman*, 1954-56; Herman E. Talmadge, *Segregation and You* (Birmingham: Vulcan Press, 1955).

9. Neil R. McMillen, *The Citizens' Council: A History of Organized Resistance to the Second Reconstruction, 1954-1964* (Urbana: University of Illinois Press, 1971), 81.

10. Letter of Eugene Cook to Bert Struby, 31 August 1955; Cook to B. Struby, 16 September 1955; Cook to "Dear" 16 September 1955; Georgia Archives, Box 2 Location # 2982-03. Department of Education; Negro Education Division; Subject Files, Director of Negro Education Series; Box 2; Segregation File.

11. Georgia Mitchell, Series 1, Reel 35, 1955, Southern Regional Council Papers. Atlanta University Center, Atlanta. Also see "The Attack on Free Opinion," n.d., Series 16, Reel 218, and "Attorney General Cook's Criticism of SRC," 2 October 1955, Series 1, Reel 35, Southern Regional Council Papers; SRC Newsletter, 1 November 1955, Series 1, Reel 54, Southern Regional Council Papers.

12. *Southern Regional Council Newsletter*, 1 November 1955; *Southern School News*, November 1955, 1; Eugene Cook, *The Ugly Truth about the NAACP* (Atlanta: [Georgia Commission on Education?], 1955); Also see *The Truth Versus Ugly Lies about the NAACP* (New York: National Association for the Advancement of Colored People, January 1957).

13. Bolster, "Civil Rights Movements," 132.

14. Walter F. Murphy, "The South Counterattacks: The Anti-NAACP Laws" *Western Political Quarterly*, 12 (Summer 1959), 374, 378.

15. Bolster, "Civil Rights Movements," 180.

16. Numan V. Bartley, *The Rise of Massive Resistance: Race and Politics in the South During the 1950's* (Baton Rouge: Louisiana State University Press, 1969), 111; *Southern School News*, September 1955, 16.

17. John P. Wesberry, "Georgia 'Stands Up' to Decree," *Christian Century*, 6 July 1955, 798.

18. Quote from Francis M. Wilhoit, *The Politics of Massive Resistance* (New York: Braziller, 1973), 42.

19. S. Marvin Griffin, *Interposition Address of Governor Marvin Griffin* (Atlanta: Georgia Commission on Education, 1956); *Atlanta Journal*, 6 February 1956, 1.

20. *Georgia Laws*, 1956, 38.

21. S. Marvin Griffin, "Interposition Address" (Atlanta: Georgia Commission on Education, n.d.); *Atlanta Journal*, 6 February 1956, 1.

22. James A. Mackay, "Crisis in the Public Schools, an Address," 3 November 1958, HOPE papers, Atlanta Historical Society, Atlanta, 1958.

23. Mackay interview, 26 November 1991; *Georgia Laws*, 1956, 6-15.

24. Hamilton Lokey interview, 2 April 1991.

25. Mackay interview, 26 October 1991.

26. Hamilton Lokey and M. M. "Mugsy" Smith from Fulton County, James A. Mackay from Dekalb County, Bernard Nightingale from Glynn County, Fred Bentley from Cobb County, and William B. Gunter and William M. Williams from Hall County.

27. Hamilton Lokey, "Low-Key Lokey: An Autobiography," Unpublished manuscript; Mackay, "Crisis in the Public Schools."

28. Reed Sarratt, *The Ordeal of Desegregation: The First Decade* (New York: Harper and Row, 1966), 105; Bolster, "Civil Rights Movements," 149.

29. Mark V. Tushnet, "Organizing Civil Rights Litigation, The NAACP's Experience" in *Ambivalent Legacy: A Legal History of the South*, eds., David J. Bodenhamer and James W. Ely Jr. (Jackson: University of Mississippi Press, 1984), 171-184; *Southern School News*, May 1958, 3; Wilhoit, *The Politics of Massive Resistance*, 153.

30. Wells had also served as President of the Georgia Education Exchange and the Southern Association of Colleges and Secondary Schools, posts leading to his appointment as education consultant for the Peace Corps in Libya in 1952. He also toured West Germany and evaluated the German education system for six months in 1947. *Atlanta Journal*, 21 September 1948, 27; *Atlanta Journal*, 17 October 1954, 5B; *Atlanta Journal*, 29 September 1956, 10.

31. *Atlanta Journal*, 21 September 1948, 27; Bolster, "Civil Rights Movements," 147.

32. Bolster, "Civil Rights Movements," 181.

33. Wells's title was reinstated in May 1965, two months before he died. *Atlanta Journal*, 14 March 1956, 1; *Atlanta Journal*, 22 March 1956, 32; *Atlanta Journal*, 28 March 1956, 6; *Atlanta Journal*, 29 March 1956, 10; *Southern School News*, April 1956; *Atlanta Journal*, 16 July 1965, 1, 24.

34. For more on the "New South" vision, see Thomas V. O'Brien, "Democracy, Privilege, and Schooling in Georgia: Testing the Effects of Politics and Markets." *JAI Series in Advances in Educational Policy* (forthcoming).

35. John Egerton, *Speak Now against the Day, The Generation Before the Civil Rights Movement in the South* (New York: Knopf, 1994), 565-6.

36. Bartley, *The Rise of Massive Resistance*, 345; For insights into McGill's views on communism see Harold H. Martin, *Ralph McGill, Reporter* (Boston: Little Brown, 1973).

37. *Atlanta Constitution*, 1 April 1956, reprinted in Michael Strickland et al. *The Best of Ralph McGill: Selected Columns* (Atlanta: Cherokee, 1980), 100-111.

38. *Georgia Laws*, 1956, 6, 314, 397, 753; Bartley, *The Rise of Massive Resistance*, 75.

39. The politically ambitious Lyndon B. Johnson (Senate Majority Leader, Texas)—who not only sensed he needed to maintain good relations with non-Southern Democrats but also sought higher office—surreptitiously found a way to avoid the Manifesto and was not asked to sign it. Albert Gore and Estes Kefauver (both from Tennessee) refused to sign it. Bartley, *The Rise of Massive Resistance*, 116; Lewis M. Killian, *White Southerners*, 2nd ed. (New York: Random House, 1985), 121; Dewey W. Grantham, *The South in Modern America: A Region at Odds* (New York: HarperCollins, 1994), 210; Sarratt, *The Ordeal of Desegregation*, 41; Wilhoit, *The Politics of Massive Resistance*, 51-55; Benjamin Muse, *Ten Years of Prelude: The Story of Integration Since the Supreme Court's 1954 Decision* (New York: Viking, 1964), 63.

40. James A. Mackay, "Private School Plan, Ticking Time Bomb," *Emory Wheel*, 2 February 1956, 2.

41. James W. Vander Zanden, *Race Relations in Transition: The Segregation Crisis in the South* (New York: Random House, 1965), 41; Neil R. McMillen, *The Citizens' Council: A History of Organized Resistance to the Second Reconstruction, 1954-1964* (Urbana: University of Illinois Press, 1971), viii. McMillen has written the most useful and complete historical analysis of the Councils. Much of what follows in the next several pages is based on his study.

42. Quote from McMillen, *The Citizens' Council*, viii. McMillen traces the birth of the Council to Mississippi shortly after *Brown*, where it grew and spread into other states in the Deep South. He argues that the movement peaked across the Deep South in 1956 and 1957 (12 to 24 months later than Vander Zanden found its climax), but by 1960 it had all but dried up. A related movement, The Citizens' Councils of America, started in 1956 and elected Roy V. Harris as it first president. The Citizens' Councils of America sought to unify the region and revitalize resistance in the early 1960s, but by the mid-decade it too was "scarcely more than a paper organization." McMillen, 137. My examination of the Roy V. Harris papers finds that this organizational decline accompanied loss of power and the political decline of Roy V. Harris between 1957 and 1961. Roy V. Harris Collection, Richard B. Russell Jr. Memorial Library, University of Georgia, Athens, GA.

43. Bodenhamer also sat on the Georgia Baptist's Convention's executive committee. Len G. Cleveland, "Georgia Baptists and the 1954 Supreme Court Desegregation Decision," *Georgia Historical Quarterly* 59 (Summer? 1975), 107-117; *Southern School News*, January 1955, 1; McMillen, *Citizens' Council*, chapter 5; Wilhoit, *The Politics of Resistance*, 115.

44. McMillen, *Citizens' Council*, 79-85.

45. McMillen agrees with Bartley that the lack of grassroots support in Georgia was not related to a softening on the issue of race. Noting that Georgia was the "cradle of the Klan" and the "political habitat of such symbols of racial bigotry as Tom Watson and Eugene Talmadge," McMillen contends that white Georgians were every bit as racist and intolerant of social change as their white neighbors in Mississippi and Alabama. McMillen and Bartley argue that Georgia failed to organize a resistance movement because leaders of the movement tended to be political bosses who already had an influential voice in state government. In effect, the SRCG was superfluous. See McMillen, *Citizens' Councils*, chapter 5; Bartley, *The Rise of Massive Resistance*, chapter 6. What both scholars overlook, however, was how the county-unit system magnified the political power of the state's rural

political leaders and their constituents. A true reading of the popular opinion in Georgia—an opinion that took into account the growing post-war middle class—would likely be more moderate than either scholar indicated.

46. Roy Vincent Harris Collection, Scrapbook, Box 2, Richard B. Russell, Jr. Memorial Library, University of Georgia, Athens.

47. Sarratt, *The Ordeal of Desegregation*, 302. Some have argued that the NAACP and Urban League also pursued class-based campaigns. For more on class conflict among blacks, see Robin D.G. Kelley and George Lipsitz, *Race Rebels: Culture, Politics, and the Black Working Class* (New York: The Free Press, 1996); Karen Ferguson, "The Politics of Exclusion: Wartime Industrialization, Civil Rights, Mobilization, and the Creation of an Underclass in Atlanta" (paper presented at The Second Wave: Southern Industrialization, Georgia Institute of Technology, 5 June 1998).

48. Sarratt, *The Ordeal of Desegregation*, 302; Wilhoit, *Politics of Massive Resistance*, 101-103; Vander Zanden, *Race Relations in Transition*, 40.

49. Vander Zanden, *Race Relations in Transition*, 40-41. Sarratt notes that after a resurgence in the 1920s the Klan had lapsed into impotence. Prior to 1954 "only a few splinter groups from the Atlanta-based Invisible Empire survived, chief among them the Association of Georgia, headed by Dr. Samuel J. Green of Atlanta." Sarratt, *The Ordeal of Desegregation*, 302-303. In 1946, Green and his followers symbolically announced the Klan's post-World War II revival at an initiation ceremony a Stone Mountain, the second birth place of the Klan. Three years later Green died. "Subsequent in-fighting led to factionalism and the emergence of several independent organizations." Bartley, *The Rise of Massive Resistance*, 202; Sarratt, *The Ordeal of Desegregation*, 302-303.

50. Bartley, *The Rise of Massive Resistance*, 202-203, 207; *Southern School News*, January 1955, 16; Sarratt, *The Ordeal of Desegregation*, 302.

51. Bartley, *The Rise of Massive Resistance*, 206, 208; Wilhoit, *The Politics of Massive Resistance*, 101-110. Harold H. Martin, *Ralph McGill, Reporter* (Boston: Little Brown, 1973), 126-128, 152; Richard Kluger, *Simple Justice* (New York: Vintage, 1977), 25; Benjamin E. Mays, *Born to Rebel* (Athens: University of Georgia Press, 1971), 73; Woodward, *The Strange Career of Jim Crow*, 143.

52. Bartley argues that there was an "element of psychological and tactical expediency in the public attack on the Klan. Neobourbons, he maintains, could assault "extremists," including both the NAACP and the Klan, and thus strengthen their conservative positions." This, of course, was what many members of the Citizens' Councils desired. Wilhoit offers a different evaluation. He maintains that the actions of the Klan were detrimental to the conservative position because the Klan brought "about a degradation of the South's traditional conservatism by equating tradition with mindless fanaticism and total reaction." Bartley, *The Rise of Massive Resistance*, 206; Wilhoit, *The Politics of Massive Resistance*, 110. In Atlanta two bombings (in 1958 and 1960) helped to mobilize moderates who opposed violence and lawlessness. This in turn led them to side with liberals and integrationists. See Melissa Fay Green, *The Temple Bombing* (New York: Fawcett Columbine, 1996); *Atlanta Constitution*, 13 December 1960. Thus, Wilhoit's interpretation, as we will see, seems better supported by the evidence when explaining the Georgia case in the late 1950s and early 1960s.

53. Edward D. Ball, ed., *A Statistical Summary, State by State of Segregation-Desegregation Activity Affecting Southern Schools from 1954 to Present Together with Pertinent Data on Enrollment, Teacher Pay, Etc.* (Nashville: Southern Education Reporting Service, 1958), 9, 18; Sarratt, *The Ordeal of Desegregation*, 16.

54. Ball, *op cit.*, 9; Sarratt, *op cit.*, 16.

55. Joseph R. McCarthy was, of course, the father of "McCarthyism." A conservative United States Senator from Wisconsin (1947-1957), McCarthy achieved national prominence and power with his sensational and unsubstantiated accusations against those he termed "Communists." After the Senate condemned him in 1954, his influence steadily declined. See Judith S. Levey and Agnus Greenhall, eds., *The Concise Columbia Encyclopedia* (New York: Columbia University Press, 1983), 499; Albert Fried, *McCarthyism: The Great American Red Scare* (New York: Oxford University Press, 1997). McCarthyism, which Woodward characterized as a "paranoid intolerance" of any opinion to the left of McCarthy, was still strong in Georgia in 1957. This was due, in part, to four publications—Herman E. Talmadge's *Segregation and You* (1955), Joseph W. Holley's *Education and Segregation* (1955), Eugene Cook's *The Ugly Truth about the NAACP* (1955) and Charles J. Bloch's *State's Rights and the Law of the Land* (Atlanta: Harrison, 1958)—all of which tried to link racial desegregation to the spread of Communism.

56. Bolster, "Civil Rights Movements," 142; *Southern School News*, October 1957, 15.

57. *Southern School News*, August 1957, 2; *Atlanta Journal*, 28 May 1957, 1, 14; *Southern School News*, December 1957, 13.

58. *Southern School News*, November 1957, 9.

59. T. V. Williams was the father of new GCE chief T.V. Williams Jr.

60. *Atlanta Journal*, 26 November 1956, 39; *Southern School News*, July 1957, 9; *Southern School News*, November 1957, 9.

61. *Atlanta Journal*, 7 March 1960, 2; *Southern School News*, July 1957, 9; *Southern School News*, November 1957, 9.

Chapter 7

Cracks in the Wall

There are already minds and schools closed in the South. There will be more. But I firmly believe those who take this action are trampling out the vintage where the grapes of wrath are stored. I mean no irreverence when I say that while public education may be crucified on a cross of willful decision to end it, it will rise again out of the wreckage. But a whole generation of children will suffer grievous and lasting discrimination.

–Ralph McGill, 1958

In the summer of 1957 massive resistance appeared to be an impervious barrier to any school desegregation. Several factors were at work, however, putting fissures in the wall. Some of these factors were working outside of Georgia or universally across the South. For example, the NAACP was experiencing repeated successes in the federal courts; and more blacks, especially in urban areas, were attempting to vote. Also, a black direct action campaign had begun which sought to bring about desegregation of public facilities through nonviolent mass protest.[1] White massive resistance movements in other states also began to suffer some defeats. By the fall of 1957 the state of Arkansas experienced a showdown with the federal government over school desegregation in Little Rock. Within Georgia, the opening of community dialogue about the school/race issue would also prove to be a significant erosive force against the wall of massive resistance.

A Change of Guard

While the NAACP continued its battles in the courts, a bus boycott in Montgomery, Alabama, marked the emergence of an alternative mode of action within the civil rights movement. A year-long boycott of city buses was triggered by actions of a black NAACP secretary named Rosa Parks, who refused to give up her bus seat to a white passenger.

Parks's action gave Dr. Martin Luther King, Jr. his first opportunity to test his theory of nonviolent protest.[2] King's methods were quite different from the NAACP's legal campaign in fundamental ways. He stressed nonviolent, mass protest and persuaded blacks in Montgomery that it was their duty to protest, assuring them that God was on their side.[3] Blacks successfully organized and walked or carpooled instead of riding segregated city buses. The cost of the loss of ridership eventually forced the city bus system to desegregate. The bus boycott focused national attention on segregation and brought forth in King a leader of national stature.[4]

In a few years King's method of employing nonviolent, mass protest would become a compelling force for desegregation across the South. But in Georgia in 1956 and 1957, nonviolent protest was still a fledgling movement. In Atlanta in January 1957 a group of black ministers boarded a city bus and sat in white seats. Five of them were eventually arrested.[5] The plans for mass protest, however, were abandoned in favor of pursuing litigation.

Meanwhile, between 1954 and 1957 the black and biracial movements in Georgia to nullify segregation was understandably cautious. Massive Resistance had reached its zenith in this period, and the NAACP was fighting "a defensive battle for its own survival."[6] Although the NAACP continued to pursue desegregation suits in higher education,[7] the elementary and secondary school action stalled. Indeed, in Atlanta A.T. Walden, the lawyer who had directed the group's legal campaign in the state, appeared to have returned to the pre-*Brown* strategy of pursuing litigation only with respect to higher education. He had not acted on *Aaron v. Cook* for well over a year, giving federal district court Judge Frank Hooper a reason to dismiss the case for lack of prosecution.[8]

For "Colonel" Walden, the 72-year-old patriarch of the Georgia black legal community, the U.S. Supreme Court's *Brown* decision may have been a national victory for black civil rights, but it was not necessarily an achievement that would readily translate into equality for Georgia's blacks, especially in a climate of massive resistance. He, like the moderate Atlanta mayor William Hartsfield, was concerned with preserving the peace in the community and maintaining the harmonious relationship in Atlanta between the black community and the white power structure. His approach, however, had not been effective at bringing about the desegregation of schools.

In August 1957, two full years after the NAACP had petitioned the Atlanta system for a speedy end to segregation, the Atlanta School Board and its aging matriarch, Superintendent Ira Jarrell, issued their study entitled "Learning and Teaching in the Atlanta Public Schools." Jarrell's foot-dragging strategy for postponing action on Walden's petitions had borne three years of fruit, due to the comprehensiveness of the study she commissioned and the timing of its release. The study, which had tested some 25,000 pupils and 3,000 teachers in Atlanta, was released too close to the start of the 1957 school year, thus frustrating black efforts to desegregate and sheltering segregation in the system for at least another term.[9]

Walden's tolerance of Jarrell's prolonged study project reflected his comfort and rate of success in working out Georgia's racial problems within the doctrine of separate-but-equal. His legal and political activities in the late 1940s and early 1950s had brought about major improvements in the black community, ranging from the installation of street lights and swimming pools for blacks, to less police brutality in black neighborhoods and the equalization of salaries for black public school teachers.[10] His efforts in 1948, along with the efforts of John Wesley Dobbs, a powerful black Republican, to organize and register 17,000 black voters in Atlanta gave the city's blacks enough political power to influence any elected municipal office.[11]

Brown, however, had changed the rules for how blacks would make gains toward achieving first class citizenship. In effect, it trumped Walden's conservative means of bringing about improvements in the black community in general and in black education in particular. The new formula for racial equality was desegregation. To carry out their campaign for desegregation, black Georgians would need new leadership.[12]

By 1956 the 'old guard' leadership in the black community began passing the torch to the younger, less conservative leaders.[13] Taking over the legal struggle for Walden were two bright young lawyers named Eugene E. ("E. E.") Moore Jr. and Donald Hollowell. Walden remained as the symbolic head of the black legal community and continued to function as liaison between the Atlanta mayor's office and the black community. However, Moore and Hollowell—working with Thurgood Marshall and Constance Baker Motley at the NAACP national office—took over the litigation.[14] Like Walden, Moore and Hollowell believed that the "American Creed" of liberty, equal opportunity, and individualism could be brought into congruence with realities of Southern life.[15] Moore and Hollowell also firmly believed that litigation could be effectively used as an instrument to transform societal injustices. Unlike Walden, Moore and Hollowell did not put much stock in this happening within the *Plessy* doctrine.

As a graduate of Howard Law School and a protégé of James M. Nabrit Jr.,[16] Moore recalled being groomed for civil rights litigation from the moment he stepped onto the Washington, D.C., campus:

Of course they [Nabrit, Charles Houston, and others on the Howard Faculty] stressed those [civil rights] questions . . . and I developed an interest in those things. . . . We were always doing something to eradicate the system of segregation.[17]

In 1956 Moore filed a suit in federal court on behalf of four blacks who contended that they had been denied admission to Georgia State College of Business Administration (now Georgia State University) in Atlanta because of their color. The case, *Hunt v. Arnold*, centered on the legality of a new university system admissions policy that required applications to be accompanied by the endorsement of two alumni. The plaintiffs argued they could not obtain endorsements because they did not know any alumni of the all-white college, and that the "social pattern" did not permit them an opportunity to know such whites. The court agreed with plaintiffs that the Board of Regents had put the alumni recommendation requirement in place to keep black students out. Although the court declared the policy unconstitutional, the Board of Regents was able to continue to exclude the plaintiffs based on other grounds. Although the case did not lead to admission for the plaintiffs, the *Hunt* case marked the emergence of bolder strategy within Georgia's black legal community.

Little Rock

In the fall of 1957 a showdown occurred in Little Rock, Arkansas. Little Rock became the home of one of the most publicized school desegregation incidents. That January the once moderate governor of Arkansas continued to attend to his 1956 campaign pledge to resist school desegregation. By August 1957 the federal courts had ordered Central High School in Little Rock desegregated. As tensions mounted, Governor Orval Faubus accused the federal government of "cramming integration down our throats."[18] Adding to the furor were Georgia Governor Marvin Griffin and Roy V. Harris, who, in spite of their political differences, united to encourage defiance.[19]

On 22 August Griffin and Harris flew to Little Rock, and, at a Citizens' Council dinner, called upon Arkansas to join Georgia in the defense of segregation. On 2 September, after pledging that he would let city officials deal with the problem, Faubus ordered the National Guard to prevent desegregation in Little Rock. For twenty days the Guard maintained segregation at Central High School, while the Eisenhower administration stood by indecisively. By 20 September the federal district court had enjoined Faubus and the National Guard from obstructing the desegregation process, at which time Faubus promptly removed the National

Guard then flew to a Southern governors conference on Sea Island. Before leaving, Faubus predicted that violence would result if Central High attempted desegregation.[20]

The governor's predictions proved clairvoyant. With a few state police, nine black students entered Central High on 23 September 1957. By noon a white mob had grown so large and loud that the state police removed the blacks from the school. The situation remained explosive.[21] Eisenhower federalized the national guard and sent in the 101st Airborne Division. On 25 September, with troop escort, the "Little Rock Nine" permanently desegregated Central High School. The troops stayed on for the remainder of the school year.[22] *Brown* and *Brown II* had its first major ground skirmish with a defiant state government and had won an important victory.

The Little Rock episode proved to be a sobering lesson to Georgia's political leaders who had rallied behind the policy of massive resistance. It was now clear that defiance of a federal court order to begin desegregation would not be tolerated by the federal government. Eisenhower, after two years of indecisiveness, had finally sent a clear signal that Southerners would have to either accept the implications of the *Brown* decision and allow for the start of desegregation in their public schools, or get out of the education business altogether. White Georgians, if and when confronted with a similar suit, would have to choose between their public schools and segregation. Black Georgians would have to find some way to bring about compliance with *Brown* without jeopardizing a public school system that, although still separate and still unequal, was improving.

In the end, the white South would have to weigh its commitment to segregation against its commitment to public education. But for the moment, with no litigation pending at the elementary and secondary level in Georgia, the school crisis was still something to read about and monitor in other Jim Crow states.

Voices of Moderation

By late 1957 there were several other worries on the minds of Georgia's state leaders besides the image of little white children sitting next to little black children in public schools. For one, federal district court Judge Boyd Sloan refused to dismiss *Hunt v. Arnold*.[23] Second, in spite of a record-setting, 121-hour filibuster, the Eisenhower administration had managed to get through Congress the civil rights bill, demonstrating the inability of Southern Congressmen to resist federal legislative pressure. Southern legislators did, however, manage to water down the bill with amendments that deleted any enforcement powers of the new Civil Rights Commission.[24]

Perhaps more worrisome to the state politicians at the time was the emerging reality of the so-called black bloc vote in Georgia, which, if organized, could function as a "spoiler" in local and state elections. The black vote in Atlanta had increased to well over ten thousand registrations since Georgia's white primary was struck down in 1946 in *Chapman v. King.*[25]

It was the power of the black vote in Atlanta that persuaded William B. Hartsfield, the incumbent mayor, to moderate his views on race. Shortly after the white primary was struck down in 1946, Atlanta's black leaders approached Hartsfield requesting streetlights for a certain area. The mayor told them to come back and see him when they had ten thousand votes, which they did. The group of leaders, known as Hartsfield's "Kitchen Cabinet," got the streetlights.[26] Later, in 1952, Hartsfield established a biracial committee in the city that sought to understand better the issues related to black expansion there. By the late 1950s Hartsfield's personal views on race may have converged with his political positions. Morris Abram, a friend of Hartsfield's and an Atlanta attorney who spearheaded the litigation against the county-unit system, recalled that Hartsfield, with the help of several drinks, "delivered himself of opinions on race far exceeding the limits that Southern conservatism permitted its politicians." Abram recalled, "It seemed that a civil rights activist was lurking within my cagey friend." Abram recalled that Hartsfield interrupted himself to say, "you know, this is damn heady stuff we've been talking here tonight. I wonder where I got all these ideas. Well, I don't suppose I'd have gotten them if the niggers hadn't got the right to vote. . . . Well, it doesn't matter now, wherever I got them I now believe them and I'm stuck with them."[27]

In December 1957 Atlantans, largely through the power of the black ballot, re-elected Mayor William B. Hartsfield, over Lester Maddox, a flamboyant segregationist. Maddox's campaign centered on the claim that Hartsfield was controlled by the NAACP, an organization to which Maddox said he would never sell his birthright. However, Hartsfield's moderate message was more appealing to nearly two out of every three Atlanta voters.[28] Hartsfield, who had quietly opened the city's golf courses to blacks in 1956, campaigned on the view that Atlanta deserved racial understanding and not racial hatred. Hartsfield believed that Atlanta, through his leadership, would lead the South in peaceful progress and toward understanding—regardless of the state's coiled posture. "We don't want the hatred and bitterness of Montgomery or Little Rock," he said. "I'm not asking anybody to surrender anything. I'm not trying to integrate anybody. I'm not trying to destroy the traditions of the South. But no public official can do other than to cling to the law." What Hartsfield did not emphasize was that, unlike Governor Griffin, he chose to "cling" to federal and not state law.[29]

Also, across Georgia a new black organization called the Southern Christian Leadership Conference (SCLC), headed by Martin Luther King Jr., the young, charismatic leader, began an enthusiastic black voter registration drive that set its goal at registering 300,000 blacks, twice the number that was then registered. The drive, called the "Crusade for Citizenship," set as its ambitious objective to teach illiterate blacks how to read and write enough to get registered. The move was perhaps brought on by the seemingly glacial progress that the NAACP had been making on the desegregation front. It was also supported by a timely Southern Regional Council study, which estimated the potential black vote in the South. King, an Atlanta native, who had been catapulted into the national spotlight as a result of his leadership of the 1955 and 1956 Montgomery, Alabama, bus boycott, was also considering moving the SCLC headquarters to Atlanta. The power of the emerging threat of the black "bloc vote" was, without a doubt, a significant factor in changing the political and social landscape in post-*Brown* Georgia.[30]

Editors' View of the South

Less worrisome to state politicians, but no less important to the history of Georgia's response to *Brown*, were the increasingly loud white voices urging state leaders to reconsider the state's massive resistance policy and to develop policies that were fair to all Georgia's citizens. During the summer of 1957, John A. Griffin, an Emory professor, began planning a course designed to generate community dialogue about problems confronting the South. Griffin, a sociologist by training, had started adult education at Emory in 1951. In 1952 he organized a course around the film *Cry the Beloved Country*, the story of apartheid in South Africa. The participants in the course also viewed and discussed other controversial films about social injustices in various parts of the world. Griffin, a native Georgian, who had worked on the Ashmore Project in the summer and fall of 1953, reasoned that if he should teach about other countries' social, political, and economic inequities, perhaps he could also address social injustices at home. Yet in Georgia at the time there had been little if any community dialogue about the South's own system of apartheid.[31]

During the early summer of 1957, Griffin contacted some of the best known moderate editors in Georgia and the South and invited them to speak about the region's problems, particularly the issues of race, segregation, and public schools. By midsummer, however, word of Griffin's planned course reached the Emory administration. The topic of Griffin's course was soon taken up by the university's board of trustees, who agreed to allow Griffin to proceed with the course but directed him to invite editors from both sides of the segregation issue. Although the liberal professor was reluctant to give the segregationists a platform, he decided to go on with the lectures, reasoning that some two-sided discussion was better than none at all.

By 1957 many of Georgia's leading newspapers had grown more conservative on the race issue. Roy Harris's *Augusta Courier* segregationist viewpoint represented the extreme conservative view on the issue of segregation.[32] In 1957 Harris was a member of the Board of Regents (which explains a good deal of their actions in the *Hunt v. Arnold* case), the president-elect of the States Rights' Council of Georgia (SRCG) and soon-to-be president of Citizens' Council of America, a national federation that sought to direct the network of state and local Citizens' Councils.

The ardent segregationist used his weekly paper to advance his theories on how to resist *Brown*. Writing in the *Courier*, Harris proposed yet another plan to preserve segregation and "save the public schools of Georgia." Under the Harris plan the state and local authorities would cut off all money to school systems that desegregated. When this happened, he reasoned, private citizens would set up a corporation to run private schools. Harris's idea was that public schools would be saved in all those counties where no attempts were made to desegregate, but they would be abolished in places like Atlanta and Savannah where litigation was likely.[33]

Middle-of-the-road tabloids disagreed with Harris's editorials on the race issue but argued openly for continued segregation. The *Columbus Ledger*, the *Macon News and Telegraph*, and the *Savannah Morning News* argued that Georgia could solve its race problem on its own. The Macon paper went so far as to suggest that all the leaders of the state—except those from the extremist organizations like the NAACP, the Klan, and the SRCG—meet and begin to find solutions to the race-school issue that confronted Georgians.

The *Courier* and its stance on segregation were also challenged by the three moderate Atlanta newspapers—the *Constitution*, the *Daily World*, and the *Journal*—and by the Gainesville *Daily Times*, a progressive daily published and edited by Sylvan Meyer.[34]

In September 1957 Griffin began teaching an eight-week adult night course called "Editors' View of the South." The fall series, conducted on the Emory University campus at the height of massive resistance in Georgia, was one of the first discussions of the school-race issue in the post-*Brown* Deep South to fully explore the views of both segregationists and moderates. The course featured lectures by editors of stature from across the South, including Harry Ashmore from the *Arkansas Gazette*, Ralph McGill from the *Atlanta Constitution*, Sylvan Meyer from the *Gainesville Times* (GA), Reed Sarratt from the *Winston-Salem Observer*, James Jackson Kilpatrick from the *Richmond News Leader*, James Hall from the segregationist *Montgomery Advertiser* and Thomas Waring from the *Charleston News and Courier*.

Kilpatrick, Hall, and Waring argued for continued segregation. The 37-year-old Kilpatrick, a native of Oklahoma, had been the editor of the *News Leader* since 1951. A zealous resister to *Brown*, Kilpatrick had succeeded in becoming more "Virginian than Virginia."[35] Thomas Waring presented a pro-segregation paper that he had already published in *Harpers*, discussing the feasibility of maintaining segregation and public education and the role of the press in managing and controlling the popular debate.

McGill, Ashmore, Sarratt,[36] and Meyer argued for compliance with the *Brown* decision.[37] Of all the moderates, Meyer was by far the most forthright. The native Atlantan had lived in the South his whole life, except for a tour of duty in World War II. In 1947 he became editor of the *Times*, a small daily newspaper serving the 43,000 people in the north Georgia piedmont area. Speaking at Griffin's 1957 symposium, Meyer warned Georgians that they "may be in the danger of killing the institution of liberty in order to preserve the dead [institution] of segregation." He added that he had made a personal decision to ignore the color line in all aspects of Southern society. He also believed in eliminating the assignment of children to schools on the basis of race. In answering the argument that the Constitution permits states to manage their own school systems and to continue segregating by race, Meyer asserted that the "Constitution serves the individual first and foremost," and not the states or the federal government. Responding to the popular myth that nearly all of the South's blacks preferred segregation by race, Meyer said:

> Who knows what the Negro wants? I believe the Negro doesn't even know what he wants, and again I say, it doesn't make any difference what he wants. The question is what he deserves. He deserves a clean set of books, self-respect that can never come to him when the law books of his state set him apart from other Americans.[38]

Meyer warned his audience that the Georgia legislature had tied the hands of localities and had passed dangerous laws that did not allow for Georgia "to bend with the winds of change." He asserted the press had a moral and ethical role to play in the impending crisis. The local press, he advised, must guide public thinking, prevent chaos at the community level, encourage blacks and whites to communicate, and editorialize quickly before local opinion crystallizes. Thus, according to Meyer, the press had a leadership role to play in encouraging Georgians to embrace the ideals of freedom, democracy, equality, and liberty.

McGill was much less blunt in his remarks than Meyer. In his speech, McGill spent a very long time avoiding the topic of desegregation in the South, lecturing instead about the economic history of the South and its relationship to the Civil War. Then he introduced his gradualist argument, contending that the U.S. Supreme Court did not violate the Constitution but only "reinterpreted it." He went on to say that there were alternatives to defiance, like segregating by gender, as Texas planned. He pointed out that the feeling in north Georgia was that the few blacks they had up there "could just sit those kids over in the corner of the school room and nobody would care." He pointed out, however, that under the present state laws in Georgia, local school systems had no authority to keep their public school open. Reminding his audience that the Virginia private school plan had been knocked down by the Virginia Supreme Court earlier that year, he rejected the legality of the Georgia private school plan:

> [It] hasn't got a chance. . . . We ought not delude ourselves. It seems to me that a very phoney bill of goods has been sold, namely that integration—I don't know anyone that's demanding integration, a person would be a fool to demand integration now in the Deep South—would mean amalgamation. I think too much of both races to think a law keeps them from running to the marriage courts. Yet, it's the overwhelming force in this—mongrelization and amalgamation. Integration doesn't mean amalgamation.[39]

Although McGill discounted the threat of "mongrelization" and "amalgamation," he displayed an elevated concern about violence and mob action. Two months earlier McGill had watched in horror the nationally televised coverage of events that one political commentator affirmed "brought shame to the nation."[40] McGill, with the image of the Little Rock mobs in his mind, felt remorse about how the white mob had acted, and he hoped it would never happen again. Thus, it is not surprising that for McGill in 1957, avoiding chaos was even more important than keeping the public schools open.

His choice, however, had implications. He warned against a desegregation suit in Georgia at the present time. He said,

> I'd rather see Georgia, which needs public education as much or more than any other state . . . close its schools rather than go into a period of violence and mob action. I'm confident that [the state] will close the schools if it comes to that. And if it comes to that I hope they close them without any violence. I am hopeful that before that comes, we could avoid in the Deep South filing a suit

about a school, say for two or three years, and the process, which had begun in Arkansas and Oklahoma, and North Carolina, and Tennessee, could progress. I happen to know that some of the cities in North Carolina are making plans for next fall. They're going ahead.[41]

Griffin's course on the "Editors' View of the South" marked the emergence of dialogue within the white community about the school/race issue. This dialogue would prove crucial in bringing down the wall of massive resistance. It was a dialogue moved forward by abhorrence of violence and by a belief in public education. But, while the propaganda of public education promoted schools as the ideal of an American democratic meritocracy, the reality embraced and allowed for race and class privileging.

The Ministers' Manifesto

Building on the moderates' initiatives, which together suggested there were alternatives to following the state's "rabble rousing politicians," eighty white Atlanta ministers, representing all the major Protestant denominations, came out with a six-point statement that outlined their views on race relations. On 3 November 1957 the group released what became known as the "Ministers' Manifesto," a declaration which advanced community action and dialogue on race relations in general and the survival of Georgia's public schools in particular. The manifesto called for an end to all racial prejudice, obedience to the law, preservation of the public schools, protection of free speech, maintenance of communication between the races, and a prayer that difficulties might be resolved.[42] In an effort to get their message to others in the state, the ministers sent thousands of copies to the United Church Women in Atlanta and to the executive committee of the United Church Women of Georgia. The enveloping theme of the manifesto was that all Americans had a responsibility to obey federal law, specifically the 1954 *Brown* decision, regardless of how they felt about the ruling. Above all, the declaration stressed that the public school system in Georgia must not be destroyed. The institution of public education, it argued,

[is] essential to the preservation and development of our democracy. To sacrifice that system to avoid obedience to the decree of the Supreme Court would be to inflict tremendous loss upon multitudes of children whose whole lives will be impoverished as a result of such action. It would also mean the economic, intellectual and cultural impoverishment of our section, and would be a blow to the welfare of our nation as a whole.[43]

The manifesto was well received by middle-class religious moderates. Of course, there were many who disagreed with its theme. George O. King, a Methodist minister from East Point, a small town in the metropolitan area, reflected the views of most legislators and many white Georgians. King reasoned that segregation was not a moral issue, but rather a social issue, and if disrupted would lead to "confusion and strife."[44] Yet for many other Georgians the Ministers' Manifesto was like a breath of fresh air. Atlanta's black ministers, who rounded out Atlanta's old guard leadership, applauded the action and praised their white colleagues for their display of courage and their promotion of good will. Martin Luther King Sr., pastor of Ebenezer Baptist Church and now distinguished as "Daddy King," joined Morehouse President Benjamin Mays and William Holmes Borders, a powerful Northern-educated preacher who pastored at Wheat Street Baptist Church, by predicting that the proclamation "would result in a good deal for all in the South."[45] The Atlanta dailies gave positive coverage to the manifesto. Motivated by the emergence of a new viewpoint, the *Journal/Constitution* began soliciting public opinion on the school/race issue. The paper ran a series that reported the various perspectives of citizens in the state.[46]

Nor was the positive response confined to Atlanta. In December 1957, thirty-three ministers from Columbus, a small city on the Alabama line, signed an identical six-point manifesto. Community discussions, that for years had been considered too sensitive, began in Georgia in the late winter of 1957 over the issues of segregation, Christianity, and public schools. Desegregation versus segregation still was not a debatable topic in the white community. But the issue of public schools versus hastily arranged quasi-private schools was. It would be the strength of the argument for public education that would become the wedge to divide the apparent monolith of white opinion and bring about token desegregation.

The Atlanta NAACP Files Critical Suit

It was within this context that the NAACP abandoned A. T. Walden's three-year petition strategy. On 11 January 1958 the Atlanta chapter of the NAACP filed *Calhoun v. Latimer*, which charged that the Atlanta School Board was operating a racially segregated system. The suit set in motion the litigation that would push Georgians to choose between their system of segregation and their system of elementary and secondary public schools. *Calhoun* was the second lawsuit attacking segregation in the public elementary and secondary schools in eight years and the first filed in Georgia at that level since the *Brown* decision.[47]

Immediate action to the suit varied. Mayor Hartsfield said Atlanta would adhere to the motto inscribed on the Georgia state seal, which said "Wisdom, Justice and Moderation." He declared that peace must be kept and that he would fight to keep Atlanta from "becoming another Little Rock." Ralph McGill, writing in the *Atlanta Constitution*, joined Hartsfield but added that the court action was "ill-timed ill-advised, and a grave disservice to both races." C.A. Scott, publisher of the *Atlanta Daily World*, the city's black newspaper, wrote that lamenting about the timing of the suit was beside the point. He called for resolving the suit in a spirit of support for law and order.[48] Attorney General Cook said that in his opinion the suit would "totally disrupt" the state School Building Authority's (SBA) construction of new Atlanta schools. Cook also indicated that his office would take more state action against the NAACP and its members by enforcing the law of barratry that had been tightened up in 1957.[49]

Governor Griffin was not surprised by the suit. Speaking to the General Assembly, Griffin said that he did not think the action would require any new legislation, but he vowed that any usurpation of state powers by the federal government would be fought through legal means and "with all [the state's] resources. In a move that the Atlanta dailies interpreted as a slap at Atlanta Mayor William Hartsfield, the governor departed from his advance text to explain that the suit had been encouraged by "race-mixers," including "persons in high places [who] put themselves on record as moderate or middle-of-the-road."[50]

The General Assembly and 1958 Race for Governor

Calhoun v. Latimer was filed only three days before the Georgia General Assembly convened on 13 January. *The Southern School News*, a regional monthly newspaper, predicted a further buildup of legislation to circumvent the attempt to desegregate the public schools. But, for the first time in over nine years, the politics of a gubernatorial race—not segregation—preoccupied the legislature. The General Assembly, perhaps out of routine, did take time to pass its yearly resolution condemning the federal government. This time they censored President Eisenhower's use of federal troops in Little Rock. The lawmakers also modified an earlier act that empowered the governor to suspend school attendance in the event of forced desegregation.[51]

The gubernatorial race featured a growing row between Governor Marvin Griffin and Lieutenant Governor S. Ernest Vandiver. Governor Griffin, who was ineligible to run for a second term, supported Roger Lawson, the former chairman of the state highway board and Georgia Rural Roads Authority (GRRA). When Griffin asked the General Assembly to extend the bond limit to the GRRA by $50 million, Vandiver supporters labelled the proposal a "slush fund" for Lawson and rallied to defeat it in the House. The House action crushed Lawson's gubernatorial hopes.[52] While Vandiver continued to defend segregation and the county-unit system in this speeches, he also campaigned on promises to provide economy and honesty in state government and to promote industrial development in the state. By April 1958, however, race quickly became the dominant campaign issue.[53] Reverend William T. Bodenhamer, a Baptist minister and staunch segregationist, who also served on the state board of education, resigned as executive secretary of the States' Rights Council of Georgia (SRCG) to prepare to run against Vandiver. Bodenhamer became Vandiver's only serious opponent when Lawson dropped out of the race. While Bodenhamer never posed a real threat to Vandiver throughout the campaign, he and his advisor Revenue Commissioner T.V. "Red" Williams Sr., did influence the severity of the lieutenant governor's rhetoric against segregation. Bodenhamer accused Vandiver of several unsubstantiated violations of the color line, such as serving blacks barbecue in the same lines as whites at one of his rallies.[54]

Vandiver took the political goading too seriously. He later admitted that he was "too thin-skinned" to laugh off the accusations.[55] So by May 1958, he had resorted to the vintage race rhetoric reminiscent of former governor Herman Talmadge, saying "there is not enough money in the federal treasury to force us to mix the races in the classrooms of Georgia."[56] Vandiver's inability to rise above Bodenhamer's accusations that he was "weak on segregation" led to his infamous campaign pledge, "Neither my child nor yours will ever attend an integrated school during my administration, no not one."[57]

The choice between Vandiver and Bodenhamer for Georgia voters in the Democratic primary (which was tantamount to the election) was not a difficult one, in spite of the candidates' attempts to "out-seg" each other.[58] Vandiver won over 83 percent of the popular vote and carried 156 of 159 counties. On 13 January 1959, Vandiver, at age forty, was sworn into office. In his inaugural address, the new governor said his administration would make continued segregation one of his top priorities. Not budging from his campaign pledge "no not one," he said

> The people of Georgia and their new governor say to the U.S. Supreme Court that we will fight [desegregation] where ever it raises its ugly head, in these very streets, in every city, in every town, and in every hamlet—until sanity is restored in the land. . . . Georgians are determined to stand by their rights and traditions, whatever the cost.[59]

The Temple Bombing, Moderates, and Spread of Popular Support for Continued Public Education

Shortly before Vandiver replaced Griffin as the state's top executive and Georgia's most powerful segregationist, two important but unrelated developments were taking place in Atlanta. Collectively, the developments signaled the entry of the large numbers of the states' moderates into the politics of race and schooling.

Triggering involvement of moderates was the bombing of a Jewish synagogue in Atlanta. In the early morning hours on 12 October, a bomb made of fifty sticks of dynamite ripped apart the city's oldest and wealthiest synagogue. The blast caused tremendous destruction and was so loud it was said to have woken Governor Griffin. It was not the first bombing in the South since *Brown*, nor was it the most violent. Indeed, the explosion was not intended for the "darker race" and no one died. Still, until that moment, Atlanta had maintained its image as an oasis of moderation and "A City Too Busy to Hate." In the summer and early fall of 1958 Atlanta was "a city of flowering trees and wide avenues, of soda fountains and air-cooled movie houses," wrote Melissa Fay Green, and a place where "buildings stayed on their cornerstones, school children returned home happily from school, and black ministers arose in the morning unscathed from their beds."[60] But by the morning rush hour the word was out that Atlanta, caught by surprise, had stumbled into the violent fray of white supremacist extremism. In "a perverse way," observed Green, the Temple bombing, "heralded the beginning of social change."[61] It compelled to action many of the state's characteristically reluctant moderates. Perhaps more pivotal than the Sinister Seven's Declaration for Public Education, the Ministers' Manifesto, and the litigation unfolding in federal courts, the Temple bombing forced moderates to mobilize in support of decency, law and order, racial tolerance, and ultimately public schooling.

In the fall of 1958 Professor John A. Griffin was at it again, this time with a course entitled "Crisis in the Schools." Griffin recalled in 1991 that "it was the only course [he] ever taught that the press covered." The coverage stood as testimony that the press sensed an awareness that something potentially monumental was brewing in Atlanta. Griffin invited Southern Education Reporting Services chief Edward Ball, SRC President James McBride Dabbs,[62] ex-Florida Governor Millard Caldwell, Dekalb County Representative James Mackay, Assistant Attorney General Robert H. Hall, Georgia Governor Marvin Griffin, and Senator Richard B. Russell to speak.[63] The day after the temple bombing and in a sober manner, Ball presented facts and statistics about the glacial progress of desegregation in Southern schools. The following week Dabbs, a lifelong resident of the Deep South, argued that only by dropping the color line could blacks achieve first-class citizenship. The last speaker in October was the former governor of Florida Milliard Caldwell, a militant segregationist who presented a vicious attack against the U.S. Supreme Court.

James Mackay and Robert Hall, both keen lawyers, were the first Georgians to participate in Griffin's seminar. Hall, an aloof, soft-spoken gentleman, who had also taught law at Emory's Lamar School of Law, was one of Georgia's most reasoned segregationists.[64] Unlike the obvious distortions published by Herman Talmadge[65] and Roy Harris, Hall's thoughtful, historically based legal prose presented an intellectual obstacle to racial integration. In 1954, prior to the *Brown* decision, Hall had carefully documented that even those black and white Georgians who befriended the Republican Party during Reconstruction understood that their ratification of the Fourteenth Amendment would not abolish segregation. Hall wrote "Could this group have contemplated or understood the Fourteenth Amendment would abolish segregation when [in 1870] they ratified the Fourteenth Amendment and established segregated schools in the same session of the General Assembly?" Hall ended his pro-segregationist argument by asserting that, regardless of how *Brown* was decided, all Georgia leaders were "equally honest and equally desirous in various ways of securing one end—the best education possible for all of its children," in effect arguing for serious consideration of the private school plan.[66] Speaking at Emory, Hall emphasized that state law required implementing a private plan. He concluded that the plan would work.

In rebuttal, Mackay pointed out that the private school plan was a "No school plan" and argued that Georgians needed to come up with a "Some school plan." Mackay had been an outspoken opponent of the private school plan from the moment Herman Talmadge placed it in the political arena in 1953. As a liberal in a sea of conservatives in the General Assembly from 1951 to 1963, Mackay had argued against the private school plan in 1954 and again in 1956. Mackay was born and raised in the South, but unlike many of his colleagues, neither he nor his family defended the "Southern Way of Life." Indeed, it was largely through his family's encouragement and commitment to Christian values that Mackay drew his strength to stand up to accusations of being a "Communist" and a "nigger-lover."[67]

Speaking at Emory, Mackay turned not to God, but to politics. Attacking Hall's adherence to state law, Mackay linked the concept of "home rule" and local government control to the school/race issue. "Local government, local control, keeping government close to the people is a Georgia tradition which should be second to none," he said. "We, in the local communities, do not think our schools should be run from Washington, or from the State capitol." He pointed out that, because of existing legislation, the governor was required to close the schools in the event of a federal decree. Mackay argued that the 1959 General Assembly had a duty to pass legislation giving complete control to local school boards and allow them to arrange for referenda so "the people themselves" could decide on the fate of the public schools. The speech won acclaim in all of the local dailies, and Mackay's position became known as the "Parental Choice Plan."[68]

In Atlanta in late 1958 there was growing public awareness and apprehension among moderates about the possibility of public school closings.[69] With the temple bombing serving as an alarm clock, parents of school-age children began to realize that the *Calhoun* suit, together with the private school plan, would trigger the closing of the public schools throughout the state.[70] That fall the school/race debate was no longer an abstract issue; it was a reality which could have major impact on the organization of society and the instruction of children. In September 1958, nine public schools in Virginia that had begun to desegregate under federal court orders were closed by the governor pursuant to an act by the General Assembly prohibiting racially desegregated schools. The governor's action, to the dismay of many parents, left 12,700 Virginia children out of school for the first half of the 1958-59 school year.[71] That same September Arkansas Governor Faubus issued an order closing the four senior high schools of Little Rock. The Little Rock schools stayed closed for the entire 1958-59 year.

During early fall, shortly after the school year began, small groups of worried parents began to meet to discuss the real possibility of school closings. Fall brings about feelings of nostalgia, and many, no doubt, recalled last fall's scholastic beginning: Atlanta had had a routine, even serene start, but in Little Rock there had been disgraceful mayhem. Many had not forgotten stories in the local newspapers one year earlier that put their governor and former House speaker in the eye of the Little Rock storm. As historian Paul Mertz noted, "by late 1958 there was reason for alarm."[72] One of the outcomes of the Little Rock episode was a federal circuit court ruling that public schools could not be turned over to private management.[73] Muriel Lokey,[74] a woman who became very active in the growing movement to preserve the public schools, recalled that some parents were even talking about teaching their children at home, an idea that made Lokey, the mother of five, cringe. Most of the parents she talked to agreed that closing the public schools "just wasn't right" and that the facts about the situation had to be made available to the community.[75] In the wake of the temple bombing and as interest heightened in the Atlanta area, M.M. "Mugsy" Smith, a member of the Georgia General Assembly and one of the "Sinister Seven," spoke at a Parent Teacher Association meeting at the Spring Street Elementary School in Atlanta.[76] Echoing the position Mackay had taken at Emory, Smith proposed that the people in each school district should have the right to vote on whether they wanted to continue their public schools. He then joined Mackay in proposing an outright repeal of all of Georgia's massive resistance laws.

The speeches by Smith and Mackay received good publicity, reverberating throughout Georgia, particularly in Atlanta. Mayor Hartsfield announced, "It is time for action. All Georgia has today is a plan for no schools whatsoever." Four days after Smith spoke, the eighty ministers who had signed the Ministers' Manifesto the previous year reaffirmed their commitment to their six-point declaration. They were joined by an additional 232 minsters, bringing the total of signatures up to 312, which accounted for more than one-half of all the white clergy in Atlanta.[77]

On the same day outgoing Governor Marvin Griffin, speaking at Emory University in John Griffin's "Crisis in the Schools" course, reaffirmed his belief "that any attempt to integrate would be met with unprecedented resistance." First, the Governor reiterated his belief that the *Brown* decision had violated Georgia's "sacred right" to administer its system of public education. Next, he reacted to the parental-choice plan as a move by Hartsfield to end segregation. "The mayor of Atlanta cannot throw in the towel for me or any other Georgian," he remarked. "Let's not have any scalawags or political traitors on the segregation question. Let's not play roll over, Rover."[78]

The Governor's remarks did not impress the Emory faculty. On 30 November 1958, 250 of the 335 full-time faculty released a statement to the press in which they expressed opposition to public school closings anywhere in the United States. They called attention to the "irreparable damage" that would result from the state's policy of shifting to a private system in the event of desegregation. Linking the prevailing Cold War to public education, the statement went on to say that even a brief interruption of schooling would result in a decrease of trained specialists, thereby allowing "communists to gain in the battle of education." Further, they contended, that closing the schools would have negative economic and social consequences on business, industry, and the welfare of children. The statement ended by declaring that "although private schools [had] contribute[d] greatly to education for democracy, . . . history and . . . experience clearly indicate[d] that the major part of the educational load can be adequately borne only by the public school system."[79]

Two weeks later seventy-three faculty members at Agnes Scott College, a small private women's college in Decatur, published their own petition. Their statement declared that closing the public schools would be a "great disaster" and would contribute to the spread of illiteracy throughout the South. The substitution of private school, it said, would be "haphazard at best."[80] Not to be outdone by the professors, 419 physicians in the metropolitan area came out with their own manifesto, "urging whatever steps are necessary to prevent the closing of the public schools."[81]

By December discussion over the fate of the public schools was transcending the race issue. Hamilton Lokey, James Mackay, Mugsy Smith, and former Atlanta League of Women Voters President and liberal activist Eliza K. Paschall, and others picked up on the shift in moderate opinion and lectured statewide for continued public education and local control.[82] *Atlanta Journal* correspondent Harold Davis did a five-part series on the move to private schools in Virginia, concluding that many legal and practical problems had resulted. Editorials and letters to the editor on the school/race issue proliferated in most of Georgia's newspapers. One distressed woman wrote in that "nothing would make the [communists] happier than for our public school to be abandoned." Another praised the ministers, the Atlanta dailies, and Mayor Hartsfield, arguing that it was cowardly to remain neutral on the school issue, and concluded by quoting Dante: "The hottest places in hell are for those who in times of moral crisis preserve their neutrality." As Muriel Lokey later recalled, "there was something going on. There was something in the air. And we all wanted to be part of it."[83]

Although the tenor of the debate had changed, most white Georgians, moderates included, still preferred segregation. Many whites condemned the declarations that called for continued public education. By late 1958, however, the segregation debate had a very important factor linked to it—public education. The extent to which it would influence the outcome of the debate would depend on how well the public school argument was articulated by those who soon would no longer be called "integrationists" or "Communists" or "nigger-lovers," but rather "open schools advocates."

Help Our Public Education, Inc. Organizes

On 9 December 1958, Muriel Lokey, along with two other parents, Frances Breeden and Maxine Friedman, took an important step in being part of the movement to save the public schools. They chartered Help Our Public Education Inc. (HOPE), a nonprofit parents' group that sought "to give direction, guidance, information, and program to all citizens of Georgia who desire to continue the operation of the public schools of this state."[84] HOPE set a simple goal: To keep all the public schools open. HOPE deliberately steered clear of the issue of segregation, pledging instead to promote enthusiastically the open schools movement.[85]

New Massive Resistance Measures Cannot Quell the
Open Schools Movement

HOPE's activities captured the attention of Atlanta's dailies, and they were also noticed by Governor S. Ernest Vandiver. Vandiver stated, "I have no patience with those who are now coming out in the open and demanding that the races be mixed in the classrooms in the schools of Georgia, contrary to the laws and the constitution of this state." Angered by Atlanta's white moderates, Vandiver ranted that they were "running up the flag of surrender over the capital city and displaying a defeatist spirit."[86]

Like the governor he replaced, Vandiver's bite proved to be as bad as his bark. One day after Vandiver's inauguration and on his recommendation, the Georgia General Assembly passed six measures that strengthened the state's policy of massive resistance. The first two measures gave the governor the discretion to close a single public school or a single unit within the state educational system. Both measures were designed to give Vandiver more precision in stamping out desegregation at a particular school site without closing an entire system. The third measure advanced the private school plan by giving taxpayers tuition tax credits on their payments toward the organization and operation of private schools. A fourth measure prohibited the use of ad valorem taxes for racially mixed schools. The fifth measure permitted state executive arm to designate and pay the fees of legal counsel involved in school litigation.[87] It put into law a practice that governors had been following since 1950.

The sixth measure had a specific purpose. On 9 January 1959, only a few days before Vandiver's inauguration, federal district court Judge Boyd Sloan ruled in *Hunt v. Arnold* that Georgia State College of Business Administration could no longer refuse the admission of qualified blacks. This was the first ruling handed down by a federal court against public school segregation in Georgia. Sloan's action gave Vandiver his first opportunity as governor to live up to his campaign promise to prevent school desegregation. On the day of his inauguration, before the college could admit the students, Governor Vandiver suspended registration indefinitely. Then with the cooperation of the legislature, Vandiver pushed through a thinly veiled segregation measure prohibiting admission of students who were over the age of twenty-five.[88] Since the only black plaintiff who had not been excluded on other grounds was over twenty-five, she was denied admission. Vandiver had put his first plug in the massive resistance dike, but the barrier was showing signs of impending collapse.

The black response to *Hunt* and to Vandiver's actions was characteristically calm and dignified. The serene Donald Hollowell, who tried the case alongside E.

E. Moore, said he had expected the color line to fall. In the tradition that had been established by A. T. Walden, John Calhoun, former president of the Atlanta NAACP, who had been harassed relentlessly by the state attorney general's office, commented that:

> Negroes want their rights, but we in Atlanta are not crying for immediate changes. We are willing to work in harmony with whites to lessen tension and make the transition amicably.[89]

Unwittingly, Senator Herman Talmadge contributed to weakening the barrier of massive resistance. In January 1959 he spoke on the U.S. Senate floor, asking for support for constitutional amendments that would return the control of schools to local authority. Talmadge's intention was to remove the federal government from interfering with the public school system, so that racially segregated schooling could continue in Georgia. Talmadge reasoned that if control could be returned to the local level, the NAACP legal campaign would be slowed down to a crawl across the Deep South, especially in Georgia.[90] If control over public schooling was at the county level in Georgia, litigation would have to take place in 159 counties!

But in his address Talmadge stressed the importance of public education. He also argued that "the U.S. Supreme Court's decision is an 'accomplished fact' that will remain so until it is either reversed by the Court itself or it is nullified or modified by the Congress or the people." The *Atlanta Constitution* picked up on the phrase "accomplished fact" and praised the senator for his "courage and character" in being the first Deep South senator to call for moderation and acceptance of the law.[91]

In the face of Vandiver's resistance, but with the "encouragement" of Senator Talmadge, HOPE persisted. In its first year it sought to better define its policies, build up a statewide organization, and most important, to educate the public about the gravity of the school crisis and thus attempt to influence the legislature to repeal the private school plan.[92] In early 1959 HOPE's founders, Lokey, Breeden, and Friedman, hired Elizabeth Davis, a former Girl Scouts executive, to be their full-time director and to run an office in downtown Atlanta. They also recruited several attorneys, including Muriel's husband, Hamilton Lokey, Dekalb representative James Mackay, former U.S. Attorney James Dorsey, and Randall Lanier to analyze state and federal school laws and court decisions. HOPE appointed a public information committee, began promoting public discussions on the school crisis, set up a speakers' bureau, and began distributing free printed material.[93] In addition, the group recruited Mrs. Frances Pauley, a former state president of the

Georgia League of Women Voters, to coordinate the development of a statewide HOPE network.[94]

On the advice of its team of lawyers, HOPE chose to stay neutral in arguments over desegregation. As Frances Pauley explained at a speaking engagement in March 1959:

> HOPE will not enter into the controversy of segregation vs. integration. It will say that we want . . . public schools operating legally. When this means desegregation in some places then HOPE Inc. will say it will be accepted. We will work to keep the schools from closing, but in the event a school is closed anywhere in Ga. we will work to reopen it as a public school.[95]

As E.E. Moore, who represented the plaintiffs in *Calhoun*, recalled:

> [HOPE] did not focus on the idea that the schools would be desegregated. Instead the focus was centered around the idea of keeping the schools open, which targeted the moderate white community. This was an ingenious tactic.[96]

One scholar has argued that by placing the survival of the public schools as their top priority, HOPE "skillfully avoided the segregation-integration argument, while at the same time implicitly accepting some degree of desegregation."[97] It was this tactic that enabled HOPE to emerge as a critical force in the battle to save the public schools in Georgia. However, an internal struggle developed during the group's three-year campaign. The issue focused on whether HOPE should remain an all-white organization or whether it should welcome blacks.

For tactical reasons, HOPE deliberately stayed white. As Muriel Lokey explained:

> [HOPE chose to be] white people persuading white people. . . . It was seen as a tactical necessity, but it was not easy for some of us to endorse. We continued to wrestle with this during the whole time of our existence. At our executive meetings . . . people refused to join with us because of this policy. People left us because of that policy. People worked with us in spite of that policy. We never put it to rest.[98]

One liberal integrationist who worked with HOPE in spite of this policy was Frances Pauley, a Decatur, Georgia, native. In 1954, at the time of the *Brown* decision, Pauley vowed never to be part of any organization that excluded blacks. She also made it her policy to get better acquainted with blacks in Decatur and Atlanta by joining biracial organizations and interacting with blacks socially. After struggling with HOPE's all-white policy, and on the advice of NAACP attorney

Donald Hollowell, she made a "pragmatic exception," and joined the organization.[99]

HOPE's decision to stay all-white, however, was more complex than it might first appear. It was complicated in part by an earlier race-related controversy in a local organization with overlapping membership. Two years earlier in March 1956, shortly after the annual meeting of the Atlanta League of Women Voters (ALWV), 14 members of the ALWV, including the president, three vice-presidents, the treasurer, the secretary and five directors, resigned because Eliza Paschall succeeded in deleting from the organization's by-laws a clause requiring racial segregation. Those who resigned feared that Paschall would actively recruit blacks to join the ALWV. In their resignation statement, the women wrote, "We feel the integration of our league at this time will raise so many problems that the effectiveness of the Atlanta League will be seriously impaired and that we can no longer function in the political life in our communities."[100] Effectiveness aside, HOPE organizers realized in the wake of the ALWV controversy that many of the women they sought to attract to their cause harbored a definite sense of their racial superiority. Working for continued public education alongside like-minded blacks was unthinkable. One behind-the-scenes HOPE organizer candidly put it this way: "You see, we have two groups within the organization, segregationists who are dedicated, yet want the schools to remain open, and moderates. We must reconcile them."[101] Thus, with consternation, HOPE leaders put in place a similar policy, and managed to achieve focus and unity of purpose, but the choice was not without consequences. HOPE was never able to see the survival of the public school system through black eyes or incorporate the black perspectives. This shortcoming affected the timing, duration, and integrity of the group's work and compromised their otherwise courageous crusade.

On 4 March 1959, HOPE organized a rally at the Tower Theater in Atlanta. Over 1,500 people attended. Billy Wilson, an open schools advocate from Little Rock, Ralph McGill, editor of the *Constitution*, Atlanta Mayor William B. Hartsfield, Georgia legislator Mugsy Smith, and *Gainesville Times* editor Sylvan Meyer pledged their support at the rally for keeping the public schools open.[102] Muriel Lokey recalled Meyer's speech in which he used the phrase "It's mind changing time in Georgia," a slogan that HOPE used many times in the next two years.[103]

In March 1959 the atmosphere of intolerance had not abated. HOPE often encountered antagonism, even threats, and the group was sometimes labeled a communist organization. HOPE found it necessary to take numerous security precautions but generally managed to keep its good humor about its opponents. Eugene Jones, a 34-year-old physicist and one of HOPE's original charter members, supervised the security for the rally. Jones obtained help from four undercover Atlanta police officers and hired seven Pinkerton security guards. He also enlisted the help of nearly one hundred volunteers.[104] Jones, a native Atlantan and Georgia Tech graduate, took other security precautions such as changing the time and location of HOPE's public meetings and doing background checks on suspicious volunteers.

In a 1991 interview Jones recalled that in 1959 the FBI sent an undercover agent to HOPE's downtown office to investigate activities while posing as a volunteer. Jones recognized the agent but said nothing at the time. The next week, however, he went to the local FBI office and requested that they send over another guy, because the one they had sent was "a hell of a worker and we could use another one."[105]

Shortly after the "Fill the Tower with HOPE" rally, the segregationists, led by Roy Harris and Peter Zack Geer, Vandiver's executive secretary, organized their own rally for continued segregated education. It mostly attracted members from a newly formed and poorly organized segregationist organization called Metropolitan Association for Continued Segregated Education (MACSE).[106] At this rally Harris and Geer continued their calls for resistance to school desegregation at all costs. Years later Hamilton Lokey recalled that Harris, in his ruthless fashion, urged the crowd to show:

> 'Rastus' McGill, Ham Lokey and the other 'nigger-lovers' the error of their ways by phoning them at three o'clock in the morning and 'letem have it.' The very next morning, right at 3:00 A.M. my phone rang. . . . All I could hear was heavy breathing. . . . When I hung up a thought struck me—Roy Harris was spending the night at the Henry Grady Hotel. . . so I put in a call for him. . . . Roy came on the line rather sleepily. [After] I identified myself, [I told] him 'Roy, one of your boys just called me, like you told him to, and I thought you'd like to know he's on the job. Each time one of those guys calls on me, I'll report to you. Good night, Roy.'[107]

Not long after the rallies, and largely due to the efforts of Frances Pauley, HOPE branches opened in Gainesville, Marietta, Jonesboro, Rome, Athens, Macon, and Savannah.[108] Notably absent from the HOPE rallies were the state's business leaders and representatives from community power structures in Atlanta, Athens, Savannah, Macon, and Columbus. Most businessmen, it seemed, would not work openly work with moderate groups. To be sure, some Atlanta and Athens businessmen helped moderate efforts behind the scenes. Some had secretly and anonymously funneled thousands of dollars to the HOPE campaign. Still, as one moderate noted, without open support from business and local government, even the best orchestrated effort would falter.[109]

In April 1959 HOPE received a major boost when former Governor Ellis Arnall threatened to return to state politics to save the public schools. As historian Numan Bartley described it, Arnall, "like a modern Rip Van Winkle, arose from a long political slumber to demand that the schools be kept open. 'Should they be closed,' threatened Arnall, 'I will run for governor in 1962, and I will be elected.'"[110] Arnall had served as governor of Georgia from 1943-1946, winning the office from incumbent Eugene Talmadge, the "wild man from Sugar Creek" and Herman's late father. In the 1942 primary Arnall made education (and not race) the central issue of the campaign and charged that Governor Talmadge, through reckless actions, had brought disgrace to the people of Georgia. In 1941 Talmadge had fired the Dr. Walter D. Cocking, Dean of the School of Education at the University of Georgia, after Cocking suggested implementing a biracial demonstration school on the campus. After Cocking was fired the state's flagship university lost its regional accreditation. It is widely accepted that Arnall won the office by making political hay out of the issue.[111]

By 1959 Arnall, fifty-one years old and thirteen years out of state politics, declared that he believed in segregation but only favored "as much segregation as was possible under the law."[112] He articulated an increasingly more popular position that a large degree of segregation could be maintained without abandoning the public school system.

Meanwhile biracial efforts continued to press for social justice for blacks. Their goals included open schools but went much further, to include school and societal desegregation. Biracial organizations like the Greater Atlanta Council on Human Relations (GACHR), an affiliate of the Georgia Council on Human Relations (GCHR, formerly Guy Wells's GICI) and the Southern Regional Council (SRC), functioned as the magnets and pulled in liberals from the state.[113] The GACHR had quietly desegregated the Atlanta public library and eliminated segregated rest rooms at the city airport.

The GACHR ran a workshop on desegregation and the public schools in April 1959 that drew 200 participants. The morning symposium featured an update of the regional circumstances by Paul Anthony of the Southern Regional Council and Benjamin Mays. The afternoon sessions explored the legal aspects of segregation, the economic consequences of school closing and community education. Donald Hollowell, by now the de facto leader of the local NAACP, and a liberal white attorney Randall Lanier, who counseled HOPE, led the legal session, while Jim Montgomery, the business editor of the *Atlanta Constitution*, led the economic session, and Edward Weaver, a professor at Atlanta University, Harry Boyte, executive secretary of the GACHR, and Nan Pendergrast led the community education discussion.[114]

The tone of the discussion reflected the participants' determination and frustration. Desegregation of the public schools seemed beyond their reach. The GACHR had attempted but failed to persuade the Atlanta school board to prepare for desegregation. A discouraged Eliza Paschall, GACHR's most energetic member, wrote that Council's work with the Atlanta school board was the most disappointing effort of the year. "The Board," she wrote, "has taken the position that it will do nothing until faced with an actual court order to desegregate."[115]

Hooper Rules in Calhoun v. Latimer

By June 1959, after a seventeen-month wait, Atlanta's NAACP finally got a hearing in a federal case against the Atlanta School Board, the *Calhoun* case. During the trial Vandiver warned that if the courts ordered desegregation, he would have no choice but to close down the public schools. Attempting to shift the burden of school-race issue onto the shoulders of the judiciary, the governor expressed hope that "the federal courts will not force the closing of a single school."[116]

After hearing testimony, Judge Frank Hooper[117] issued an order requiring the the Atlanta School Board to submit a plan. He wrote,

> Even the most ardent segregationists have now acknowledged that the Brown decision is the law of the land. . . . For this Court to declare as law that which is not law would be not only a futile gesture, but a great dis-service to our people. It would add to the confusion already existing in the public mind.[118]

Hooper asserted that the Court was under no duty and had no power to order integration, but was compelled "to enjoin racial discrimination." The plan to accomplish that goal, he said, must originate with the School Board. He did not tell the Board exactly what the plan should include, but stated:

> [T]he Court...assumes, that any plan submitted would contemplate a gradual process, which would contemplate a careful screening of each applicant to determine his or her fitness to enter the school to which application is made. The Supreme Court has said that school authorities must proceed with 'deliberate speed' toward the elimination of racial discrimination, and this Court interprets the expression 'deliberate speed' to mean such speed as is consistent with the welfare of all our people, with the maintenance of law and order, and with the preservation if possible of our common school system. The custom and practice of maintaining separate schools for Negroes and whites has existed in

this state for many years, with the approval of the highest courts of the land, and it cannot rapidly and suddenly be ended.[119]

In his order, Hooper illustrated his concept of "deliberate speed." He did not require the Atlanta School Board to finally submit a plan until January 1960. Meanwhile, with all attention focused on the *Calhoun* litigation that summer, two black Atlanta college students, encouraged by the local NAACP, started a relatively quiet campaign against segregated higher education in Georgia. On 15 July Charlayne Hunter and Hamilton Holmes applied for admission at the University of Georgia (UGA).[120] After a quick rejection because of "limited facilities," the students reapplied in August for the winter term, only to be told that applications were not being accepted for future quarters. That fall Hunter returned to Wayne University in Detroit, and Holmes attended Morehouse College in Atlanta, for their third semester of college. However, both students continued to inform the university that they desired to transfer, and they continued to ask for advice on the application process.[121]

Although Hooper's ruling in the *Calhoun* case was perceived by many blacks as more of the same old delay tactics, the ruling served as a catalyst to HOPE organizers. HOPE believed that Hooper's time table for a desegregation plan would mean the crisis could come as early as January 1960. As Vandiver conferred with his legal advisors, HOPE organized statewide speaking engagements, bombarding citizens and legislators throughout the state with the pro-public schools argument. Sylvan Meyer, Eliza Paschall, (Nan Pendergrast, an eloquent HOPE volunteer with a delightful Georgia accent), Frances Pauley, Hamilton Lokey, Ralph McGill, James Mackay, Mugsy Smith, and several others were recruited to speak from "Rabun Gap to Tybee Island."

HOPE's aim was to get legislators to repeal the private-school plan and consider legislation that would allow for local school boards to deal with desegregation at the community level. In addition to speeches throughout the state, HOPE also reached Georgians through its open schools newsletter. This vehicle, within a year of its charter, had a circulation of 20,000.

By the end of 1959 HOPE had succeeded in making criticism of statewide school closings possible and discussions of alternatives respectable.[122] The once small group of worried mothers had changed the rhetoric of the segregation-integration argument by emphasizing massive resistance's conflict with the tradition of public education. HOPE gave focus, direction and drive to white moderates who favored compliance with *Brown* and challenged those who favored segregation but also valued public education. HOPE had built a sturdy platform on which to orchestrate its now formidable movement against massive resistance.

Notes

1. Joseph L. Bernd, *Grass Roots Politics in Georgia: The County Unit System and the Importance of the Individual Voting Community in Bi-factional Elections, 1942-1954* (Atlanta: Emory University Research Committee, 1960); Taylor Branch, *Parting the Waters: America in the King Years, 1954-1963* (New York: Simon & Schuster, 1988), 228-33.

2. Branch, *op. cit.*, 143-205; Reed Sarratt, *The Ordeal of Desegregation: The First Decade* (New York: Harper and Row, 1966), 325.

3. David J. Garrow, *Bearing the Cross: Martin Luther King, Jr. and the Southern Christian Leadership Conference* (New York: William Morrow, 1986); *Eyes on the Prize.* "No Easy Walk: 1961-1963," series produced by Henry Hampton, Blackside Inc., 1986, videocassette.

4. Branch, *op. cit.*, 203; C. Vann Woodward, *The Strange Career of Jim Crow*, 3rd ed. (New York: Oxford, 1974), 169.

5. Paul D. Bolster, "Civil Rights Movements in Twentieth Century Georgia" (Ph.D. diss., University of Georgia, 1972), 171; Martin, *William Berry Hartsfield*, 118-119; Donald L. Grant, *The Way It Was in the South: The Black Experience in Georgia* (New York: Birch Lane Press, 1993), 390.

6. Bolster, *op. cit.*, 132.

7. The *Ward v. Board of Regents* suit arose when Horace Ward was denied admission to the University of Georgia Law School in September 1950. The impending suit was postponed when Ward went into the armed forces. Upon his return to civilian life in 1956 he again applied and was rejected at the University of Georgia and entered Northwestern Law School. In 1957 Federal District Court Judge Frank Hooper found Ward had not exhausted all administrative remedies and also ruled the case moot since Ward was already in law school. *Ward v. Regents of the University System of Georgia*, 191 F. Supp. 491 (ND Georgia 1957); Bolster, *op. cit.*, 163, 171-172; *Southern School News*, June 1960, 16. See, also, *Hunt v. Arnold*, 172 F. Supp, 847 (ND Ga 9 Jan. 1959).

8. Hollowell interview, 18 July 1991; *Southern School News*, June 1956, 16; Richard Kluger, *Simple Justice* (New York: Vintage, 1977), 137; Mark V. Tushnet, "Organizing Civil Rights Litigation, the NAACP's Experience" in *Ambivalent Legacy: A Legal History of the South*, eds., David J. Bodenhamer and James W. Ely Jr. (Jackson: University of Mississippi Press, 1984), 174.

9. The study itself, however, produced more evidence that the tradition of separate-but-equal schooling had not produced separate-but-equal achievement between the races. The study was conducted by the Educational Testing Service (ETS) in Princeton, New Jersey. ETS found that a representative sample of black pupils and teachers scored much farther behind the national average in all categories—including reading, arithmetic in the lower grades, science, English, encyclopedic knowledge—in the upper grade pupils and for the teachers, compared to the sample of white pupils and teachers who scored only slightly behind the national average. Researchers also found that as black pupils progressed through the grades the gap between their scores and the national norm increased. The report pointed out that there was a wide variation and a considerable overlap in the distribution of scores between blacks and whites. The study concluded by noting that the category where the most

overlap was shown was the "Non-Verbal Reasoning" section, which the researchers referred to as an "unschooled area." For a summary, see *Southern School News*, September 1957, 16; Melvin W. Ecke, *From Ivy Street to Kennedy Center: A Centennial History of the Atlanta Public School System* (Atlanta: Atlanta Board of Education, 1972), 344.

10. C.A. Scott interview, 13 October 1991; Virginia H. Hein, "The Image of a 'City Too Busy to Hate': Atlanta in the 1960's." *Phylon* 33 (Fall 1972), 205-221; David N. Plank and Marcia Turner, "Changing Patterns in Black School Politics, Atlanta, 1872-1973," *American Journal of Education* 95 (August 1987), 584-608; Philip Noel Racine, "Atlanta's Schools: A History of the Public School System 1869-1955" (Ph.D. diss., Emory University, 1969), chapter 10.

11. Martin, *William B. Hartsfield*, 50; Plank and Turner, *op. cit.*, Scott interview, 1991. For more on Dobbs, see Gary M. Pomerantz, *Where Peachtree Meets Auburn: The Saga of Two Families and the Making of Atlanta* (New York: Scribner, 1996).

12. Hornsby describes Walden as the "New South's first black political boss ... who wheeled and dealed in the councils of [Atlanta's] white leadership." O'Brien argues that several local black activists—including William Boyd and Grace Hamilton—did not trust Walden with Civil Rights litigation in the late 1940s and early 1950s. Bolster suggests that Walden initially hampered the local chapter's legal battle against school segregation. Walden may have done so because of the possible implications of pressing for desegregation in 1955—which included the elimination of public education for whites and blacks. Walden, a pragmatist, no doubt, wanted both desegregation and public education, but given the choice between the two, he probably would have taken separate-but-equal public education in Georgia (in spite of *Brown*) over racial desegregation in Georgia and no public education. Alton Hornsby Jr., "A City That Was Too Busy to Hate," in *Southern Businessmen and Desegregation*, eds. Elizabeth Jacoway and David Colburn (Baton Rouge: Louisiana State University Press, 1982), 125; Thomas V. O'Brien "*Aaron v. Cook* and the NAACP Strategy in Georgia before *Brown*," *Journal of Negro Education* (forthcoming); Bolster, *op. cit.*, 156, 159.

13. Numan V. Bartley, *The Creation of Modern Georgia*, 2nd ed. (Athens: University of Georgia Press, 1983), 217.

14. Constance Baker Motley passed the bar in 1948 and worked within the "inner circle" staff of the NAACP national office. She later became the first black woman appointed to the federal bench. Constance Baker Motley, *Equal Justice Under Law* (New York: Farrar, Straus and Giroux, 1998); Jack Greenberg, *Crusaders in the Court: How a Dedicated Band of Lawyer Fought the Civil Rights Revolution* (New York: Basic Books, 1994).

15. Gunnar Myrdal, *An American Dilemma: The Negro Problem and American Democracy* 2 vols. (New York: Harper & Row, 1944), but compare to Paul M. Gaston, *The New South Creed: A Study in Southern Mythmaking* (Baton Rouge: Louisiana State University Press, 1940).

16. Nabrit, born in Americus, Georgia, joined the Howard Law School faculty in 1936 and organized the first civil rights course in the country, turning Howard "into a clearinghouse for the legal fight that picked up full momentum as the Thirties lengthened." Nabrit later became the President of Howard. Kluger, *Simple Justice*, 127; Moore interview, 5 November 1991.

17. Moore interview, 5 November 1991.

18. Quote from Sarratt, *The Ordeal of Desegregation*, 18.

19. Harris managed Fred Hand's unsuccessful campaign for governor against Griffin in 1954.

20. Bartley, *The Rise of Massive Resistance*, 266-8.

21. Shortly after the mob action Faubus commented that Griffin and Harris had "contributed to the situation." Griffin replied he was pleased to promote "pro-segregation unity." *Southern School News*, October 1957, 15.

22. *Eyes on the Prize*, "Fighting Back: 1957-1962," series produced by Henry Hampton, Blackside Inc., 1986, videocassette.

23. The state had argued that the case should be dismissed because plaintiffs failed to exhaust administrative remedies available in the admissions process. The remedies, which were put in place to avoid desegregation, were virtually impossible to exhaust.

24. Branch, *Parting the Waters*, 220; Emmet John Hughs, *The Ordeal of Power, A Political Memoir of the Eisenhower Years* (New York: Dell Publishing, 1963), 210; Kluger, *Simple Justice*, 754.

25. *Chapman v. King*, 154 F2d 460 (5th Cir. 1946); cert. denied 327 US 800 (1946). See also *Smith v. Allwright*, 1944, in which the Supreme Court declared Texas's white primary to be unconstitutional. *Chapman* and *Smith* were struck down on the same legal principle.

26. Virginia H. Hein, "The Image of a 'City Too Busy to Hate': Atlanta in the 1960's," *Phylon* 33 (Fall 1972), 209; Harold H. Martin, *William Berry Hartsfield, Mayor of Atlanta* (Athens: University of Georgia Press, 1978), 48.

27. Morris B. Abram, *The Day Is Short: An Autobiography* (New York: Harcourt Brace, 1982), 122-123.

28. *Southern School News*, January 1958, 5; Martin, *William Berry Hartsfield*, 128.

29. Martin, *William Berry Hartsfield*, 129. Griffin and Hartsfield were political foes. They repeatedly locked horns over issues related to race and suffrage.

30. *Southern School News*, November 1957, 9; Margaret Price, *The Negro Voter in the South* (Atlanta: Southern Regional Council, September 1957); Branch, *Parting the Waters*, 265-266.

31. Griffin interview, 12 November 1991; *Southern School News*, November 1957, 9.

32. Sarratt, *The Ordeal of Desegregation*, 189.

33. *Southern School News*, December 1957, 13.

34. Weltner interview, 17 September 1990; *Crisis in the Schools*, audiotapes of lectures in "Editors' View of the South" (Fall/Spring, 1957-58), Special Collections, Woodruff Library, Emory University, Atlanta, audiocassettes.

35. Benjamin Muse, *Virginia's Massive Resistance* (Bloomington: Indiana University Press, 1961), 20. In 1962 James J. Kilpatrick condensed his pro-segregationist editorials in a book called *The Southern Case for School Segregation* (New York: Crowell-Collier Press, 1962).

36. Sarratt, a moderate, directed the Southern Educational Reporting Service from 1961 to 1966. The Service published *Southern School News* and statistical summaries of school desegregation activity in the wake of *Brown*. He is also the author of *The Ordeal of Desegregation*, which I have cited extensively.

37. Randolph L. Fort, ed. "Crisis in the Schools," *Emory Alumnus* 35 (February 1959), 4-12; *Crisis in the Schools* audiotapes, *op. cit.*; Griffin interview, 1991; *Southern School News*, November 1957, 9.

38. *Crisis in the Schools* audiotapes, *op. cit.* Many writers and scholars have addressed the idea that there was widespread black preference for segregation. For further discussion of black divergence of opinion on segregated education, see, for example, Harold Cruse, *Plural But Equal: Blacks and Minorities and Minorities in America's Plural Society* (New York: William Morrow, 1987); Derrick Bell, "Serving Two Masters" in Kimberle Krenshaw, et al., eds., *Critical Race Theory* (New York: New Press, 1995) 5-19.

39. *Crisis in the Schools* audiotapes, *op. cit.*

40. Hughs, *The Ordeal of Power*, 210.

41. *Crisis in the Schools* audiotapes, *op. cit.*

42. *Atlanta Constitution*, 12 November 1957, 2; *Atlanta Journal/Constitution*, 3 November 1957, 1, 6A; *Southern School News*, December 1957, 13.

43. *Atlanta Journal/Constitution*, 3 November 1957, 6A.

44. *Southern School News*, January 1958, 5.

45. *Southern School News*, January 1958, 5.

46. Martin, *William Berry Hartsfield*, 133; *Southern School News*, January 1958, 5.

47. *Calhoun v. Latimer*, 377 US 263 (1964).

48. *Atlanta Constitution*, 14 January 1958, 4; *Southern School News*, February 1958, 4.

49. *Atlanta Constitution*, 14 January 1958, 1; *Southern School News*, February 1958, 4. The SBA was still building school plants under the separate-but-equal philosophy and had spent an estimated 55% of its $158 million on black facilities. Governor Griffin estimated that since 1951 over 314 school plants had been completed, amounting to 6,527 new classrooms. He also said that 363 school additions had been completed. *Atlanta Constitution*, 15 January 1958, 8. There is no evidence that school building decreased in the period after the *Calhoun* suit was filed.

50. *Southern School News*, February 1958, 4.

51. Sarratt, *The Ordeal of Desegregation*, 15.

52. *Atlanta Constitution*, 14 January 1958, 1, 11; Charles Pyles, "S. Ernest Vandiver and the Politics of Change," in *Georgia Governors in an Age of Change: From Ellis Arnall to George Busbee*, eds. Harold P. Henderson & Gary L. Roberts (Athens: University of Georgia Press, 1988), 144-145.

53. Ann E. Lewis, "S. Ernest Vandiver, 73rd Governor of Georgia," *Georgia Magazine* (February-March 1959), 9. As early as the summer of 1957 Vandiver and Lawson had been exchanging blows on the school/race issue. Lawson accused Vandiver of being soft on segregation and an advocate of "gradual integration." Vandiver, however, was no friend of the Negro. He countered by demanding that Lawson check his record, which clearly demonstrated his willingness to maintain segregation, the county unit system (which was considered the bulwark of segregation) and the "Southern Way of Life." *Southern School News*, August 1957, 2.

54. *Southern School News*, May 1958, 3; *Southern School News*, June 1958, 3; *Southern School News*, September 1958, 12. Clarke interview, 1991; H. Lokey interview, 1991; S. Ernest Vandiver, "Vandiver Takes the Middle Road," in *Georgia Governors in an Age of Change: From Ellis Arnall to George Busbee*, eds. Harold P. Henderson & Gary L. Roberts (Athens: University of Georgia Press, 1988), 158-9. In a 1991 interview Hamilton Lokey remembered suggesting to Vandiver in 1958 that he possibly could put an end to Bodenhamer's political attacks by pointing out that Bodenhamer, the self-proclaimed preserver of segregation, allowed his own son to attend an integrated school. Bodenhamer's son was a cadet at West Point at the time. Vandiver never acted on Lokey's suggestion.

55. Clarke interview, 1991; Vandiver, "Vandiver Takes the Middle Road," 159.

56. *Southern School News*, June 1958, 3.

57. Vandiver, "Vandiver Takes the Middle Road," 158. For a good study of Southern politicians' campaign rhetoric during this period, see Earl Black, *Southern Governors and Civil Rights: Racial Segregation as a Campaign Issue in the Second Reconstruction* (Cambridge, MA: Harvard University Press, 1976).

58. Pyles, "S. Ernest Vandiver and the Politics of Change," 146.

59. *Atlanta Journal*, 13 January 1959, 1, 4.

60. Melissa Fay Green, *The Temple Bombing* (New York: Fawcett Columbine, 1996), 6.

61. Green, *The Temple Bombing*, 7.

62. At the time Dabbs was the President of the Southern Regional Council and had just completed a book entitled *The Southern Heritage* (1958). The book examined race relations in the South in detail and ended with a plea for desegregation. Dabbs, who was born and lived in South Carolina, later published three other books about the South. They are: *The Road Home* (1960), *Who Speaks for the South?* (1964), and *Haunted by God* (1972).

63. Russell initially agreed to speak but backed out at the last minute, citing the tense gubernatorial battle that was presently unfolding in the state. Russell did not want his personal views on the school/race issue to impact negatively on his good friend and nephew-in-law, S. Ernest Vandiver. Vandiver was married to Russell's niece, Sybil Elizabeth.

64. Other segregationists considered to be constitutional scholars and authorities on the legal basis of segregation were Charles J. Bloch of Macon and R. Carter Pittman of Dalton.

65. Talmadge did publish one legalistic argument for the continuation of segregated schools. Herman E. Talmadge, "School Systems, Segregation and the Supreme Court," *Mercer Law Review* 6 (Spring 1955), 189-201.

66. Robert H. Hall, "Segregation in the Public Schools of Georgia," *Georgia Bar Journal* 16 (1954), 420, 126.

67. Mackay interview, 1991. Mackay was born in Alabama in 1919, the son of Methodist minister Edward G. Mackay a native of Northern Ireland, who emigrated to the Georgia as a young man and graduated from Emory College in Oxford, Georgia, in 1910. Mackay's mother was born in China, the daughter of Southern Baptist Missionaries. In 1951, Herman Talmadge published that MacKay was "on the payroll of the Rosenwald Fund Foundation, which devotes its energy to creation of equality between negroes and whites." *The Statesman*, 17 May 1951, 2.

68. Randolph L. Fort, ed. "Crisis in the Schools," *Emory Alumnus* 35 (February 1959), 4-12; *Atlanta Journal*, 18 December 1958; Mackay interview, 1991; James A. Mackay, "Crisis in the Public Schools, an Address," 3 November 1958, HOPE papers, Atlanta Historical Society, Atlanta.

69. Paul E. Mertz, "HOPE, Inc. and School Desegregation in Georgia" (paper presented at the 54th meeting of the Southern Historical Association, Norfolk, VA., November 1988), 3.

70. Muriel Lokey, videotape of "The Civil Rights Revolution Symposium," for the Institute for Continuing Legal Education (1989) University of Georgia, Athens, videocassette Recording no. 12.

71. The school closings prompted the formation of "Save Our Schools" (SOS) committees in several communities in Virginia and Arkansas. The SOS organizations attempted to rescue what one group of concerned citizens called the South's "lost class of 1959." Agnes Scott College Papers, faculty statement on public education file, Library Archives, Agnus Scott College, Decatur, GA; Bartley, *The Rise of Massive Resistance*, 248; Muse, *Virginia's Massive Resistance*, chapter 16.

72. Mertz, "HOPE, Inc.," 3.

73. *Cooper v. Aaron*, 358 US 1 (1958); Mertz, *op. cit.*, 3, 19; *New York Times*, 30 September 1958, 1, 21.

74. Muriel Lokey was the spouse of Hamilton Lokey. Hamilton left the Georgia General Assembly in 1958 and opened his own law practice.

75. M. Lokey, videotape of "The Civil Rights Revolution Symposium," M. Lokey interview, 19 April 1991.

76. *Atlanta Journal*, 30 November 1958, 2; M. Lokey, videotape of "The Civil Rights Revolution," Charles Longstreet Weltner, *Southerner* (New York: Lippincott, 1965), 30-1; Weltner interview, 17 September 1990.

77. *Southern School News*, December 1958, Fort, "Crisis in the Schools," 7; *Southern School News*, January 1959.

78. Fort, Crisis in the Schools, 12; *Southern School News*, December 1958, 15.

79. Fort, "Crisis in the Schools," 5.

80. "Faculty Statement on Public Education," in Faculty Statement on Public Education File, December 1958, Library Archives, Agnes Scott College, Decatur, GA; Fort, "Crisis in the Schools," 5.

81. *Atlanta Journal*, 21 December 1958, 1.

82. *Atlanta Journal*, 16 December 1958, 6; *Atlanta Journal*, 18 December 1958, 21.

83. *Atlanta Journal*, 18 December 1958, 18; *Atlanta Journal*, 23 December 1958, 18; M. Lokey interview, 2 April 1991.

84. M. Lokey videotape of "The Civil Rights Revolution," Mertz, "HOPE, Inc. and School Desegregation in Georgia," 1; Frances Breeden interview, 21 June 1995; Maxine Friedman interview, 12 July 1995.

85. Bolster, "Civil Rights Movements," 152-155; Sarratt, *The Ordeal of Desegregation*, 315.

86. Bartley, *The Creation of Modern Georgia*, 214-5.

87. *Southern School News*, February 1959, 10.

88. *Atlanta Journal*, 11 January 1959, 1; Bolster, "Civil Rights Movements, 164-5; *Southern School News*, February 1959, 10.

89. *Atlanta Journal*, 10 January 1958, 1.

90. Robert Sherrill, *Gothic Politics in the Deep South* (New York: Grossman, 1968), 52; Talmadge interview, 1991.

91. Bartley, *The Rise of Massive Resistance*, 333-4; Sherrill, *Gothic Politics*, 52-3, 62; Harold H. Martin, *Ralph McGill, Reporter* (Boston: Little Brown, 1973), 155.

92. Mertz, "HOPE, Inc. and School Desegregation in Georgia," 6.

93. M. Lokey, videotape of "The Civil Rights Revolution"; Mertz, "HOPE, Inc. and School Desegregation in Georgia," 6; Pendergrast interview, 17 January 1991; Sarratt, *The Ordeal of Desegregation*, 315.

94. Pauley interview, 15 October 1991. Also see Frances Freeborn Pauley Papers, Series 4, Box 1 (HOPE), Series 2, Box 1 (League of Women Voters), Special Collections, Woodruff Library, Emory University, Atlanta.

95. As quoted in Mertz, "HOPE, Inc. and School Desegregation in Georgia," 6-7; M. Lokey interview, 2 April 1991; Mertz, Pendergrast interview, 1991.

96. Moore interview with Lynette Elise Wolfe. Notes only. Atlanta, 6 December 1990.

97. Quote from Mertz, "HOPE, Inc. and School Desegregation in Georgia," 6,7; Also see Paul E. Mertz, "'Mind Changing Time All Over Georgia' HOPE, Inc. and School Desegregation," *Georgia Historical Quarterly* 77 (Spring 1993), 41-61.

98. M. Lokey, videotape of "The Civil Rights Revolution."

99. Hollowell interview, 1991; Pauley interview, 1991; Mertz, "HOPE, Inc. and School Desegregation in Georgia," 7.

100. *Atlanta Journal*, 30 March 1956, 1; Pauley interview, 1991. Also see Eliza K. Paschall Papers, Series 3, Box 14 (Atlanta Public Schools), Box 20 (HOPE), Box 21 (League of Women Voters), Special Collections, Woodruff Library, Emory University, Atlanta.

101. *Atlanta Daily World*, 6 November 1959, 1.

102. Bolster, "Civil Rights Movements, 152; Jones interview, 6 May 1991; Sarratt, *The Ordeal of Desegregation*, 315.

103. M. Lokey, videotape of "The Civil Rights Revolution"; Lokey interview, 1991.

104. Jones interview, 1991; Pauley interview, 1991.

105. Jones interview, 1991; Pauley interview, 1991.

106. MASCE was never a significant factor in rallying support for continued segregation. By late 1959 it was replaced by another poorly organized insignificant segregationist group called Georgians Unwilling to Surrender (GUTS), headed by Lester Maddox, an Atlanta restaurant owner and politician.

107. H. Lokey, interview 2 April 1991; M. Lokey, videotape of "The Civil Rights Revolution."

108. Bolster, "Civil Rights Movements," 152; Mertz, "HOPE, Inc. and School Desegregation in Georgia," 9; Sarratt, *The Ordeal of Desegregation*, 315; *Southern School News*, July 1959, 2.

109. Beverly Long interview, 1995.

110. Bartley, *The Creation of Modern Georgia*, 215.

111. Sue Bailes, "Eugene Talmadge and the Board of Regents Controversy" *Georgia Historical Quarterly* 53 (Fall 1969), 409-423; William Anderson, *The Wild Man from Sugar Creek: The Political Career of Eugene Talmadge*, (Baton Rouge: Louisiana State Press, 1975), 196-204; Harold Paulk Henderson, *The Politics of Change in Georgia: A Political History of Ellis Arnall* (Athens: University of Georgia Press, 1991), 36-39.

112. *Southern School News*, June 1959, 16.

113. Liberal members of the SRC, Anti-defamation League, League of Women Voters, HOPE, NAACP, National Council of Christians and Jews were among the participants at workshop held at the Central YWCA at 72 Edgewood Avenue in Atlanta.

114. Eliza Paschall papers, # 532, Series I Box 1, Special Collections, Emory University, Atlanta, GA.

115. Eliza Paschall papers, # 532, Series I Box 1, Special Collections, Emory University, Atlanta, GA.

116. Sarratt, *The Ordeal of Desegregation*, 235; *Southern School News*, July 1959, 2; Bolster, "Civil Rights Movements," 161; H. Mark Huie, Sr., "Factors Influencing the Desegregation Process in the Atlanta School System, 1954-1967" (Ph.D. diss., University of Georgia, 1967), 29.

117. Hooper, a former Georgia legislator, was no stranger to civil rights cases. He presided over *Ward v. Board of Regents* and handled another civil rights case that originated in 1957, when 20 black ministers from Atlanta boarded Atlanta's buses, occupied "white" seats, and were later arrested. Typical of Hooper's civil rights cases, litigation moved slowly. On 9 January 1959 Hooper ruled in favor of the ministers, but gave no injunctive relief. *Atlanta Constitution*, 10 January 1959, 1; *Atlanta Journal*, 9 January 1959, 1; Bolster, "Civil Rights Movements," 163, 171-172; *Southern School News*, June 1960, 16.

118. *Calhoun v. Members of the Board of Education of the City of Atlanta*, 188 F. Supp. 401 (N.D. Ga, 1959).

119. *Calhoun v. Members of the Board of Education of the City of Atlanta*, 188 F.Supp. 401 (N.D. Ga, 1959).

120. *Southern School News*, August 1959, 4; Calvin Trillin, *An Education in Georgia* (New York: Viking, 1964), 11; Charlayne Hunter-Gault, *In My Place* (New York: Farrar Straus Girioux, 1992).

121. Bolster, "Civil Rights Movements," 165; Trillin, *An Education in Georgia*, 4. Hooper, in the *Ward* case, made it clear to the NAACP (who counselled Holmes and Hunter) that all administrative remedies needed to be exhausted.

122. Bolster, "Civil Rights Movements, 153; Mertz, "HOPE, Inc. and School Desegregation in Georgia," 10.

Chapter 8

Making Concessions, Maintaining the System

> *The impulse in American society, as far as I can tell from my experience in it, has essentially been to ignore me when it could, and then when it couldn't intimidate me; and when that failed, to make concessions.*
>
> —James Baldwin, 1963

Vandiver's Dilemma

By mid-January 1960 federal district court Judge Frank Hooper had approved a plan for gradual desegregation of four Atlanta high schools. The plan was similar to Alabama's pupil placement plan and desegregated one grade per year, starting at the top with grade twelve. It authorized local school administrators to use psychological tests and other "nonracial" criteria in placing black students in four white Atlanta schools.[1] The plan fell far short of providing blacks open access. Conspicuously absent from the plan—and the major point of contention for E. E. Moore and Constance Baker Motley—was a starting date. Nevertheless, in Judge Hooper's view, the plan complied with the requirements of the *Brown* decision by voiding segregation, and with the spirit of *Brown II* by making a "reasonable start."[2]

Even though there was no starting date for the Atlanta school desegregation plan, its approval by the federal district court made it clear to Governor S. Ernest Vandiver that he would soon have to make a decision between closing the schools and abandoning massive resistance. His decision would not be an easy one. The political landscape had changed dramatically since his 1958 campaign for governor on the "no not one" pledge. Now the cracks in Georgia's massive resistance wall had grown deep and quite obvious. He was aware of the outrage across the South

171

among moderates, liberals, and intellectuals generated by public school closings in Virginia and Arkansas.[3]

Vandiver had appointed a group of well-respected lawyers to travel around the South and confer with the governors and attorneys general of other states.[4] They had informed him of a growing body of federal and state legal precedents voiding other states' massive resistance policies. The most devastating blow to massive resistance had come from the U.S. Supreme Court in the fall of 1958 in *Cooper v. Aaron*, a case which had grown out of the Little Rock episode. Affirming an Eighth Circuit decision, an angry Court in a special session held that *Brown* was the "supreme law of the land," and that a state cannot "bar children on racial grounds from attending schools where there is state participation through any arrangement, management, funds or property." As Jack Greenberg, one of NAACP attorneys concluded, the opinion demolished legal maneuverings by the state for turning public schools into private schools.[5] Four months later in Virginia (and ironically on the birthday of Robert E. Lee), the federal judiciary again expressed its intolerance for massive resistance. A three-judge federal court, citing the equal protection clause of the fourteenth amendment, told Virginia's lawmakers that if they chose to close one "public school or grade therein," they would have to close all the public schools in the state. On the same day the Virginia Supreme Court of Appeals ruled that laws providing for public school closings, cutting off state funds at desegregated schools, and tuition grants for private schools violated the state constitution.[6] The courts, in short, indicated that evasive schemes, borne by the state, aimed at circumventing *Brown* would not be tolerated in Arkansas and Virginia, and presumably throughout the South.

Vandiver also felt the pressure of the growing black direct-action campaign. In the wake of the Montgomery bus boycott, nonviolent mass protest competed vigorously with the steady but slow court-oriented methods of the NAACP. By 1960 nonviolent tactics emerged in the South as the method of choice in the struggle for racial equality. The alternative movement for racial equality led by Dr. Martin Luther King, Jr. was at the center of a storm of controversy. Vandiver feared Dr. King's move from Montgomery to Atlanta in January 1960. He declared, "[w]herever M.L. King, Jr. has been there has followed in his wake a wave of crimes including stabbing, bombings, and inciting of riots, barratry, destruction of property and many others. . . . For these reasons, he is not welcome to Georgia. Until now, we have had good relations between the races."[7] (Vandiver did not acknowledge, of course, that the violence that followed King was committed by whites who were supported and encouraged by the climate of resistance.)

Vandiver's difficulties in planning his strategy for handling the Atlanta school desegregation plan were exacerbated by the generally positive public reaction to the Atlanta school pupil placement plan. The *Atlanta Constitution* embraced the plan because it minimized integration. The paper also praised the Atlanta School Board for presenting a compromise plan rather than insisting on complete segregation or closed schools. The slightly larger *Atlanta Journal* editorialized that it was the only answer to the school crisis. The *Augusta Chronicle*, long criticized by Roy Harris as being too moderate, suggested that the plan, with no starting date, gave all Georgians—and "not a small group of state officials"—time to decide between abandoning the schools or keeping them with token integration. The *Macon Telegraph* and *Macon News* liked the plan but doubted that the Georgia General Assembly would clear the way for its implementation.[8]

The ever optimistic *Atlanta Daily World*, the state's black daily, expressed gratification that the Atlanta school board had set as its primary objective to keep the school system open. Conservative blacks with a voice inside the power structure, like editor C.A. Scott and Rufus Clement, President of Atlanta University (and the only black serving on the Atlanta board), also endorsed the plan. Clement realized it was a compromise for the plaintiffs, but, as so many of the black leaders had done earlier, endorsed it because it did not immediately threaten the public school system. "A civilized society can neither grow nor be sustained in a nation or community which prefers ignorance to knowledge," he said.[9]

There was some negative reaction to the plan. As might have been expected, Roy Harris excoriated the plan in the *Augusta Courier*. Harris's opinion was seconded by the Bainbridge *Post-Searchlight*, which lambasted the prevailing logic that to allow a little "token integration" would be the best way to maintain de-facto segregation.[10] Vandiver, who had run on a strict segregation platform, could not now be certain that the private-school plan enjoyed widespread popular support and approval.

The unified support for massive resistance that had formerly dominated the legislature also began to erode in early 1960. According to state representative James M. Mackay, who seemed to have a good feel for the mood in the legislature, there had been a shift in the General Assembly in favor of new methods of resistance which could travel under a guise of "local control."[11] The local control option was favored by moderates, because it would avoid a statewide school closing and because it might allow for some desegregation at the option of the local school boards.

The shift in rhetoric put Governor Vandiver on the defensive. At a press conference on the eve of the 1960 legislative session, Vandiver emphatically denied he was an advocate of public school closures. He maintained his public support of massive resistance but began to have private reservations about the wisdom of the private school plan.[12] Even within his inner circle of political advisors, there was no agreement on the proper course of action.

This dissension prompted an exchange between Roy Harris and James S. "Mr. Jim" Peters, the new behind-the-scenes political boss, chairman of the State Board of Education, and former chairman of the state Democratic Party. In late December 1959 Roy Harris drafted an editorial in the *Augusta Courier* responding to the Atlanta School Board's "token integration" plan and its generally positive reception around the state. Harris argued that no form of integration could be tolerated in Georgia. "If one little Negro is entitled to go to Henry Grady High School in Atlanta," reasoned Harris, "then all the Negroes are entitled to go to some high school with the whites." Harris went on to call for continued resistance, and he praised two segregationist leaders in the state—Charles Bloch, a powerful Macon attorney, and U.S. House Representative James C. Davis from Stone Mountain—for countering HOPE's statewide open schools campaign with their own pro-segregation speeches.[13]

Two days later, in a private letter, Peters responded to Harris's call for continued massive resistance. In his letter Peters asserted that the school/race issue would be a dominant political issue in the 1962 governor's race. Peters wrote:

> I am convinced that Ellis [Arnall] and the proponents of integration are delaying their move [to announce his candidacy] to 1961 with the hope and prayer that Gov. Vandiver will close the schools down. . . . This would create the issue which they want. . . .Given 12 months with our schools closed to register 600,000 Negroes and to convince the mothers and fathers the only way to re-open is with him as governor. Ellis will indeed be difficult to defeat . . . . [W]e would lose control of government and entrench Ellis Arnall and the integrationists in the control of the government for decades to come.[14]

Peters went on to reason that some form of integration was inevitable, that the only question left was whether this integration will be under the control of the "friends of segregation or the proponents of integration." Then, disagreeing with Harris's appraisal of the public's commitment to segregation at all costs, he wrote:

> I do not agree with you as to the public sentiments. In fact, it is changing and will change much faster between now and September 1962 unless Herman Talmadge and his friends find a better answer to this problem than the closing down of the public schools system, leaving 75,000 teachers and other employees idle, more than three quarters of a million children who will not be able to get into any kind of school playing on the streets and growing up in ignorance.[15]

Peters's private letter to Harris was made public in January 1960, exposing the fact that some of Vandiver's closest advisors were discussing in private the possible long-term political consequences of abandoning the schools. Adding to Vandiver's troubles was the now growing public perception that his position on desegregation was mere rhetoric.

When the General Assembly convened for the 1960 session, a core of open-school advocates, led by James Mackay, took the offensive in suggesting legislation. Mackay, in what he later considered a rearguard action, introduced a resolution in the House that would strike the segregation phrase from the Georgia Constitution, paving the way for his parental-choice plan. His plan would allow localities the discretion to abandon the public schools or maintain them.[16] His was a proposed shift from compulsory massive resistance to permissive atomized resistance—that would save the public schools. He was not concerned, or even perhaps aware, that the shift would change only the canvas of resistance. No longer would it be painted in the easy-to-discern language of state law, but sketched ephemerally in the elusive policies of local systems.

The act, if approved, would also profoundly reduce well-established patterns of state executive power. For Vandiver this was all too troubling. He did not want to be remembered as the governor who caved in on segregation and squandered the power of the state's highest office. Yet he also abhorred the violence and mean-spirited resistance witnessed in Little Rock, Montgomery, and scores of other communities across the South. More immediately, he had no clear indication on how the voting public stood on the school/race issue. The temple bombing had galvanized the will of moderates, and HOPE had mobilized them. Vandiver realized that up to this point, he had not completely fallen out of favor with moderates. Most still believed he could save Georgia from raw strife and bring about change in a dignified manner.

Vandiver was caught in a political thicket. He wanted to avoid being outmaneuvered by Mackay and labeled "soft on segregation," as he had been during his gubernatorial campaign. He also hoped to shift the burden of choosing between abandoning massive resistance or the public schools to another set of shoulders. Harris, the old political boss, argued for more overt defiance, while Peters, the new patriarch, argued for some form of passive resistance.

On the advice of Griffin Bell, his chief of staff, Vandiver took the "middle of the road."[17] Vandiver supported two measures that demonstrated his support for the private-school plan. These were a bill allowing for the sale of school buildings to private corporations and a bill prohibiting levying taxes for any school (private or public) that desegregated. But, to avoid tying his own hands on the school/race issue, he grasped at the only political option available to him. Acting on Bell's suggestion, Vandiver introduced a measure that created the General Assembly Committee on Schools, commonly called the "Sibley Commission" after its chairman, John Adams Sibley.[18]

The seventy-one-year-old Sibley was a respected and distinguished lawyer, banker, and businessman and was a leading member of the Atlanta establishment. Having grown up in the Georgia Black Belt and having served as a judge in Baldwin County, Sibley also had great credibility among rural county elites.[19] A business progressive with strong personal appeal, Sibley had a sense of what it would take to keep Georgia moving forward economically and socially. Vandiver could not have chosen a person who better exemplified New South thinking or who was more likely to provide a rationale for saving the schools. Vandiver directed the Sibley Commission to hold public hearings in each of Georgia's twelve congressional districts to ascertain whether the people desired any modification of the private school plan and to report these findings by 1 May 1960.[20]

The school/race debate in the 1960 meeting of the General Assembly ended in somewhat of a stalemate. The segregation clause remained in the Constitution, and Vandiver pushed through the General Assembly the tax prohibition bill. Vandiver's school sale proposal did not pass, but his Sibley Commission measure did. The Commission would become an important factor in the ultimate choice between adhering to massive resistance or maintaining the public school system.

The Sibley Commission Hearings

The creation of the Sibley Commission was greeted with both hope and skepticism. Segregationists expected that during the proceedings the governor would come to his senses and follow the traditional course of bold talk and apartheid policy laid down by Herman Talmadge, S. Marvin Griffin, and Vandiver's political mentor, Richard B. Russell. Liberals and the NAACP saw the commission as either a vehicle to build a stronger case for defiance, or as Vandiver's only alternative to evade a politically difficult decision. Nevertheless, HOPE and other moderate groups who favored continued public education took the work of the commission seriously. Frances Breeden told a HOPE supporter in early February 1960 that HOPE would "flood" the hearings "with sentiment for uninterrupted education" so that state leaders realize "that there are thousands of Georgians who are willing to 'stand up and be counted.'"[21]

In an attempt to persuade two of the state's most powerful segregationists to endorse a modification of the state's private school plan and set the tone for the upcoming hearings, open-school advocates, claiming to represent 535,000 supporters, visited the homes of Senators Richard B. Russell and Herman Talmadge. Russell, who perhaps had underestimated the strength of the open-schools movement, remarked, "I can't believe you people are here to tell me to keep the schools open." Yet, neither he nor Talmadge gave any encouragement to the delegations. Talmadge said he favored both segregation and public education. Russell remarked that Georgia should "defend segregation to the last extremity."[22]

In March 1960 the Sibley Commission went to the ten congressional districts and held twelve hearings to find out how "the people" felt about public school desegregation and to give them an opportunity to air their views on the impending crisis.[23] The pace at which hearings took place was nothing short of remarkable. Starting on 3 March 1960 in south Georgia, Sibley and the other eighteen committee members zigzagged back and forth across the state, hearing several hours of testimony an average of every other day. The Commission heard testimony of 1,578 Georgians, who, as Claude Sitton, a correspondent for the *New York Times* described them:

> included Negroes and whites, farmers in galluses and sweat-stained khakis, businessmen in Ivy League suits, lanky mountaineers from the Blue Ridge hill country, cattlemen from the pines and palmetto flatlands, teachers fresh from the classroom and suburban housewives. Their views ranged from the thundering 'never!' of the States Rights' Council to the equally adamant demand for 'desegregation now' from members of the NAACP."[24]

Chairman Sibley, an intelligent, grandfatherly type, proved to be an acceptable commission chairman to blacks, white segregationists and white moderates. Often infusing the hearings with his own unique blend of dignified and folksy humor, he allowed both blacks and whites to feel at ease giving testimony. At the start of each hearing he gave a short, matter-of-fact presentation of the history of the crisis facing Georgians. And he ended his chat with his distillation of the two choices Georgians had. As Sibley saw it, the people could either (1) leave the state laws as they were, maintain rigid segregation, but risk public school closures, or (2) modify the existing laws so as to allow local authorities to deal with desegregation in a way that they felt was appropriate. (Notably absent from his list of options was open access for black students.)

Whites who testified were asked their name, occupation, their affiliation and their answer to the choices laid out. Throughout each hearing Sibley, with gavel in hand, reminded those in attendance to refrain from any applause, cheering, or booing. During white testimony Sibley often added humor and personal stories about himself and his family to diffuse tension and avoid shouting matches and chaos. In an exchange with a farmer in south Georgia, Sibley asked how many grandchildren the man had, and added, "That's always important to the chairman, because the chairman has seven children and ten grandchildren!" At another hearing, after an ardent segregationist, educated at "integrated" schools in Ohio, gave emotional testimony for no modification of the state's segregation laws, Sibley replied, "I have often understood that the worst kind of Rebel in the world is a converted Yankee. We are glad to have you down here." When a Methodist minister from Columbus prepared to read a statement endorsed by fifteen other pastors—including Baptists, Sibley interrupted him to say, "Excuse me Doctor, but I'm glad to know that the Methodists and the Baptists are on such good terms that the Methodists can speak to the Baptists."[25]

Sibley usually gave blacks who testified the same level of courtesy he gave whites. He exuded an air of gentility and civility that stood in sharp contrast to the defiant postures of Talmadge, Bodenhamer and Harris. As he had with whites, he referred to witnesses as "Mr." or "Mrs." But, instead of giving blacks a choice between a modification of the state laws or leaving the laws as they were, Sibley often shifted the choices. Blacks were asked to give their personal preference for segregation or integration. For example, while taking testimony from a black minister, Sibley asked, "I want to know your real convictions of what you think is best for your own race and the white race on this school question, whatever it may be. In your opinion, is it better for the colored children in the South to have separate schools, or whether to have integrated, mixed schools?" In an exchange with another black testifier, Sibley asked, "Do you think a Negro teacher is in a better position to educate a Negro pupil than a white teacher?" Perhaps Sibley was attempting to find out the truth behind one of the prevailing myths of the time that most blacks in Georgia preferred enforced segregation. On the other hand, he may have been trying to persuade blacks that segregated education was the best kind for both races.

While most open-school advocates appreciated Sibley's tone, the hearings did not have an auspicious beginning.[26] At the first meeting in Americus, dozens of people, both white and black, and very few with school-age children, testified in favor of continued segregation and the private-school plan. This alarmed HOPE organizers, who quickly set off to make sure a respectable number of open-school advocates testified before the committee.[27] HOPE's efforts were not in vain. At the eleven remaining hearings, five had majorities for favoring local option, five had majorities favoring "school closings, if necessary," and one was evenly divided.[28] The outcomes were related to two factors: the size of the black population in the districts and the strength of HOPE support in the area. In south Georgia, for instance, where HOPE had made few friends and where blacks generally outnumbered whites, most testimony favored the private school plan. In north

Georgia, where HOPE support was strong and where there were fewer blacks, testimony favored local option.[29] Upon review of the testimony, 64 percent (1,003 witnesses) supported no change in state laws, while 36 percent (575 witnesses) favored modifying the laws to keep the public schools open, even if it required token integration. The 1,003 witnesses who supported no change in policy claimed to represent 74,978 people, while the 575 witnesses favoring open schools maintained they represented 45,432 people.[30] Although 64 percent of the witnesses preferred no change in the segregation laws, the hearings legitimized the position held by white open-school advocates by giving them equal time and consideration to express their viewpoint. At the same time, the hearings had the effect of further distancing the open-schools position advocated by HOPE from the integration position advocated by the NAACP. It was at this critical moment in the school debate that the goal of open access for blacks was subordinated to the white middle-class self interest in continued public education.

While the Sibley Commission hearings went forward, other pressures on Vandiver continued to mount in the tumultuous spring of 1960. March came in like a lion when black college students at Atlanta University Center published in three Atlanta dailies "An Appeal for Human Rights," a full-page declaration that they were enlisting in the sit-in movement. The statement was unequivocal in its insistence on immediate rights and pointed to inequalities and injustices in education, jobs, housing, voting, hospitals, entertainment, restaurants and law enforcement. Eloquently laced with allusions to Christian morality and democratic idealism, the statement ended with a vow "to use every legal and non-violent means at our disposal to secure full citizenship rights as members of this great Democracy of ours."[31]

Mayor William T. Hartsfield's quick public praise of the appeal only heightened the pressure on Vandiver. Vandiver had tussled with the mayor over matters of race a few times before, notably during his term as Lieutenant Governor. As in the past, Hartsfield took the higher road and put the forty-two-year-old governor on the defensive. In a snap reaction that at once put down the quality of schooling at AUC, invoked the allusion that the Georgia Negro was happy in his place, and tied the origin of the appeal to foreign, "anti-American propaganda," Vandiver angrily judged the "skillfully prepared" "paid advertisement" to be a statement "calculated to breed dissatisfaction, discontent, discord and evil."[32]

Six days later, black students staged sit-ins at Atlanta lunch counters; seventy-seven students were arrested under the anti-trespass law. Two days later Vandiver suffered a heart attack that hospitalized him through the rest of the month and kept him out of his office until the beginning of May.[33]

The Sibley Commission Report

By the end of April the Sibley Commission had completed its study and had written a summary of its findings. The majority report, written by John Sibley and endorsed by ten other committee members, began by attacking *Brown*. It declared that the decision was "utterly unsound on the facts...a usurpation of the legislative function...[and] a clear and present danger to our system of constitutional government." Nevertheless, it continued, "we must recognize the decision exists; that it is binding on the lower federal courts; and it will be enforced." The report recommended alternatives to closing the public schools, such as local option and freedom-of-choice options to parents, despite the fact that a majority of those who testified favored no modification of the segregation laws. The freedom-of-choice recommendations gave "assurances that no child w[ould] be required to go to school with a child of different race, except on a voluntary basis," and included a provision for pupil transfers and direct tuition grants where no suitable institution was available.[34] The majority report also declared that private schools could not, as a practical matter, educate the masses of children in the state. It argued that the plan of leasing the existing public schools to private organizations would be held invalid by the federal courts.

The majority report concluded with a simple lesson in cause-and-effect for the people of Georgia. Until the release of the report, Georgians had been told that it was the federal government, the NAACP, outside agitators, moderates, and Communists that were closing the schools. Sibley placed the responsibility of closing the schools squarely in the lap of all Georgians, saying:

> If the schools are closed, the step should be taken as a deliberate choice, with the expectation that the state will go out of the school business permanently, except for providing tuition grants or scholarships, and that the people will resort to private schools. Closing the schools otherwise is a useless gesture and can cause nothing but confusion, great economic loss, and utter chaos to the administration of the school system.... Those who insist upon total segregation must face the fact that it cannot be maintained in public schools by state law. If they insist upon total segregation everywhere, they must be prepared to accept eventual abandonment of public education.[35]

Sibley had written the report in a way that sought to appeal to all the members of the committee, who he hoped would endorse his recommendations unanimously. Following the lead of state legislature, he had condemned the U.S. Court and asserted states' rights. He advised continuing public schooling in ways that would preserve the creed of segregation. But for nearly half of the committee members,

Sibley's advice to break with the state's unwavering ten-year policy of open defiance, that dated back to *Aaron v. Cook*, was simply too much too fast. The minority report, signed by nine committee members, six of whom were state legislators from rural counties, argued for Georgians to continue "exert[ing] every influence to maintain segregation," including moving to a private system "as a last resort."

In spite of the last-ditch resistance recommendations in the minority report, it was Sibley's majority report calling for local option that caught the attention of most Georgians. The "Sibley Report," as it was later called, was an official statement that the private school plan would not protect the system of segregation and would needlessly sacrifice the public schools. Closing the schools would be only a symbolic gesture toward preserving segregation; it would not serve the practical interests of any group. Without public schools an important avenue of upward mobility for Georgia's emerging middle class would be cut off. Interests of upper-class Georgians would also be harmed as the lack of public schools would destroy Georgia's New South image. The interests of business and industry, which had shaped the development of a segregated, class-based public school system, would not be served by closing the schools. Those interests would best be served by providing a rationale and support for the minimum change to the status quo. Far from recommending open access for black students to white schools, the Sibley Commission advised Georgians to maintain their public schools and employ other means of resistance.

The Date for Desegregation Finally Set

Judge Frank Hooper had been waiting for the Sibley Commission's report before setting a date for the initiation of the Atlanta desegregation plan. On 9 May 1960, just twelve days after the release of the report, Hooper ordered the Atlanta school desegregation plan to go into effect 1 May 1961 and not May 1960, as many had expected. Admitting he was troubled about the situation, he said the delay he built into the order would be the "last chance" he would give to state leaders and Georgians to avoid statewide school closures.[36]

Although white moderates may have found merit in Hooper's extrapolation of the "deliberate speed" clause in *Brown II*, the national office of the NAACP was disturbed by Hooper's built-in delay. Indeed, a promise for eventual equal protection under the laws was carrying less and less weight by 1960 in Georgia, especially in light of the black direct-action campaign and student protests that had arrived in Atlanta and Savannah that spring.

Constance Baker Motley, who had assumed the role as lead attorney for the *Calhoun* case, said that because of the delay, the ruling would be appealed. Citing recent legal precedent, Motley argued that the U.S. Supreme Court or the Fifth Circuit Court of Appeals had never held that a state legislature had the power "to say when and if a desegregation plan should go into effect."[37] As tempers flared in the courthouse, A.T. Walden, who had been sitting in on the case with Motley and Moore, moved in to diffuse the tension. Siding with Motley, Walden pointed out that an order dependent on legislative action would have to be appealed. Walden suggested, however, that if the formal order, which Hooper had not yet written, upheld Motley's argument that implementation of the plan should not depend on what the legislature does, then no appeal would be necessary.[38]

Hooper, taking the black patriarch's advice into account, formally placed in the record statements that the school desegregation plan would become effective in Atlanta on 1 May 1961, no matter what the legislature did or did not do. Six years and six months after the *Brown* decision, Georgia finally had a time and a place for the process of desegregation to begin.

"Mind Changing Time in Georgia"

In the meantime, HOPE was delighted with the Sibley Commission's majority report. Just as HOPE had wished, the report placed public schools above segregation. The fact that Sibley had recommended pupil placement, freedom-of-choice, and other atomized resistance measures aimed at minimizing desegregation was deeply troubling to a handful of HOPE members and supporters, particularly Frances Pauley and Eliza Paschall. But for the many of the moderates who dominated the organization, it hardly registered that the majority report contained seeds of a new and far more resilient form of resistance.

Their battle to save the public schools was far from over. HOPE sensed that the Sibley report, together with Hooper's ruling, needed to be bolstered by community action. Specifically, they would have to rally popular opinion to persuade the legislature to repeal the private school laws.

HOPE's message was now being heard and evaluated by several of the state's most respected segregationists. Ardent segregationists were also aware of the trends in litigation in other states and began to shift their positions on the private school plan and other segregation laws. Speaking at the annual Georgia Bar Association (GBA) Convention in Savannah, Newell Edenfield, president of the GBA and counsel for the defendants in *Calhoun*, called for repeal of the state's segregation laws. Edenfield remarked that he spoke "as a segregationist" and not as an "open school advocate" or a "token integrationist," although he stressed the importance of keeping the public schools open.[39] Reviewing the recent case law around the South, Edenfield concluded that litigation in states that had segregation laws inevitably resulted in a "blanket injunction" against segregated schools. On the contrary, in litigation in states where segregation laws no longer existed, such as Alabama and North Carolina, blacks consistently lost their appeals for blanket relief. Atomized resistance would be much more difficult for black plaintiffs to fight in the courts.

Buck Murphy, one of Vandiver's legal advisors and chief counsel for the defendants in *Calhoun*, agreed with Edenfield. So did James S. "Mr. Jim" Peters, chairman of the State Board of Education, who stepped out publicly from behind his "Dear Roy" letter to argue openly for adoption of Sibley's recommendations.[40]

While support for the private school plan was eroding, the open-schools movement was experiencing a groundswell of support, especially in Atlanta and in north Georgia, where blacks were fewer and HOPE was strong. Beverly Downing, who headed the HOPE chapter in Athens, wrote in the summer of 1960 that she was "immensely surprised and delighted to find so much interest and enthusiasm" about keeping the schools open and was convinced that HOPE "could really do something about the situation." Frances Breeden from the Atlanta chapter wrote John Sibley that "the reception [HOPE] was getting would hearten you as it does us." HOPE organizers believed that the fall of 1960 was "mind changing time all over Georgia."[41]

In September 1960 HOPE adopted a phrase used by Judge Hooper and launched "Operation Last Chance" to win legislative support for Sibley's majority report.[42] The initiative was designed to rally popular support for the Sibley report before the legislature convened in January 1961.[43] HOPE strategists believed that if public opinion shifted enough, lawmakers might be persuaded to repeal the private school bills and thus keep the tradition of public schooling alive. Another goal of the operation was to solicit open-schools statements from the state business community.[44] Many of Atlanta's white business leaders had joined the growing chorus, calling for the retention of public education, even with desegregation.[45] As early as 1959 members of the Atlanta Chamber of Commerce had echoed HOPE's call for keeping the schools open but other major business groups around the state—as late as 1961—remained silent on the issue. HOPE sought to gain the support of business leaders statewide, convinced that the legislators would never change the laws without pressure from their business constituents.[46]

By October HOPE was joined in the crusade by three persistent opponents to the private school plan, the Active Voters, The Georgia League of Women Voters, and the United Church Women. The cooperating organizations planned a series of meetings all over the state that focused on the theme "The School Bells Toll for You." Joining James Mackay, Hamilton Lokey, Mayor Hartsfield, and Mugsy Smith on the open-school lecture circuit were two former last-ditch resisters: Jim Peters and, from Dalton, U.S. Congressman Erwin Mitchell.[47]

Open-Schools Movement Appears More Acceptable in Light of the Black Direct-Action Campaign

Certainly one factor contributing to the pace at which white Georgians were changing their minds about the private school plan was the increasing momentum of the black civil rights movement.[48] The arrival in Atlanta in February of 1960 of Martin Luther King Jr., an acknowledged leader of the civil rights movement, was no doubt a critical factor. Having accepted copastorship with his father at the Ebenezer Baptist Church in February 1960, King moved to Atlanta at a timely moment. His presence augmented Atlanta's emerging direct-action movement.

As head of the Southern Christian Leadership Conference (SCLC), King sought not only the desegregation of schools but also the elimination of all racial restrictions. King's leadership ignited the entire black community, not only in Atlanta and the South, but nationwide, and served to help blacks recognize and demand their rights as U.S. citizens. In early 1959 the SCLC held its first nonviolent workshop at Spelman College in Atlanta. There King trained participants in the techniques of peaceful protest.[49]

King's arrival in 1960 temporarily created a rift in the black community. In the 1950s Atlanta's established black leadership had maintained "generally effective control over the emerging black protest."[50] Unlike blacks from other cities, Atlanta's blacks had developed a political alliance with the white municipal power structure and business community. Through bloc voting and "wheeling and dealing," at City Hall, blacks had become a major political force in Atlanta.[51] Blacks had made significant progress within the separate-but-equal restriction. Because the reinvigorated civil rights movement—with its broader goal of immediate, open access—threatened this vehicle of progress, many of Atlanta's established black leaders sought to control it. But with the arrival of King and direct action movement, the tight control the black "bourgeois" had over the black community began to loosen.[52]

Simultaneously, the student movement, inspired by the success of the lunch counter sit-ins in Greensboro, began to take root in Georgia.[53] Students in Atlanta successfully organized and staged the state's first sit-in at Rich's department store in Atlanta. A few days later students from Savannah State College followed with a sit-in strike at lunch counters in downtown Savannah. Although King had supported and participated in sit-in movements in other cities, he was silent about Atlanta student activism. Students, committed to their course of continued activism, went on to organize the Student Non-Violent Coordinating Committee (SNCC) the following summer.[54]

Meanwhile, white power structure in the city, with some support from the old guard black leaders, moved to reduce the impact of student activism. The conservative *Atlanta Daily World* failed to give this movement coverage or support. An alternative black paper, the *Atlanta Inquirer*, started in 1960 by student activist Julian Bond, covered the sit-ins and was a more enthusiastic supporter of the new direction that the civil rights movement took.[55]

Most biracial organizations in Georgia were quick to support the goals of the direct-action campaign. At a joint meeting in April, the Greater Atlanta Council of Human Relations (GACHR) and the Georgia Council of Human Welfare (GCHW) declared that segregation was immoral. Through published reports and workshops both councils bolstered their efforts to hammer home the theme that a just society is an integrated one. Ironically, it was black members of the councils, many of them old guard, who hesitated to openly support the sit-in movement, stalling a resolution supporting the student demonstrations until October 1960.[56]

As historian Numan Bartley noted, "[t]he direct-action campaign infuriated massive resistance politicians."[57] As protests continued, and as students were arrested and brought to court, Governor Vandiver demanded the black colleges also take disciplinary action against them. The protests were also attacked by some of the more moderate whites in Atlanta. Ralph McGill, for example, forcefully came out against the sit-ins, arguing that the campaign was ill-timed and threatened progress in the open-schools movement.[58]

For several tense months elders of both races expressed their reservations about the direct action movement. Atlanta student leaders, determined to persevere, reluctantly met behind closed doors at the Atlanta University Center with college presidents Benjamin Mays, Rufus Clement, and James Brawley. The presidents, in turn, met with Mayor Hartsfield, Rich's owner, Richard H. Rich, and other downtown businessmen. The elders urged patience, the students demanded results.[59]

Then came another ugly reminder that violent racism continued to exist in Atlanta. On the morning of 12 December, almost two years after the temple bombing and well into the Christmas season, another bomb exploded at English Avenue Elementary School, a Negro elementary school in the northwest corner of Atlanta. Like the temple bombing, it was a monstrous blast, destroying a first grade classroom and damaging six other classrooms, but injuring no one. Newspapers reported that the school's auditorium also was marred and windows from a dozen nearby homes had been blasted out by the explosion.[60] The bombing left no middle ground for moderates and old guard blacks to bicker about the sensibility of peaceful protest tactics.

McGill used his front-page column in the *Constitution* to recreate the tragedy and to make the point that the currents of social change pushing through Georgia could not be averted, even by intimidation. He compared the perpetrators to the Nazis who "tended Hitler's gas furnaces" and placed the blame not only on the Atlanta Klan—whose leader days earlier had advocated destroying the schools to stem change—but also on the shoulders of the governor, legislators, and Citizens' Council resisters like Roy Harris. "Men and women in high places who organize groups to resist court orders and never surrender," the angry moderate charged, "their hands were there just the same." In the end," McGill, concluded, "there will be education for all children. Bombers prove nothing by bombing, or by destroying a school or church. God still lives. Learning still remains."[61]

The bombing, along with the presence of Martin Luther King Jr. and the emergence of the direct-action campaign in Atlanta and Savannah, cast the open-schools movement in a new light. HOPE's goals no longer appeared radical, but comparatively mainstream. McGill had now connected massive resistance and violent hatefulness. King's nonviolent methods gained new stature in the white community because of the comparison. The student movement assumed the position of the left fringe, thus further legitimizing the open-schools movement, which, in its goals and methods, was tame by comparison.[62]

Focus of School Crisis Shifts to University of Georgia

In the spring of 1960, Charlayne Hunter and Hamilton Holmes, who had been waiting for final administrative action on the denial of their applications to the University of Georgia, pushed ahead with a lawsuit against the Board of Regents. NAACP attorney Donald Hollowell handled the case.[63] The litigation, known as *Holmes v. Danner*, began in August 1960, three months after the Sibley Commission reported to the legislature. At that moment HOPE, the NAACP, and many Georgians believed that the state's defiant policy and the federal judiciary desegregation mandate would come to loggerheads in Atlanta because of the *Calhoun* case. James Mackay, for example, thought any action in the massive resistance arena would "wait for the actual showdown—or shutdown—[of Atlanta's public schools] in the fall."[64]

Less than a month after the school bombing and with all eyes on the *Calhoun* case in Atlanta, an unexpected turn of events occurred in another federal courtroom in Macon. On Friday, 6 January 1961, Judge William T. Bootle found that Charlayne Hunter and Hamilton Holmes would have been admitted to the University of Georgia (UGA) in the fall of 1960 if they had been white.[65] In a ruling that caused Governor Vandiver to conference with his legal advisors all weekend, Bootle ordered Hunter and Holmes admitted to the university immediately.

The shift of focus of the desegregation battle from the elementary and secondary schools of Atlanta to the University of Georgia put additional pressure on Vandiver not to close the schools as the 1956 private school plan legislation required him to do. Vandiver was well aware of Eugene Talmadge's blunder which brought disgrace to the state and its revered flagship university in 1942. Support for closing the university would be almost nil. On the other hand, popular and political opinion favoring keeping the public schools open was at an all-time high.[66]

At 9:30 in the morning on Monday, 9 January 1961, Attorney General Eugene Cook and Buck Murphy appeared in Judge Bootle's courtroom in Macon to ask for a stay pending appeal of the decision. Also present were NAACP attorneys Donald Hollowell and Constance Motley. Bootle, citing that "every litigant has a right of appeal," granted a stay of his order pending an appeal to the Fifth Circuit Court of Appeals.[67] That same morning, Hunter and Holmes were on the University of Georgia campus in Athens and were prepared to register for spring semester classes.[68]

Back in Atlanta on the same day, the General Assembly anxiously awaited word on whether Bootle had granted the stay. At 10:30 a.m., upon learning of the stay, the legislators reacted with loud applause. Vandiver gave his scheduled opening address to the legislature at noon. In statement, buried in the middle of a very routine state-of-the-state address, Vandiver said, "we cannot abandon public education." The declaration drew applause from an otherwise quiet gathering of lawmakers. Vandiver then called on the lawmakers to pass a "child-protection amendment" that, he explained, would guarantee every child the "God-given right" to attend public schools of their choice. Alluding to the university crisis, Vandiver pointed out that he had not cut off any state aid to the university. But he did not outline any course of action to keep the university open.[69] Vandiver's speech confused lawmakers, the media, segregationists, and open-school advocates alike. In commenting about Vandiver's state-of-the-state speech, one legislator said, "I never heard a man talk so much and say so little about a problem that has to be solved."[70]

Public confusion continued into the next day when the *Atlanta Constitution* falsely reported in a front-page headline that Vandiver had closed the schools. But, as Jack Spalding, an astute correspondent for the *Atlanta Journal*, wrote, the significance of Vandiver's speech was what he left "unsaid"—that massive resistance was doomed.[71] At 2:30 the previous afternoon, one hour after Vandiver's address, Fifth Circuit Judge Elbert Tuttle rescinded Bootle's stay. Vandiver quickly dispatched Georgia Attorney General Cook to the U.S. Supreme Court in Washington to seek a stay of Tuttle's order pending appeal.[72] Meanwhile, that afternoon in Athens, Charlayne Hunter and Hamilton Holmes registered for classes.

On the evening of 9 January Vandiver wrote a letter to the General Assembly saying that, under the private school plan, he was required to cut off funds to the University of Georgia. He termed it the "saddest duty of [his] life" to recognize that state law now required him to do so. He went on to call the private school plan a "roadblock" and an "albatross," which "if allowed to stand strips us of remaining safeguards."[73] He called for the repeal of the fund-cutting requirement, saying:

> If allowed to remain in the law, its effect will be to close the doors of Georgia's hallowed halls, to cease bringing learning and enlightenment to over 7,500 young men and women pursuing a higher education, jeopardize their credits, create unrest among one of the most outstanding faculties in America and otherwise create harmful results without accomplishing anything. Such wanton disregard of the learning process, I am sure you will agree with me, would be unthinkable.[74]

The next day, 10 January, Vandiver sent a telegram to Bootle in which he excoriated him for "attempting to take over the executive and legislative processes." On 11 January, in what turned out to be the dying gasp of the state policy of open defiance to federal law, a small group of legislators introduced a package of seven bills designed to maintain segregation.[75]

In spite of all the gestures—the telegrams, dispatching the attorney general to Washington, the letter, and the introduction of a new package of segregation bills—Vandiver knew of the overwhelming public support for open-schools —especially at the University of Georgia. His moves were calculated to demonstrate that every means of appeal had been exhausted before he formally proposed to the legislature the repeal of the private school plan and other massive resistance measures.

Meanwhile, tension mounted on the Athens campus and resulted in a "riot." Hunter and Holmes had attended classes for two days amidst relative calm. Then, on Wednesday night, 11 January, after the university lost to Georgia Tech in an overtime basketball game, angry students converged on Hunter's dormitory and began throwing bricks and chanting vulgar slogans. Police were called in to quiet the crowd. After about an hour, the Athens fire department arrived with fire hoses, and the riot ended.[76] UGA officials removed Hunter and Holmes from the university and brought them back to Atlanta—ostensibly for safety reasons.

Bootle was not intimidated. On 12 January, one day after the disturbance, he ordered Hunter and Holmes readmitted. Bootle also enjoined Vandiver from cutting off state funds to the university.[77] Hunter and Holmes returned to classes on Monday, and there were no more riots. Bootle's and Tuttle's decisive actions changed not only the time and place for the showdown but also the level of public schooling at which desegregation would first occur in Georgia. This was the first desegregation in public education in the state's history. Bootle and Tuttle had played hardball with state government and had won a major battle.

Although the federal judiciary had admitted two blacks to the state's revered university and enjoined the governor from cutting off state funds to the school, most of Georgia's school segregation legislation remained intact. Further, there was no guarantee that breaking the color line in higher education would translate into its disappearance at the high school or elementary level.

Massive Resistance Legislation Repealed

The question was now starkly presented. Would Georgia abandon its public schools or its policy of massive resistance? On 18 January 1961, in a speech that was broadcast by radio and television, Vandiver made Georgia's choice. Appearing before a joint session of the General Assembly, he proclaimed that both public schooling and segregated education must be preserved. But, he said, the current legislation is insufficient protection against federal "usurpation of state authority."[78] He asked the legislature to repeal the laws setting up the private school plan, saying, "The time is at hand, therefore, to seek new and better defenses—to perfect alternative plans—to act with courage and resolve—to act decisively—to determine to carry on legal resistance with every means available to us. We must discard rusty and defective safeguards."[79]

Vandiver's speech against massive resistance confirmed what many had been speculating about for months. Vandiver had probably known for some time that desegregation, though politically unpopular, was inevitable, and that massive resistance to it was legally futile. He also believed that public education could not be sacrificed, even temporarily, without major political reverberations. In this sense, it was fortuitous for Vandiver, the legislature, and the other "friends of segregation" that the school/race showdown occurred at the University of Georgia and not the Atlanta public schools. Closing the Atlanta public schools, though still controversial, could have been more easily justified because it would not have directly and instantly linked each legislator to the responsibility. Closing the schools in Atlanta might have been written off by many rural members of the legislature as a necessary slap in the face to city slickers and a good place for Vandiver to take a symbolic stand in the schoolhouse door.

A strike against Georgia's oldest and most respected institution, however, would have had immediate repercussions. Closing the University of Georgia would swiftly put some white students from every county in Georgia out of school, angering parents across the state. Closing the state's revered university could then be used as a potent political weapon in any county race for the General Assembly or the governorship, as Ellis Arnall had demonstrated in 1942. Moreover, the university showdown could not be readily linked with the sit-in movement or to Martin Luther King Jr. in Atlanta. Nor could it be connected with big-city moderates like William Hartsfield, the old-guard blacks in Atlanta, Ralph McGill, and HOPE. Vandiver and his legal advisors could not have designed a better scenario in which to muster the most possible support for the surrender of massive resistance. With all legal avenues exhausted, no one to blame, and nothing to gain, Vandiver bade massive resistance farewell.

Following his speech, Vandiver's administration introduced four bills that politicians called either an "open schools" package or a "defense package."[80] Specifically, the bills would repeal the law that prohibited the expenditure of state or local funds for desegregated schools. They would also repeal the acts providing for tuition grants and the closing of schools, the provision allowing the governor to close a single school system ordered to desegregate, and the provision that prohibited ad valorem taxes for racially mixed schools. No proposal was made to repeal the laws that applied to segregation generally or the acts that set up the machinery for disposing of public school property.[81] The package also contained new provisions, including a bill to "secure the constitutional rights of school children to attend private schools of their choice" and a new tuition grant program. The package also included provisions for local pupil placement boards, which would make it more difficult to litigate school issues in the federal court by setting up extensive procedures for local appeals. Another provision set up local option procedures for closing and reopening public schools in desegregation crises.[82]

While the legislature was considering the governor's package, state leaders received an additional reason to go along with Vandiver. They received a telegram signed by 986 of the state's leading businessmen calling on them to keep the schools open. The telegram was prompted by the work of H. E. Benson, a prominent business leader in Athens and the father of HOPE organizer, Beverly Downing.[83] Business leaders had finally acted on behalf of the schools, but their late entry into the battle which had been under way for two full years revealed more about their desire to be on the winning side than their moral courage. Meanwhile, public opinion strongly favored the package. The voices of racist extremists were all but drowned out by the chorus of open school advocates, business leaders, and white moderates. Thirteen days after Vandiver's speech, the legislature voted overwhelmingly to pass the package of bills presented by the Vandiver administration.[84] Collectively, the bills ushered out massive resistance and ushered in atomized resistance.

The public schools would not close. Neither would they allow black students open access.

Atlanta Schools Begin Token Desegregation

Even as massive resistance crumbled, Atlanta's leaders braced themselves for the possibility of more violence that had rocked the city twice in the past three years. A well-publicized episode of resistance in New Orleans the previous year only served to reinforce their convictions to make the transition peaceful and uneventful. Judge Hooper had ordered that four Atlanta high schools begin desegregation in September 1961. Atlanta's business leaders and middle class, now fully behind open-schools, determined they had a critical role to play in avoiding another "Little Rock" or a "New Orleans" and set off to uplift the image of the city. Atlanta Mayor William B. Hartsfield had supported the open-schools movement from its genesis. Hartsfield had observed the University of Georgia crisis very closely and, shortly after the crisis, had ordered the "entire city government" to place itself "squarely behind the preservation of public education."[85] He set off to build the road toward peaceful school desegregation in the city he sloganed as "too busy to hate." He worked closely with the police department, black community leaders, civic groups, Ralph McGill and others in an all-out effort to ensure peaceful compliance with Judge Hooper's order. On the directive of Hartsfield, Atlanta Police Chief Herbert T. Jenkins had conducted a study of desegregation in other Southern cities. He also educated his police force, requiring his officers to read books about civil rights, racial violence and law enforcement.[86]

While most Atlantans, indeed most Americans, looked on in admiration of the city's graceful preparation for token desegregation, the facelift did not fool everyone. "Actually, what we have demonstrated," lamented Eliza Paschall, "is that we have a good police department and that we don't want to hurt our business."[87]

In the meantime, the Atlanta School Board and its new Superintendent, John Letson, turned to the issue of how to desegregate their system. Letson oversaw the preparation of procedures for the application and transfer of black students to white schools. Far from being a simple mechanism for open access, the procedures were difficult and tedious. Of the 268 students who applied for transfer, only 10 were approved.[88] Perhaps more than any other single piece of evidence, the Atlanta plan proved that Georgia had discovered more insidious ways to avoid compliance.

For liberals and the NAACP the Atlanta plan was a sobering document, and a omen that the real battle was only beginning. Long frustrated with the Atlanta board's foot-dragging antics, Eliza Paschall, now the executive secretary of GACHR, had written the school board president in April to urge genuine desegregation.[89] Paschall pressed him to answer questions on board desegregation policy and sent copies of her correspondence to all board members, but her efforts were ignored. "It [the desegregation plan] was certainly a victory," recalled Donald Hollowell, "but it didn't mean we were finished."[90]

With the fall of massive resistance, HOPE leaders felt that their primary goal had been accomplished. They continued operating, however, joining forces with the mayor's office, the police department, the press, and other civic groups to work for the orderly desegregation of the Atlanta public schools. Under the name Organizations Assisting Schools in September (OASIS), they combined forces with 53 organizations in the summer of 1961 to "create a climate of dignified acceptance of desegregation in the fall."[91] Maintaining the same basic organizational policy on integration as HOPE, OASIS by and large excluded the city's blacks from participating in the orchestration of the token desegregation, which included meetings and discussions with schoolteachers, principals, and civic groups.[92] The exclusion of blacks from planning for the Atlanta school desegregation illustrated the limits and missed opportunities of the Georgia campaign to save the public schools and foreshadowed the difficulties that lay ahead.

On 30 August 1961, nine black students entered four previously all-white Atlanta high schools. Mayor Hartsfield, Police Chief Jenkins, and OASIS had prepared well for the event. Jenkins had ordered his force to keep away from the schools every white person not actually enrolled or employed there.[93] Hartsfield turned the city council chamber into a press room, complete with teletypes and typewriters and refreshments. The press room was in direct radio communication with each police car present at the various schools. The members of the press could monitor the arrival of the black students without actually being present at the scene.

The scene that developed for the press to describe and for the world to see was relatively calm.[94] Unlike New Orleans ten months earlier, no mobs came. No Klansmen marched. No bombs exploded. No protesters shouted or harassed the students. The peace continued. Seven years after the *Brown* decision Atlanta had accomplished the first peaceful desegregation of a public high school in the Deep South. But open access for black students to Georgia's public schools was not even on the horizon. As the press representative for OASIS recalled, one policeman broadcast from the scene, "Everything is normal. No one is eating with them. No one is speaking with them. I repeat: Everything is normal. No one is eating with them and no one is speaking with them."[95]

Given the calm that accompanied the desegregation of the Atlanta schools, OASIS and HOPE determined that their job was finished. OASIS disbanded entirely. HOPE closed its office but claimed to remain ready on "a standby basis."[96]

Public schools, which had been founded on the shifting sands of racial politics, had survived the storm. During a century of development of the public school in Georgia, however, the spread and growth of school opportunities was entangled in the politics of race and class that privileged upper-income whites. By 1961 it was clear that universal public schooling was well established and would survive. It was also clear that race and class politics had survived and would continue to play a dominant role not only in the shape and purpose of the institution but also in the larger society.

Notes

1. H. Mark Huie, Sr., "Factors Influencing the Desegregation Process in the Atlanta School System, 1954-1967" (Ph.D. diss., University of Georgia, 1967), 30-1; Moore interview, 1991; *Southern School News*, January 1960, 16. Federal courts in other jurisdictions had indicated they would permit local school authorities to use "nonracial" criteria in assigning children to public schools. Numan V. Bartley, *The Rise of Massive Resistance: Race and Politics in the South During the 1950's* (Baton Rouge: Louisiana State University Press, 1969), 249; Herbert O. Reid, "The Supreme Court Decision and Interposition," *Journal of Negro Education*, 25 (Spring 1956), 110; *Shuttlesworth v. Birmingham Board of Education*, 1958. Thus, during the late 1950s and early 1960s pupil placement laws emerged as the new legal standard for compliance with *Brown*. Pupil placement evolved into the most effective resistance measure.

2. *Calhoun v. Latimer*, 1958; *Southern School News*, January 1959, 16.

3. Public schools had closed in three districts in Virginia in September 1958, giving rise to attention by national media. Children in Prince Edward County, Virginia, did not have access to public schools for six years and became known as the "lost generation." Public schools in Arkansas were closed for six months during the 1958-59 school year. See generally, Benjamin Muse, *Virginia's Massive Resistance* (Bloomington: Indiana University press, 1961); Bartley, *The Rise of Massive Resistance*; and James W. Ely, *Crisis in Conservative Virginia: The Byrd Organization and the Politics of Massive Resistance* (Knoxville: University of Tennessee Press, 1967).

4. This group included Charles Bloch, Buck Murphy, Griffin Bell and Holcombe Perry. Griffin Bell, Clifford M. Kuhn, and W. Bost, "That's Where I Came In: An Oral Interview with Griffin Bell," *Georgia Journal of Legal History* 1 (Spring 1991), 146-7; *Southern*

School News, August 1959, 4.

5. Jack Greenberg, *Crusaders in the Court: How a Dedicated Band of Lawyers Fought the Civil Rights Revolution* (New York: Basic Books, 1994), 238-241; Bartley, *The Rise of Massive Resistance*, 249.

6. Bartley, *The Rise of Massive Resistance* 248; Muse, *Virginia's Massive Resistance*, 124.

7. Taylor Branch, *Parting the Waters: America in the King Years, 1954-1963* (New York: Simon & Schuster, 1988), 267.

8. *Southern School News*, January 1960, 16.

9. *Southern School News*, January 1960, 16.

10. *Southern School News*, January 1960, 16.

11. *Atlanta Journal*, 13 January 1960, 1.

12. *Atlanta Journal*, 26 January 1960, 1; Numan V. Bartley, *The Creation of Modern Georgia*, 2nd ed., (Athens: University of Georgia Press, 1983), 215.

13. *Augusta Courier*, 28 December 1959, 1, 3; *Atlanta Journal-Constitution*, 17 January 1960, 21.

14. *Atlanta Journal-Constitution*, 17 January 1960, 21.

15. *Ibid.*

16. *Atlanta Journal*, 20 December 1959, 4; *Atlanta Journal*, 26 January 1960, 1; Mackay interview, 1991.

17. Bell, "That's Where I Came In," 146-7; Vandiver, "Vandiver Takes the Middle Road," 159.

18. *Atlanta Journal*, 26 January 1960, 1; Sarratt, *The Ordeal of Desegregation*, 20.

19. *Atlanta Journal*, 26 October 1986, 1, 18.

20. Bartley, *The Creation of Modern Georgia*, 215; *Atlanta Journal/Constitution*, 26 October 1986, 18A; Vandiver, "Vandiver Takes the Middle of the Road," 159-60.

21. As quoted in Paul E. Mertz, "HOPE, Inc. and School Desegregation in Georgia" (paper presented at the 54th meeting of the Southern Historical Association, Norfolk, VA, November 1988), 11; Pauley interview, 1991.

22. Paul D. Bolster, "Civil Rights Movements in Twentieth Century Georgia" (Ph.D. diss., University of Georgia, 1972), 153; *New York Times*, 9 February 1960, 16; Lokey interview, 1991; Pauley interview, 1991; Pendergrast interview, 1991.

23. John Adams Sibley Papers, Boxes G8-G10; Special Collections, Emory University, Atlanta, GA.

24. *New York Times*, 8 May 1960, 66.

25. Sibley papers, Boxes G4-G10, G15, Special Collections, Emory University.

26. Mertz, "HOPE, Inc. and School Desegregation in Georgia," 11; *New York Times*, 4 March 1960.

27. M. Lokey, videotape of "The Civil Rights Revolution," Pauley interview, 1991.

28. Mertz, "HOPE, Inc. and School Desegregation in Georgia," 12, 25; *New York Times*, 3 April 1960.

29. *New York Times*, 3 April 1960; Sibley papers, Boxes G4-G10, G15, Special Collections, Emory University.

30. Mertz, *op. cit.*, 25.

31. "An Appeal for Human Rights," reprinted in David Garrow, *Atlanta, Georgia, 1960-1961* (Brooklyn: Carlson, 1989), 187.

32. Jack L. Walker, "Sit-Ins in Atlanta: A Study in Negro Revolt," reprinted in Garrow, *Atlanta, 1960-1961*, 67.

33. After his heart attack, Vandiver remained quiet and aloof about the Commission's work. Upon release of the recommendations, the governor, who was returning from a two-week respite in Florida and Jekyll Island, denied rumors that he would call a special session of the legislature to act on the majority report. *Atlanta Constitution*, 31 March 1960, 41, 7; 14 April 1960, 2; 28 April 1960, 1.

34. John A. Sibley, Report to the General Assembly, *The General Assembly Committee on Schools, Majority and Minority Report*, 28 April (Atlanta, 1960); Quote from James A. Mackay, "Will Georgia's Public Schools Close?" *Emory Alumnus* 36 (December 1960), 4-7, 39.

35. Sibley, *General Assembly Committee on Schools*.

36. *Southern School News*, June 1958, 16; *New York Times*, 10 May 1960, 25.

37. *New York Times*, 10 May 1960, 25.

38. *Southern School News*, June 1960, 16.

39. *New York Times*, 27 May 1960, 14; *Southern School News*, July 1960, 9.

40. *Southern School News*, July 1960, 9; *Southern School News*, November 1960, 2.

41. Quotes from Mertz, "HOPE, Inc. and School Desegregation in Georgia," 14, and M. Lokey, videotape of "The Civil Rights Revolution."

42. Reed Sarratt, *The Ordeal of Desegregation: The First Decade* (New York: Harper and Row, 1966), 315; *Southern School News*, November 1960, 2.

43. Mertz, *op. cit.*, 15.

44. *Ibid.*

45. Alton Hornsby Jr., "A City That Was Too Busy to Hate," in *Southern Businessmen and Desegregation*, eds. Elizabeth Jacoway and David Colburn (Baton Rouge: Louisiana State University Press, 1982), 130. The Atlanta Chamber of Commerce was led by businessman, booster, and future mayor, Ivan Allen.

46. Hornsby, "A City That Was Too Busy to Hate," 130-3; Helen Hill Miller, "Private Business and Public Education in the South," *Harvard Business Review* 38 (July/August 1960), 87; Mertz, *op. cit.*, 15.

47. Bolster, "Civil Rights Movements," 150; *Southern School News*, November 1960, 2.

48. Bartley, *The Creation of Modern Georgia*, 216-7; Julian Bond, "Julian Bond, Student, 1962," reprinted in Rose and Greenya, eds. *Black Leaders Then and Now* (Garrett Park, MD: Garrett Park Press, 1984), 25-36; *Eyes on the Prize*, "Fighting Back: 1957-1962"; Virginia H. Hein, "The Image of a 'City Too Busy to Hate': Atlanta in the 1960's," *Phylon* 33 (Fall 1972); Hornsby, "A City That Was Too Busy to Hate." Clyde W. Hall, *One Hundred Years of Educating at Savannah State College* (East Peoria Il: Versa, 1991), 74-6.

49. Numan V. Bartley, *The Creation of Modern Georgia* 2d ed. (Athens: University of Georgia Press, 1983), 196-197; Branch, *Parting the Waters*, 265.

50. As quoted in Bartley, *op. cit.*, 196-7; Garrow, *Atlanta, 1960-61*.

51. Hein, "The Image of a 'City Too Busy to Hate'"; Hornsby, "A City Too Busy to Hate," 124; David N. Plank and Marcia Turner, "Changing Patterns in Black School Politics, Atlanta, 1872-1973," *American Journal of Education* 95 (August 1987); Philip Noel Racine, "Atlanta's Schools: A History of the Public School System 1869-1955" (Ph.D. diss., Emory University, 1969).

52. Bartley, *op. cit.*, 197.

53. Bolster, "Civil Rights Movements," 193; Sarratt, *The Ordeal of Desegregation*, 327; Howard Zinn, *SNCC, The New Abolitionists* (Boston: Beacon Press, 1965), 17; Clyde W. Hall, *One Hundred Years of Educating at Savannah State College* (East Peoria, IL: Versa, 1991), 75.

54. Bartley, *The Creation of Modern Georgia*, p. 217, 220; Sarratt, *The Ordeal*, 327-8.

55. Bond, "Julian Bond, Student," 25-36; John Smith interview, 1991. Also see David J. Garrow, ed. *Atlanta Georgia, 1960-1961: Sit-ins and Student Activism* (Brooklyn: Carlson, 1989). The book contains essays by August Meier, Davis Lewis, Jack L. Walker, Eric Lincoln, Lionel Newson, William Gordon and Vincent D. Fort. "An Appeal for Human Rights" is in appendix. Walker's third essay is very good at piecing together the Atlanta sit-in movement.

56. Eliza Paschall papers, # 532, Series I Box 1, Special Collections, Emory University, Atlanta.

57. Bartley, *The Creation of Modern Georgia*, 223.

58. Bartley, *op. cit.*, 217; Walker in Garrow, *Atlanta*, 185-189.

59. Eliza Paschall papers, # 532, Series I Box 1, Special Collections, Emory University.

60. *Atlanta Constitution*, 13 December 1960, 1; *Atlanta Constitution*, 14 December 1960, 1, 4-5; *Atlanta Daily World* 13 December 1960, 1.

61. *Atlanta Constitution*, 13 December 1960, 1.

62. *New York Times*, 11 December 1960, 74.

63. Bolster, "Civil Rights Movements," 165; *Southern School News*, February 1961, 1.

64. James A. Mackay, "Will Georgia's Public Schools Close?" *Emory Alumnus* 36 (December 1960), 6; Mertz, "HOPE, Inc. and School Desegregation in Georgia," 14; Benjamin Muse, *Ten Years of Prelude: The Story of Integration Since the Supreme Court's 1954 Decision* (New York: Viking, 1964), 223.

65. Bolster, "Civil Rights Movements," 166; *Holmes v. Danner*, 1959; *Southern School News*, February 1961, 8.

66. Many analysts have hypothesized that prior to the showdown at the University of Georgia, the chances for abandoning massive resistance and complying with Brown were nil. These analysts have ignored the support for the open schools movement. See, Jack Bass, *Unlikely Heroes: The Unlikely Story of Southern Judges of the Fifth Circuit Who Translated the Supreme Court's Brown Decision into a Revolution for Equality* (New York: Simon and Schuster, 1981); Hornsby, "A City Too Busy to Hate; Mays, *Born to Rebel*, 207-8; Charles Pyles, "S. Ernest Vandiver and the Politics of Change," in *Georgia Governors In An Age of Change: From Ellis Arnall to George Busbee*, eds. Harold P. Henderson & Gary L. Roberts (Athens: University of Georgia Press, 1988), 149-50; Weltner interview, 1991; Francis M. Wilhoit, *The Politics of Massive Resistance* (New York: Braziller, 1973), 190-1; Calvin Trillin, *An Education in Georgia* (New York: Viking, 1964).

67. *Atlanta Constitution*, 10 January 1961, 1; Hornsby, "A City Too Busy to Hate," 126; *Southern School News*, February 1961, 8.

68. Bolster, "Civil Rights Movements," 167; Trillin, *An Education in Georgia*, 51.

69. *Atlanta Constitution*, 10 January 1961, 12; *Atlanta Journal*, 9 January 1961, 20; *Southern School News*, February 1961, 8.

70. *Atlanta Constitution*, 10 January 1961, 1.

71. *Atlanta Journal*, 10 January 1961, 25.

72. *Atlanta Constitution*, 10 January 1961, 1; *Atlanta Constitution*, 11 January 1961, 1; *Southern School News*, February 1961, 10; Trillin, *An Education in Georgia*, 45-6.

73. *Southern School News*, February 1961, 10.

74. *Ibid.*

75. *Atlanta Constitution*, 11 January 1; *Southern School News*, February 1961, 9.

76. *Southern School News*, February 1961, 9.

77. *Atlanta Journal*, 12 January 1961, 1; Sarratt, *The Ordeal of Desegregation*, 164-5; *Southern School News*, February 1961, 8.

78. Georgia General Assembly, *Georgia House Journal* (Atlanta, 1961), 232-233.

79. *Ibid.*, 237

80. *Southern School News*, February 1961, 10.

81. *New York Times*, 1 February 1961, 26; *Southern School News*, April 1961, 16. In April 1961, the Georgia Attorney General commented that these measures were considered invalid in light of the Supreme Court precedents and the repeal of the other massive resistance measures.

82. *Southern School News*, April 1961, 16.

83. Hornsby, "A City Too Busy to Hate," 131-2; Mertz, "HOPE, Inc. and School Desegregation in Georgia," 15.

84. *Georgia Laws*, 1961, 37; Clarke interview, 1991.

85. Sarratt, *The Ordeal of Desegregation*, 170.

86. Harold H. Martin, *William Berry Hartsfield, Mayor of Atlanta* (Athens: University of Georgia Press, 1978), 152; Sarratt, *op. cit.*, 171.

87. Letter from E. Paschall to Robert Hutchins (President, Center for the Study of Democratic Institutions), September 1961, Paschall papers, 532, box 29, folder #1, Special Collections, Emory University, Atlanta.

88. Melvin W. Ecke, *From Ivy Street to Kennedy Center: A Centennial History of the Atlanta Public School System* (Atlanta: Atlanta Board of Education, 1972), 364-8.

89. Letter from Paschall to L. J. O'Callaghan, 21 April 1961, # 532, Series I Box 1, Eliza Paschall papers, Special Collections, Emory University, Atlanta.

90. Hollowell interview, 1991.

91. *Background Atlanta: A Handbook for Reporters Covering the Desegregation of Atlanta Public Schools*, ed. Judy Neiman, (Atlanta: Organizations Assisting Schools in September, 1960), 13. M. Lokey interview, 1991; Sarratt, *The Ordeal of Desegregation*, 316.

92. Letter from Paschall to Harry Boyte and Ernest E. Lent, Jr., Unitarian Service Committee, Inc. 39 [sic] May 1961, Eliza Paschall papers, # 532 Series I Box 1, Special Collections, Emory University, Atlanta. Paschall wrote "One of my visitors last night is on

one of the committees of OASIS (Organizations Assisting Schools in Sept., Ernie) and when I said I thought there should be more Negro participation, that we cannot prepare for something by avoiding it, she said, 'But you see, our objectives are not the same . . . the Negroes are working for a desegregated community . . . . We are working for a peaceful situation in the schools.' A bit of a blow to have it said in so many words."

93. Martin, *William Berry Hartsfield*, 152-4.

94. *Atlanta Constitution*, 30 August 1961, 1; M. Lokey videotape of "The Civil Rights Revolution 1989." The following week the National Broadcasting Corporation (NBC) produced a celebratory news documentary on the Atlanta desegregation effort.

95. Quote from M. Lokey, videotape of "The Civil Rights Revolution."

96. Sarratt, *The Ordeal of Desegregation*, 316.

Conclusion

The School that Race Built

By the end of 1961, champions of the state's public system could look back and point with pride to myriad victories in the face of tremendous obstacles. They could count on seeing children in school for nearly nine months each year and higher standards for hiring and training teachers. They could celebrate a statewide equalization effort that worked toward leveling up instructional costs among counties, a comprehensive curriculum that helped prepare the young for gainful employment, a state building program that consolidated hundreds of one- and two-room school houses into modern, comprehensive plants, and a program that promised to continue the consolidation efforts. The pitiful country schools that Gunnar Myrdal had recounted in 1938, and the "education in the rough" that shocked the visiting *New York Times* education editor Benjamin Fine in 1946, had for all intents and purposes become a thing of the past.

Perhaps the most celebrated victory for the champions of the public school occurred with the first nonviolent token desegregation of a Deep South public secondary school system. As the battle developed between public schooling and Jim Crow, many observers had predicted that the commitment to segregation was stronger than Georgia's system of public education. But by the time that the school issue would finally go head-to-head with segregation, public schooling had become too important to sacrifice. The survival of the public school in the face of a direct struggle with Jim Crow segregation signaled that a new Southern institution had arrived and secured its place.

The public school that had survived and the goals it embodied, however, were more complex than most realized or were willing to admit. Notably, the school had a racial history of its own. Created from the ashes of the Civil War and secure after its battle with Jim Crow in the early winter and fall of 1961, the public school that endured was a product of the politics of race, a function of almost one hundred years of black determination to secure literacy, equality and mobility, matched step-by-step with white resistance.

The school that race created was, in part, the result of what two sociologists have recently dubbed the *racial wars of maneuver and position*.[1] Thus, public school from an early point in its development, reflected the black struggle for self-preservation and survival. By the end of World War II, the school had become entangled in a political and cultural conflict where it was used to leverage those in power to allow blacks access to the greater society. The school was thus a principal contested arena identified in the struggle for black liberation. Viewed by many blacks and whites as a democratic and egalitarian institution, the scars of race politics revealed the school's less noble nature.

The public school embodied the interests of whites, particularly whites with influence over the economy, access to the media and political officials, control and leadership roles in foundations, universities, and educational organizations.[2] Elites held goals for the public school that were at odds with and competed decisively with blacks' goals. These goals had a profound influence on school's core shape, form, and features, and served to undermine and frustrate the racial battle for position and the struggle for democratic equality. The school continued to embody elitist goals for social efficiency, social mobility and the belief in white supremacy.

In the early decades of the twentieth century, while blacks waged a war of maneuver, the school served the interests of politicians, investors and industrialists in their unrelenting drive to realize economic progress in the state. The system that developed thus promoted social efficiency, preparing children to fill particular economic and social roles. By 1961, this legacy included a full range of program offerings that sorted children by race and by class, selecting some children for college and others for the vocations, trades, and the home. Although there was increasing upward mobility within the system during the post-war expansion, the public school remained an outgrowth of an arrangement that privileged rich over poor and white over black.

In 1961 the Atlanta public schools became the site of a symbolic victory over segregation. A few black students gained access to the previously all-white schools. But the door to the white schools remained barely cracked open to blacks. Whites would continue to resist opening the door completely into the present. Whites would continue to maintain control over school finance, student assignment and the curriculum. Race segregation would persist; and where it fell, it would be succeeded by new forms of discrimination that would rise to maintain white supremacy and privilege. Tracking, ability grouping, differential discipline, and other modes of discrimination would take the place of strict segregation.

The school that race built would persist in both advancing and frustrating the black struggle for first-class citizenship.

Notes

1. Michael Omi and Howard Winant, *Racial Formation in the United States: From the 1960s to the 1990s* 2nd. ed. (New York: Routledge, 1994).

2. David Tyack and Larry Cuban, *Tinkering Toward Utopia: A Century of Public School Reform* (Cambridge, MA: Harvard University Press, 1995), 8.

Appendix A

Archival Records Consulted

Agnes Scott College Papers, Library Archives, Agnes Scott College, Decatur, GA.

Austin Thomas (A. T.) Walden Papers, Atlanta Historical Society, Atlanta.

Crisis in the Schools, audiotapes of lectures in "Editors' View of the South" (Fall/Spring, 1957-58). Special Collections, Woodruff Library, Emory University, Atlanta, audiocassettes.

Eliza K. Paschall Papers, Special Collections, Woodruff Library, Emory University, Atlanta.

Frances Freeborn Pauley Papers, Special Collections, Woodruff Library, Emory University, Atlanta.

Georgia's Political Heritage Project, Special Collections, State University of West Georgia (formally West Georgia College), Carrollton.

Grace Towns Hamilton Papers, Atlanta Historical Society, Atlanta.

Help Our Public Education (HOPE) Papers, Atlanta Historical Society, Atlanta.

Herman E. Talmadge Papers. Atlanta Historical Society, Atlanta.

John Adams Sibley Papers, Special Collections, Emory University, Atlanta.

Mauney Douglass (M. D.) Collins Papers. Georgia Department Archives and History, Atlanta.

Roy Vincent Harris Collection, Richard B. Russell Jr. Memorial Library, University of Georgia, Athens, GA.

S. Ernest Vandiver Collection, Richard B. Russell Jr. Memorial Library, University of Georgia, Athens, GA.

Southern Regional Council Papers. Atlanta University Center, Atlanta.

Appendix B

Unpublished Interviews

Breeden, Frances. 1995. Interview by author. Tape recording. Clearwater, FL, 21 June 1995.

Clarke, Harold G. 1991. Interview by author. Tape recording. Atlanta, GA, 3 March, 19 March.

Goodwin, George. 1990. Interview by author. Tape recording. Atlanta, GA, 3 November.

Griffin, John A. 1991. Interview by author. Tape recording. Atlanta, GA, 12, November.

Hollowell, Donald. 1991. Telephone conversation with author. Atlanta, GA, 18 July.

Huie, H. Mark Sr. 1991. Interview by author. No tape recording. Atlanta, GA, 1 April.

Jones, Eugene. 1991. Telephone conversation with author. Florida, 6 May.

Lokey, Hamilton. 1991. Interview by author. Tape recording. Atlanta, GA, 2 April, 19 April.

Lokey, Muriel. 1991. Interview by author. Tape recording. Atlanta, GA, 2 April, 19 April.

Long, Beverly. 1995. Interview by author. Tape recording. Atlanta, GA, 21 July.

Mackay, James A. 1991. Interview by author. Tape recording. Rising Fawn, GA, 26 October.

Maxine Friedman. 1995. Interview by author. Tape recording. Atlanta, GA, 12 July 1995.

Moore, Eugene E. 1991. Interview by L.E. Wolfe. Atlanta, GA, 6 April.

Moore, Eugene E. 1991. Interview by author. Tape recording. Atlanta, GA, 5 November.

Pauley, Frances F. 1991. Interview by author. Tape recording. Atlanta, GA, 15 October.

Pendergrast, Nan. 1991. Interview by author. Tape recording. Atlanta, GA, 17 January.

Pye, Durwood. 1991. Interview by author. Tape recording. Atlanta, GA, 27 July.

Scott, C. A. 1991. Interview by author. Tape recording. Atlanta, GA, 13 October.

Smith, George T. 1991. Interview with author. Tape recording. Atlanta, GA, 1 April.

Smith, John 1991. Interview with author. Tape recording. Atlanta, GA, 19 November.

Talmadge, Herman E. 1991. Interview by author. Tape recording. Atlanta, GA, 30 July.

Weltner, Charles L. 1990. Interview by author. Tape recording. Atlanta, GA, 17 September.

Appendix C

Principal Court Cases Cited

Aaron v. Cook, No. 3923 (1950) National Archives, East Point, GA.

Brown v. Board of Education, 347 US 483 (1954).

Brown v. Board of Education, 349 US 294 (1955).

Calhoun v. Latimer, 377 US 263 (1964).

Cooper v. Aaron, 358 US 1 (1958)

Gaines v. Canada, 305 US 337 (1939).

Holmes v. Danner, 191 F. Supp. 394 410 (MD Ga 1961).

Hunt v. Arnold, 172 F. Supp. 847 (ND Ga 9 Jan. 1959).

McLaurin v. Oklahoma, 339 US 637 (1950).

Plessy v. Ferguson, 163 US 537 (1896).

Roberts v. City of Boston (5 Cushing Reports, 1849).

Sipuel v. Board of Regents, 332 US 631 (1948).

Smith v. Allwright, 321 US 649 (1944).

Sweatt v. Painter, 339 US 629 (1950).

Ward v. Regents of the University System of Georgia, 191 F. Supp. 491 (ND Georgia 1957).

Selected Bibliography

Abram, Morris B. *The Day Is Short: An Autobiography.* New York: Harcourt Brace, 1982.

Ader, Emile B. "Why the Dixiecrats Failed," *Journal of Politics* 15 (1953): 356-369.

American Institute of Public Opinion Survey. "White Attitudes to Supreme Court and ICC Decisions" 28 February 1956, 108-109.

————. "AIPO's Summary of Reactions to Supreme Court Decision." 16 July 1954, 106-107.

Anderson, James D. *The Education of Blacks in the South, 1860-1935.* University of North Carolina Press, 1988.

Anderson, William. *The Wild Man from Sugar Creek: The Political Career of Eugene Talmadge.* Baton Rouge: Louisiana State Press, 1975.

Ashmore, Harry S. *Hearts and Minds: A Personal Chronicle of Race in America.* Cabin John, MD: Seven Locks Press, 1988.

————. *The Negro and the Schools,* 2nd ed. Chapel Hill: University of North Carolina Press, 1954.

"Atlanta Declaration," *The Crisis* (June/July 1979): 198.

Bailes, Sue. "Eugene Talmadge and the Board of Regents Controversy," *Georgia Historical Quarterly* 53 (Fall 1969): 409-423.

Ball, Edward D., ed. *A Statistical Summary, State by State of Segregation-Desegregation Activity Affecting Southern Schools From 1954 to Present Together with Pertinent Data on Enrollment, Teacher Pay, Etc.* Nashville: Southern Education Reporting Service, 1958, 9.

Barber, Benjamin R. *An Aristocracy of Everyone: The Politics of Education and the Future of America.* New York: Oxford University Press, 1992.

Bartley, Numan V. *The New South, 1945-1980: The Story of the South's Modernization.* Baton Rouge: Louisiana State University Press, 1995.

————. *The Creation of Modern Georgia,* 3d ed. Athens: University of Georgia Press, 1990.

————. *The Creation of Modern Georgia,* 2d ed. Athens: University of Georgia Press, 1983.

————. *From Thurmond to Wallace: Political Tendencies in Georgia, 1948-1968.* Baltimore: Johns Hopkins Press, 1970.

————. *The Rise of Massive Resistance: Race and Politics in the South During the 1950's.* Baton Rouge: Louisiana State University Press, 1969.

Bass, Jack. *Unlikely Heroes: The Unlikely Story of Southern Judges of the Fifth Circuit Who Translated the Supreme Court's Brown Decision into A Revolution for Equality.* New York: Simon and Schuster, 1981.

Bell, Derrick. "*Brown* and the Interest-Convergence Dilemma," in Derrick Bell, ed. *Shades of Brown: New Perspectives on School Desegregation.* New York: Teachers College Press, 1980.

Bell, Griffin, Clifford M. Kuhn, and W. Bost. "That's Where I Came In: An Oral Interview with Griffin Bell," *Georgia Journal of Legal History* 1 (Spring 1991): 141-153.

Belvin, William L. Jr. "The Georgia Gubernatorial Primary of 1946" *Georgia Historical Quarterly* 50 (Spring 1966): 37-53.

Bernard, Raymond. "The South Moves Toward Desegregation," *Christian Century* (2 October 1954): 9-11.

Bernd, Joseph L. *Grass Roots Politics in Georgia: The County Unit System and the Importance of the Individual Voting Community in Bi-factional Elections, 1942-1954* (Atlanta: Emory University Research Committee, 1960): 30.

Billington, Monroe. "Civil Rights, President Truman and the South," *Journal of Negro History* 58 (April 1973): 127-139.

Black, Earl. *Southern Governors and Civil Rights: Racial Segregation as a Campaign Issue in the Second Reconstruction.* Cambridge, MA: Harvard University Press, 1976.

Bloch, Charles J. *State's Rights: The Law of the Land.* Atlanta: Harrison, 1958.

Bodenhamer, David J., and James W. Ely, Jr, eds. *Ambivalent Legacy: A Legal History of the South.* Jackson: University of Mississippi Press, 1984.

Bolster, Paul D. "Civil Rights Movements in Twentieth Century Georgia." (Ph.D. diss., University of Georgia, 1972).

Bond, Julian. "Julian Bond, Student, 1962," reprinted in Thomas Rose and John Greenya, eds. *Black Leaders Then and Now.* Garrett Park, MD: Garrett Park Press, 1984, 25-36.

Boyle, Sarah P. "A Voice from the South," *Christian Century* (17 December 1952): 1471-1473.

Braddock, Jomills H. II, Robert L. Crain, and James M. McPartland. "A Long-Term View of School Desegregation: Some Recent Studies of Graduates as Adults," *Phi Delta Kappan* 66 (December 1984): 259-264.

Branch, Taylor. *Parting the Waters: America in the King Years, 1954-1963.* New York: Simon & Schuster, 1988, 228-233.

Broughton, James Hilliard. "A Historical Study of Selected Aspects of the Equalization of Educational Opportunity in Georgia, 1937-1968." (Ph.D. diss., University of Georgia, 1969).

Bryan, Mary Givens, ed. *Georgia Official and Statistical Register*, 1961-1962 (Hapeville, n.d.).

———. *Georgia Official and Statistical Register, 1959-1960* (Hapeville, n.d.).

———. *Georgia Official and Statistical Register, 1957-1958* (Hapeville, n.d.).

———. *Georgia Official and Statistical Register, 1955-1956* (Hapeville, n.d.).

———. *Georgia Official and Statistical Register, 1953-1954* (Hapeville, n.d.).

———. *Georgia Official and Statistical Register, 1951-1952* (Hapeville, n.d.).

Butchart, Ronald E. *Local Schools*. Nashville: American Association for State and Local History, 1986.

Chafe, William H. *Civilities and Civil Rights*. Chapel Hill: University of North Carolina Press, 1982.

Chappell, David L. *Inside Agitators: White Southerners in the Civil Rights Movement*. Baltimore: Johns Hopkins University Press, 1969.

Chirhart, Ann Short. "Torches of Light: African American and White Female Teachers in the Georgia Up Country, 1910-1950." (Ph.D. diss., Emory University, 1997).

Cleveland, Len G. "Georgia Baptists and the 1954 Supreme Court Desegregation Decision," *Georgia Historical Quarterly* 59 (Summer 1975): 107-117.

Cobb, James C. *Industrialization and Southern Society, 1877-1984*. Louisville: University of Kentucky Press, 1985.

———. *The Selling of the South: The Southern Crusade for Industrial Development* (Baton Rouge: Louisiana State University Press, 1982).

Coleman, Kenneth, ed. *A History of Georgia*, 2nd ed. (Athens: University of Georgia Press, 1991).

Cook, Eugene. *The Ugly Truth about the NAACP*. Atlanta: [Georgia Commision on Education?], 1955.

———. Attorney General of Georgia, *The Georgia Constitution and Mixed Public Schools: An Official Opinion from the Attorney General*. Atlanta, 1954.

Counts, George S. *Dare the School Build a New Social Order?* New York: John Day, 1932.

Cremin, Lawrence A. *American Education: The Metropolitan Experience, 1876-1980*. New York: Harper and Row, 1988.

Crisis in the Schools, audiotapes of lectures in "Editors' View of the South" (Fall/Spring, 1957-58). Special Collections, Woodruff Library, Emory University, Atlanta, audiocassettes.

Cruse, Harold. *Plural but Equal: Blacks and Minorities and Minorities in America's Plural Society,* New York: William Morrow, 1987.

Dawn's Shining Light: Ralph McGill and the Segregated South, produced by K. Dowdery & J. Dannenbaum, [Atlanta?] Center for Contemporary Media.

212 *Selected Bibliography*

1989. videocassette no. 31394013.

Department of Health, Education and Welfare. *Preliminary Statistics of State School Systems, 1961-62* (Washington DC, Government Printing Office, 1963).

———. *Expenditures for Education at Mid-century* (Washington DC: Government Printing Office, 1953).

Dierenfield, Kathleen Murphy. "One 'Desegregated Heart': Sarah Patton Boyle and the Crusade for Civil Rights in Virginia." 104 *The Virginia Magazine of History and Biography* (Spring, 1996) 251-284.

Douglass, Harl R., and Calvin Grieder. *American Public Education: An Introduction.* New York: Ronald Press, 1948.

Duram, James C. *A Moderate among Extremists: Dwight D. Eisenhower and the School Desegregation Crisis.* Chicago: Nelson-Hall: 1981.

Ecke, Melvin W. *From Ivy Street to Kennedy Center: A Centennial History of the Atlanta Public School System.* Atlanta: Atlanta Board of Education, 1972.

Edmonds, Ronald. "Effective Schools for the Urban Poor," *Educational Leadership* 37 (October 1979): 15-23.

Egerton, John. *Speak Now against the Day, the Generation Before the Civil Rights Movement in the South.* New York: Knopf, 1994: 311-316.

Ely, James W. *Crisis in Conservative Virginia: The Byrd Organization and the Politics of Massive Resistance.* Knoxville: University of Tennessee Press, 1976.

Eyes on the Prize. "No Easy Walk: 1961-1963." Series produced by Henry Hampton. Blackside Inc. 1986. Videocassette.

———. "Fighting Back: 1957-1962." Series produced by Henry Hampton. Blackside Inc. 1986. Videocassette.

"Faculty Statement on Public Education," in Faculty Statement on Public Education File, December 1958, Library Archives, Agnes Scott College, Decatur, GA.

Fairclough, Adam. "Race and Democracy: The Civil Rights Struggle in Louisiana." 17 Southern Changes (Spring 1995): 12-18.

Fite, Gilbert C. *Richard B. Russell, Jr., Senator from Georgia.* Chapel Hill: University of North Carolina Press, 1991.

Fleming, Harold C. "The South Will Go Along," *New Republic* (31 May 1954): 6-7.

Fort, Randolph L., ed. "Crisis in the Schools," *Emory Alumnus* 35 (February 1959): 4-12.

Fried, Albert. *McCarthyism: The Great American Red Scare.* New York: Oxford University Press, 1997.

Garrow, David J. *Bearing the Cross: Martin Luther King, Jr. and the Southern Christian Leadership Conference.* New York: William Morrow, 1986.

Garrow, David J., ed. *Atlanta, Georgia, 1960-1961: Sit-ins and Student Activism,* Brooklyn: Carlson, 1989.

Gaston, Paul M. *The New South Creed: A Study in Southern Mythmaking.* Baton Rouge: Louisiana State University Press, 1970.

Georgia General Assembly. *Georgia House Journal.*

———. *Georgia Senate Journal.*

———. *Ninety-Second and Ninety-Third Annual Reports of the State Department of Education to the General Assembly of the State of Georgia* (Atlanta, 1964).

———. *Eighty-Second and Eighty-Third Annual Reports of the State Department of Education to the General Assembly of the State of Georgia* (Atlanta, 1954).

Georgia Laws, *Acts and Resolutions.*

"Georgia, Pick the Winning Side," *Time,* 26 June 1950: 18-9.

"Georgia Suit Asks School Equality," *New York Times,* 10 August 1949.

Grant, Donald L. *The Way It Was in the South: The Black Experience in Georgia.* New York: Birch Lane Press, 1993.

Grantham, Dewey W. *The South in Modern America: A Region at Odds.* New York: HarperCollins, 1994.

Green, Melissa Fay. *The Temple Bombing.* New York: Fawcett Columbine, 1996.

Greenberg, Jack. *Crusaders in the Court: How a Dedicated Band of Lawyers Fought the Civil Rights Revolution.* New York: Basic Books, 1994.

Grieder, Calvin, and William Everett Rosenstengel. *Public School Administration.* New York: Ronald Press, 1954.

Griffin, John A. "The Harmful Impact of Segregation," *Southern Changes,* 13 (November 1991): 17-19.

Griffin, S. Marvin. *Interposition Address of Governor Marvin Griffin.* Atlanta: Georgia Commision on Education, 1956.

Hall, Clyde W. *One Hundred Years of Educating at Savannah State College.* East Peoria Il: Versa, 1991.

Hall, Robert H. "Segregation in the Public Schools of Georgia," *Georgia Bar Journal* 16 (May 1954): 417-426.

Hammer, Jane (Mrs. Philip J.), ed. League of Women Voters. *Georgia Voter,* 24 (February-revised 1954): 1-6.

Harlan, Louis R. *Separate and Unequal: Public School Campaigns and Racism in the Southern Seaboard States, 1901-1915.* New York: Atheneum, 1969.

"Harris Claims School Plan Gains Support," *Atlanta Constitution,* 5 October 1950.

Harris, Roy V. "Reaction," *Richmond County History* 7 (Fall, 1975): 75-76.

———. "Strictly Personal," *Augusta Courier,* 2 October 1950; Also in same issue,

see "Schools Are Used As Part of Plan to Force Complete Social Equality."
————. "'Education Doesn't Cost, It Pays' Dr. M.M. Collins," *Augusta Courier*, 21 March 1949.
————. "Strictly Personal: Education Essential for Prosperity, Happiness of People of Georgia," *Augusta Courier*, 10 January 1949.
————. "National Association Puts White People of Nation on Notice of Its Intention," *Augusta Courier*, 3 January 1949.
————. "Legislators Warned on Fund Needs for Georgia Schools," *Augusta Courier*, 6 December 1948.
Hays, J.E., ed. *Georgia Official and Statistical Register, 1945-1950*. Atlanta, n.d.
Hein, Virginia H. "The Image of a 'City Too Busy to Hate': Atlanta in the 1960's," *Phylon* 33 (Fall 1972): 205-221.
Henderson, Harold Paulk. *The Politics of Change in Georgia: A Political History of Ellis Arnall*. Athens: University of Georgia Press, 1991.
————. *Georgia Governors in an Age of Change: From Ellis Arnall to George Busbee*, eds. Harold P. Henderson & Gary L. Roberts. Athens: University of Georgia Press, 1988: 49-60.
Hepburn, Lawrence R. *Contemporary Georgia*. Athens: Carl Vinson Institute of Government, 1987.
Holley, Joseph Winthrop. *Education and Segregation*. New York: William Frederick Press, 1955.
————. *What If the Shoe Were on the Other Foot?* New York: William Frederick Press, 1953.
————. *You Can't Build a Chimney From the Top: The South Through the Life of a Negro Educator*. New York: William-Frederick, 1949.
Hornsby, Alton Jr. "A City That Was Too Busy to Hate," in *Southern Businessmen and Desegregation*, eds. Elizabeth Jacoway and David Colburn Baton Rouge: Louisiana State University Press, 1982.
Hughs, Emmet John. *The Ordeal of Power, A Political Memoir of the Eisenhower Years*. New York: Dell Publishing, 1963: 210.
Huie, H. Mark, Sr. "Factors Influencing the Desegregation Process in the Atlanta School System, 1954-1967." (Ph.D. diss., University of Georgia, 1967).
Hunter, Floyd. *Community Power Structure: A Study of Decision Makers*. Chapel Hill: University of North Carolina Press, 1953.
Hunter-Gault, Charlayne. *In My Place*. New York: Farrar, Straus Girioux, 1992.
Jacoway, Elizabeth, and David L. Colburn, *Southern Businessmen and Desegregation*. Baton Rouge: Louisiana State University Press, 1982.
James, Michael E., ed. *Social Reconstruction through Education: The Philosophy, History and Curricula of a Radical Idea*. Norwood NJ: Ablex, 1995.

Johnson, R. O. "Desegregation of Public Education in Georgia: One Year Afterward," *Journal of Negro Education* 24 (Summer 1955): 228-246.

Joiner, Oscar H., ed. *A History of Public Education in Georgia 1834-1976.* Columbia, SC: R. L. Bryan, 1979.

Kaestle, Carl F. "Recent Methodological Developments in the History of American Education," in *Complementary Methods for Research in Education*, ed. Richard M. Jaeger. Washington, DC: American Educational Research Association, 1988: 62-73.

Kelley, Robin D.G., and George Lipsitz. *Race Rebels: Culture, Politics, and the Black Working Class.* New York: The Free Press, 1996.

Key, V. O. Jr. *Southern Politics in State and Nation.* New York: Knopf, 1949.

Killian, Lewis M.. *White Southerners*, 2nd ed. New York: Random House, 1985: 121.

Kirp, David L. *Just Schools: The Idea of Racial Equality in American Education.* San Francisco: University of California Press, 1982.

Klarman, Michael J. "How *Brown* Changed Race Relations: The Backlash Thesis." *Journal of American History* 81 (June 1994): 81-118.

Kluger, Richard. *Simple Justice.* New York: Vintage, 1977.

Lawson, Steven F. "Freedom Then, Freedom Now: The Historiography of the Civil Rights Movement," *American Historical Review* 96 (April 1991): 456-471.

Leflar, Robert A., and Wylie H. Davis. "Segregation in the Public Schools," *Harvard Law Review* 67 (January 1954): 377-435.

Lemann, Nicholas. *The Promised Land: The Great Black Migration and How It Changed America.* New York: Knopf, 1991.

Levey, Judith S., and Agnus Greenhall, eds. *The Concise Columbia Encyclopedia.* New York: Columbia University Press, 1983.

Lewis, Ann E. "S. Ernest Vandiver, 73rd Governor of Georgia," *Georgia Magazine* (February-March 1959): 9, 12.

Lewis, Richard. "The South Isn't Solid," *New Republic*, 28 June 1954, 16.

Lokey, Hamilton. "Low-Key Lokey: An Autobiography." Unpublished manuscript. n.d.

Lokey, Muriel. Videotape of "The Civil Rights Revolution Symposium," for the Institute for Continuing Legal Education (1989) University of Georgia. Athens, videocassette Recording no. 12.

Mackay, James A. "Will Georgia's Public Schools Close?" *Emory Alumnus* 36 (December 1960): 4-7, 39.

———. "Crisis in the Public Schools, An Address," 3 November 1958, HOPE papers, Atlanta Historical Society, Atlanta. 1958.

———. "Private School Plan, Ticking Time Bomb," *Emory Wheel*, 2 February

1956, 2.

Marshall, R. "Black Employment in the South Since 1954," in E. Lander and R. Calhoun eds., *Two Decades of Change: The South since the Supreme Court Desegregation Decision.* Columbia: University of South Carolina Press, 1975: 27-47.

Martin, Harold H. *William Berry Hartsfield, Mayor of Atlanta.* Athens: University of Georgia Press, 1978: 126-128, 152.

———. *Ralph McGill, Reporter.* Boston: Little Brown. 1973: 134.

Matthews, Donald R., and James W. Prothro. "Stateways Versus Folkways: Critical Factors in Southern Reactions to Brown v. Board of Education," in G. Dietz, ed., *Essays on the American Constitution.* Englewood Cliffs NJ: Prentice Hall, 1964: 139-156.

Mays, Benjamin E. *Born to Rebel.* Athens: University of Georgia Press, 1971.

———. "Why an Atlanta School Suit?" *New South* 5 (September/October 1950): 1-3.

McCain, R. Ray. "Reactions to the U.S. Supreme Court Segregation Decision of 1954," *Georgia Historical Quarterly*, 52 (1968): 371-387.

McClain, H. G. "South Carolina's School Amendment," *New South* (February 1953): 1-8.

McCullough, David. *Truman.* New York: Touchstone-Simon and Schuster, 1992.

McGill, Ralph. "To Be of Scottish Blood," *Atlanta Constitution*, 12 October 1950.

McMillan, George. "Talmadge, The Best Southern Governor?" *Harpers Magazine* 209 (1954): 34-40.

McMillen, Neil R. *The Citizens' Council: A History of Organized Resistance to the Second Reconstruction, 1954-1964.* Urbana: University of Illinois Press, 1971.

Mertz, Paul E. "'Mind Changing Time All Over Georgia' HOPE, Inc. and School Desegregation," *Georgia Historical Quarterly* 77 (Spring 1993): 41-61.

———. "HOPE, Inc. and School Desegregation in Georgia." (paper presented at the 54th meeting of the Southern Historical Association, Norfolk, VA, November 1988).

Miles, Matthew B., and Michael A. Huberman. *Analyzing Qualitative Data: A Source Book for New Methods.* Beverly Hills CA: Sage Publications, 1984.

Miller, Helen Hill. "Private Business and Public Education in the South," *Harvard Business Review* 38 (July/August 1960): 75-88.

Moore, John Hammond. "Jim Crow in Georgia," *South Atlantic Quarterly* 66 (Autumn 1967): 554-565.

Motley, Constance Baker. *Equal Justice under Law.* New York: Farrar, Straus and Giroux, 1998.

Murphy, Walter F. "The South Counterattacks: The Anti-NAACP Laws," *Western Political Quarterly*, 12 (Summer 1959): 371-390.

Muse, Benjamin. *Ten Years of Prelude: The Story of Integration since the Supreme Court's 1954 Decision*. New York: Viking, 1964.

————. *Virginia's Massive Resistance*. Bloomington: Indiana University Press, 1961.

Myrdal, Gunnar, et al. *An American Dilemma: The Negro Problem and American Democracy*, 2 vols. New York: Harper & Row, 1944.

Neiman, Judy, ed. *Background Atlanta: A Handbook for Reporters Covering the Desegregation of Atlanta Public Schools*. Atlanta: Organizations Assisting Schools in September, 1960.

Newberry, Anthony Lake. "Without Ardor or Urgency: The South's Middle-of-the-Road Liberals and Civil Rights, 1945-1960." (Ph.D. diss., Ohio University, Athens, OH, 1982).

Norton, John K. and Eugene S. Lawler. "The Myth of Educational Equality," *American Mercury* 62 (1946): 16-23.

————. *An Inventory of Public School Expenditures in the United States: A Report of the Cooperative Study of Public School Expenditures*, 2 vols. Washington, DC: American Council on Education, 1944.

O'Brien, Thomas V. "Aaron v. Cook and the NAACP Strategy in Georgia Before Brown," *Journal of Negro Education* (forthcoming).

————. "Democracy, Privilege, and Schooling in Georgia: Testing the Effects of Politics and Markets," *JAI Series in Advances in Educational Policy* (forthcoming).

Omi, Michael, and Howard Winant. *Racial Formation in the United States: From the 1960s to the 1990s*, 2nd ed. New York: Routledge, 1994.

Orr, Dorothy. *A History of Education in Georgia*. Chapel Hill: University of North Carolina Press, 1950.

Pajari, Roger N. "Herman E. Talmadge and the Politics of Power," in *Georgia Governors in an Age of Change: From Ellis Arnall to George Busbee*, eds. Harold P. Henderson & Gary L. Roberts. Athens: University of Georgia Press, 1988: 75-92.

Peltason, Jack W. *Fifty-Eight Lonely Men: Southern Federal Judges and School Desegregation*. New York: Harcourt, Brace and World, 1961.

Perkinson, Henry J. *The Imperfect Panacea: American Faith in Education, 1865-1990*, 3rd ed. New York: McGraw Hill, 1991.

Plank, David N., and Marcia Turner. "Changing Patterns in Black School Politics, Atlanta, 1872-1973," 95 *American Journal of Education* 95 (August 1987): 584-608.

Pomerantz, Gary M. *Where Peachtree Meets Auburn: The Saga of Two Families and the Making of Atlanta*, New York: Scribner, 1996.

Popham, John N. "Negro, White Schools in the South Held $545,000,000 Apart in Value," *New York Times*, 26 January 1949.

Pratt, Robert A. *The Color of Their Skin: Education and Race in Richmond, Virginia, 1954-1989.* Charlottesville: University Press of Virginia, 1992.

Price, Margaret. *The Negro Voter in the South*. Atlanta: Southern Regional Council, September 1957.

"Private School System Urged in Georgia to 'Foil' Negro Anti-Segregation Plan," *New York Times*, 3 October 1950.

Pyles, Charles. "S. Ernest Vandiver and the Politics of Change," in *Georgia Governors In An Age of Change: From Ellis Arnall to George Busbee*, eds. Harold P. Henderson & Gary L. Roberts. Athens: University of Georgia Press, 1988: 144-145.

"Race Amendement Pushed in Georgia: Would Preserve Segregation by Turning Schools Over to Private Individuals," *New York Times*, 1 February 1951.

Racine, Philip Noel. "Atlanta's Schools: A History of the Public School System 1869-1955." (Ph.D. diss., Emory University, 1969).

Raines, Harold. *My Soul Is Rested*. New York: Putnam, 1977.

Ravitch, Diane. *The Troubled Crusade: American Education, 1945-1980.* New York: Basic Books, 1983.

Reed, Merl Elwyn. *Seedtime for the Modern Civil Rights Movement: The President's Committee on Fair Employment Practice, 1941-1946.* Baton Rouge: Louisiana State University Press, 1991.

Reid, Herbert O. "The Supreme Court Decision and Interposition," *Journal of Negro Education*, 25 (Spring 1956): 109-117.

Reitman, Sanford W. *The Educational Messiah Complex: American Faith in the Culturally Redemptive Power of Schooling*. Sacramento: Caddo Gap Press, 1992.

Rossi, Peter H. Review of *The Negro and the Schools*, by Harry S. Ashmore, *Harvard Law Review* 68 (1955): 1108-1110.

Sarratt, Reed. *The Ordeal of Desegregation: The First Decade*. New York: Harper and Row, 1966.

Sarratt, Reed, ed. *A Statistical Summary, State by State of Segregation-Desegregation Activity Affecting Southern Schools From 1954 to Present, Together with Pertinent Data on Enrollment, Teachers, Colleges, Litigation and Legislation*. Nashville: Southern Education Reporting Service, 1962.

Sherrill, Robert. *Gothic Politics in the Deep South*. New York: Grossman, 1968: 52.

Sibley, John A. Report to the General Assembly, *The General Assembly Committee on Schools, Majority and Minority Report*, 28 April (Atlanta, 1960).

Special Committee on Education. *A Survey of Public Education of Less Than College Grade in Georgia: A Report to the General Assembly of Georgia By Its Special Committee on Education* (Atlanta, 1 January 1947).

Spring, Joel. *Conflict of Interests: the Politics of American Education.* 2nd ed. New York: Longman, 1993.

Spritzer, Lorraine Nelson, and Jean B. Bergmark. *Grace Hamilton and the Politics of Southern Change.* Athens: University of Georgia Press, 1997.

St. John, M. L. "Negroes Not Paying for Schools—Harris," *Atlanta Constitution*, 9 October 1950.

————. Editorial. "Adding Color to the Issue," *Atlanta Constitution*, 11 October 1950.

Strickland, Michael, et al. *The Best of Ralph McGill: Selected Columns.* Atlanta: Cherokee, 1980.

Sugg, Redding S. Jr., and George Hilton Jones. *The Southern Regional Education Board: Ten Years of Regional Cooperation in Higher Education.* Baton Rouge: Louisiana State University Press, 1960.

"Suit to End Racial Segregation in the Schools Draws Fire," *New York Times*, 24 September 1950.

Suitts, Steve. "The Southern Regional Council and the Roots of Rural Change," *Southern Changes* 13 (September 1991): 5-12.

Swanson, Ernst W., and John A. Griffin. *Public Education in the South, Today and Tomorrow: A Statistical Survey* (Chapel Hill: University of North Carolina).

Talmadge, Herman E. *Talmadge: A Political Legacy, A Politician's Life—A Memoir,* edited by Mark Royden Winchell. Atlanta: Peachtree Publishers, 1987.

————. "School Systems, Segregation and the Supreme Court," *Mercer Law Review* 6 (Spring 1955), 189-201.

————. *Segregation and You.* Birmingham: Vulcan Press, 1955.

————. "Highlights of Governor Talmadge's Address," *County Commissioners Comments* 3 (1952): 5.

"Talmadge to Air 'Package' Tax Bill," *Atlanta Constitution*, 3 October 1950.

"Talmadge Attacks Negro School Suit," *New York Times*, 23 October 1949.

"The Georgia Approach," *Time*, 26 February 1951, 47.

"The School Suit in Irwin County," *Atlanta Constitution*, 24 October 1949.

The Truth Versus Ugly Lies about the NAACP. New York: National Association for the Advancement of Colored People, January, 1957.

Thompson, M.E. "Problems of Public Education in Georgia," *Emory University Quarterly* 3 (October 1947): 129-33.

Trillin, Calvin. *An Education in Georgia.* New York: Viking, 1964.

Tushnet, Mark V. *The NAACP's Legal Struggle Against Segregated Education, 1925-1950.* Chapel Hill: University of North Carolina Press, 1987.

———. "Organizing Civil Rights Litigation, The NAACP's Experience," in *Ambivalent Legacy: A Legal History of the South*, eds., Bodenhamer and Ely. Jackson, MS: University of Mississippi Press, 1984: 171-184.

———. "Thurgood Marshall as a Lawyer and the Campaign against School Segregation, 1945-1950." *Maryland Law Review* 40 (1981): 411-434.

Tyack, David, and Larry Cuban. *Tinking Toward Utopia: A Century of Public School Reform.* Cambridge MA: Harvard University Press, 1995.

Tyack, David, and Elisabeth Hanscott. *Managers of Virtue.* New York: Basic Books, 1982.

Tyack, David, and William Tobin. "The Grammar of Schooling: Why Has It Been So Hard To Change?" 31 *American Education Research Journal* (Fall 1994): 453-479.

Vander Zanden, James W. *Race Relations in Transition: The Segregation Crisis in the South.* New York: Random House, 1965: 40.

Vandiver, S. Ernest. "Vandiver Takes the Middle Road," in *Georgia Governors in an Age of Change: From Ellis Arnall to George Busbee*, eds. Harold P. Henderson & Gary L. Roberts. Athens: University of Georgia Press, 1988: 158-9.

Walhquist, John T., et al. *The Administration of Public Education.* New York: Ronald Press, 1952.

Wells, Amy Stuart, and Robert L. Crain."Perpetuation Theory and the Long-Term Effects of Segregation," *Review of Educational Research* 64 (Winter 1994): 531-555.

Welter, Rush. *Popular Education and Democratic Thought in America.* New York: Columbia University Press, 1962.

Weltner, Charles Longstreet. *Southerner.* New York: Lippincott, 1965: 30-1.

Wesberry, John P. "Georgia 'Stands Up' to Decree," *Christian Century*, 6 July 1955, 198.

———. "What Will It Cost to Equalize School Buildings in the South?" *New South* (January 1949): 6-8.

———. "Georgia Politicos Are Desperate," *Christian Century*, 14 February 1951, 195.

Wilhoit, Francis M. *The Politics of Massive Resistance.* New York: Braziller, 1973.

Wilkinson, J. Harvey III. *From Brown to Bakke: The Supreme Court and School*

Integration. New York: Oxford University Press, 1979.

Williams, Winston. "Herman the Unhappy," *The New Republic* (31 October, 1949): 13.

Wolcott, Harry F. "Ethnographic Research in Education," in *Complementary Methods for Research in Education*, ed. Richard M. Jaeger. Washington DC: American Educational Research Association, 1988: 185-221.

Wolters, Raymond. *The Burden of Brown*. Knoxville: University of Tennessee Press, 1984.

Woodward, C. Vann. *The Strange Career of Jim Crow*, 3rd. ed. New York: Oxford, 1974.

Yin, Robert K. *Case Study Research, Design and Methods*. Beverly Hills CA: Sage Publications, 1984.

Zinn, Howard. *SNCC, The New Abolitionists*. Boston: Beacon Press, 1965.

Index